Human Resource Management In Act

Skill Building Experiences

FIFTH EDITION

Human Resource Management In Action
Skill Building Experiences

FIFTH EDITION

LANE KELLEY
College of Business Administration
University of Hawaii

ARTHUR WHATLEY
College of Business Administration and Economics
New Mexico State University

WEST PUBLISHING CO.
St. Paul   New York   Los Angeles   San Francisco

COPYEDITOR: Sheryl Rose
COMPOSITION: Alphatype

WEST'S COMMITMENT TO THE ENVIRONMENT

In 1906, West Publishing Company began recycling materials left over from the production of books. This began a tradition of efficient and responsible use of resources. Today, up to 95 percent of our legal books and 70% of our college texts are printed on recycled, acid-free stock. West also recycles nearly 22 million pounds of scrap paper annually—the equivalent of 181,717 trees. Since the 1960s, West has devised ways to capture and recycle waste inks, solvents, oils, and vapors created in the printing process. We also recycle plastics of all kinds, wood, glass, corrugated cardboard, and batteries, and have eliminated the use of styrofoam book packaging. We at West are proud of the longevity and the scope of our commitment to our environment.

Library of Congress Cataloging-in-Publication Data

Kelley, Nelson Lane, 1937–
   Human resource management in action : skill building experiences /
Lane Kelley, Arthur Whatley.—5th ed.
      p.   cm.
   Rev. ed. of: Personnel management in action, 4th ed. c1987.
   ISBN 0-314-00030-5 (soft)
   1. Personnel management.   2. Personnel management—Problems, exercises, etc.
I. Whatley, Arthur A., 1939–   . II. Kelley, Nelson Lane, 1937–   . Personnel management in action.   III. Title.
HF5549.K344   1992
658.3—dc20
                                                                91-43633
                                                          ∞   CIP

Contents

Preface

For most of this century nations have competed with each other on the basis of capital and technology. Those with more capital were able to outspend those with less capital and thereby gain and maintain dominance in a given industry or market. So, too, those with the best technology were able to provide consumers with the latest in goods and services and in this way succeed in making their economies grow.

Beginning in the 1970s, however, the ways in which nations competed with each other began to change. Technology and capital became accessible worldwide. If organizations in the United States couldn't borrow money from U.S. financial institutions, they could get it from the West Germans or the Japanese. Anyone, from anywhere, with a sound business idea could get financing in the world's growing financial markets. Technology was experiencing similar changes. No longer could a nation keep the lid on its commercial technology. The United States quickly learned this lesson from the Japanese who would buy products containing our best technology, disassemble them and study the technology, improve upon it, and quickly manufacture and market it in competition with the original U.S.-made product, often at a lower price and at a higher level of quality.

These changes have led to a very different playing field for nations and for organizations. Worldwide, organizations are coming to realize that the key to success today is the effective management of their human resources. Examples are everywhere. Ten years ago few would have believed that the Japanese-owned plants in this country, using American workers, could compete effectively with sister plants in Japan using highly touted Japanese workers. Even more farfetched is the idea that Ford Motor Company could create a plant in Hermosillo, Mexico, using Mexican workers, and produce Ford cars which meet world-class standards.

In the Basque country of northern Spain, in a small town called Mondragon, a quiet revolution in democratic capitalism is going on based on worker ownership. Today, over one hundred industrial cooperatives employ over 19,500 people, who own the organizations in which they work. These organizations are highly successful in terms of the quality of their products and services, their profit margins, and their survival rate of over ninety-seven percent over the three decades of Mondragon's history. This spectacular performance is primarily due to the management of the employees of Mondragon.

Based on these and other examples, the conclusion we have come to is that the effective management of human resources is now the most important key to business success around the globe. We hope that this book in some way contributes to your learning about human resource management.

The book has been designed to be used in conjunction with a typical human resources/personnel management textbook or to be used by itself with readings supplemented by your instructor or initiated on your own. To ease the use of this joint textbook approach, we have constructed the matrix which appears on pages xi–xii. The matrix shows the relationship between the exercises in this book and the chapters in several other human resources/personnel management texts. We hope you find it useful. If this is the only text you will be using for the course, make use of the suggested readings provided at the end of each exercise as well as the readings provided by your instructor.

Students today insist that human resource management be made "practical" as opposed to "theoretical." It is, of course, difficult to practice real management decision making in the classroom. But it is possible to simulate, discuss and question various practices in a learning environment with your peers. The exercises in this book do just that—they require you as a student to do more than listen to the lecture or read the text. They require you to confront common human resource issues with others, make inferences based on limited information, and use theories to assist in resolving these issues. An important point for all learners to remember: learning based on experiential exercises is enhanced when combined with the relevant theories and concepts gained through reading and lectures. All learning is experiential; lasting learning is the result of experience and a contextual framework in which to interpret and make sense of the experience.

ORGANIZATION OF THE BOOK

The exercises in this book cover important issues as well as functional areas of human resource management. The term "functional" refers to those activities that managers actually do. For example, most managers recruit new employees, select employees from those recruited, train new employees, and so forth. Other exercises center around concepts and activities that are not directly performed by managers but instead are influenced by them. Managers, for example, might want to redesign the jobs that employees do in order to indirectly improve employee morale or job satisfaction.

Each exercise is independent of all others. Therefore, any combination of exercises may be used, in any order, without need for concern over continuity. It all depends on how the material for the course is organized.

Each exercise begins with Learning Objectives to be accomplished by the student as a result of completing the exercise. The Time Suggested to complete each exercise is given for the convenience of both students and teachers and is not to be interpreted as a limit for completing the exercise; rather, it is to be used for planning how class time is to be used. All of the exercises contain a set of Procedures which will guide the student through the exercise. The Introduction is followed by a Problems and Questions section (or, in some instances, role-playing situations or case studies), and, finally, a brief list of suggested readings. This uncomplicated structure will allow you to concentrate on learning rather than spending time figuring out what to do.

In summary, remember that your attitude is a very important variable in determining just how much you will benefit from this approach to learning. Consciously choose to get involved in the process. If you are asked to play a role, act out the role to the best of your ability; if you are asked to discuss a certain topic or situation, genuinely involve yourself in the discussion. By actively and enthusiastically participating in your own learning experiences you will gain a better understanding of human resource management.

ACKNOWLEDGMENTS

Special appreciation is owed to the reviewers of this 5th edition. Their opinions and criticisms have helped make this book better than it otherwise would have been. They are:

R. J. Ahlers
Florida International University

Bill Ferris
Western New England College

Herb Genfan
Ithaca College

Jeffrey Hornsby
Ball State University

Jacqueline Landau
Suffolk University

Daniel Turban
University of Missouri, Columbia

Special thanks are extended to the many students who have offered suggestions and criticisms throughout the years. There is nothing quite as useful as feedback from the end users themselves. Further appreciation is owed to the office staff members who have helped with this edition: Pam Speer and Carolyn Fowler at New Mexico State University and Naomi Wipf at the University of Hawaii/Manoa.

The West Publishing Company staff couldn't have been more cooperative and helpful. Bob Horan and Vickie Grandchamp at West Publishing were unwavering in their support and enthusiasm for the project. We couldn't have asked for two better people to help us develop this edition.

This edition is dedicated to Francie Nolan-Whatley, my wife, to Faye Kalani Whatley, my baby daughter, and to Nolan Gidley, my stepson—for all the lessons learned and lessons yet to come.—Art Whatley

The deepest appreciation to my wife Chung Nyang Kelley-Park for her support and encouragement, to the membership of the Association for Business Simulation and Experiential Learning (ABSEL) and to my friends and colleagues.—Lane Kelley

CHAPTER/EXERCISE CROSS INDEX

Numbers denote chapter in text.

	Casico, Managing Human Resources, 2/e	Schuler, Personnel and Human Resource Management	Dessler, Personnel and Human Resource Management	Mitchell, Human Resource Management and Economic Approach	Monday and Noe, Human Resource Management	Singer, Human Resource Management	Mathis and Jackson, Personnel/Human Resource Management 6/e	Werther and Davis, Human Resource and Personnel Management 3/e	Byars and Rue, Human Resource Management 3/e	Fisher, Schoenfeld and Shaw, Human Resource Management	Sherman, Bohlander and Cruden, Managing Human Resources 8/e	French, Human Resource Management 2/e
PART I — Managing the Human Resource in Organizations												
1 Corporate Cultures and the Personnel Function	2	1	1,8	1,2	1,9	1	1,2	1,2	1	1	1	1,3
2 Organization Climate	1,2	1	1,8	1,2	1,2	1,15	1,2	1	1	1	1	3,4
3 International Business and Human Resources Management	17	5	Appd*	1,2	1,2	1,17	1,22	1,2	1	1	2	4
4 Human Sexuality in the Workplace	1,2	2,5	3	1,2	3	1	1,2	2	3	1	2	5
5 An Employee Assistance Program: Alcoholism on the Job	15	13	3,9	1,2	1,2	1	1,2	2	3	9	2	20
PART II — Job Design												
6 Work Simplification	2	3	3	3	4	3	4,7	5	4	3	4	7
7 Job Descriptions	2	3	3	3	4	3	4,7	5	4	3	4	7
8 Job Design	1,4	12	3,9	3	4	3	4,7	5	4	3,9	4	7
9 Job Redesign	2	12	3	3	4	3	4,7	5	4	3,9	4	7
10 Quality Circles	1	12	3,9	3	4,9	3	4,7	5,6	4	9	4	7
PART III — Fair Employment Practices in the Workplace												
11 Landmark Cases of Title VII	3	5	2	15	3	2	5,6	3	1,2,3	4	3	6
12 Bona Fide Occupational Qualifications	3	5	2	15	3	2	5,6	3	1,2,3	4	3	
13 Application Blank	6	5	2	15	3	2	5,6	3	1,2,3	4	3	6
14 Sexual Harassment	3	5	2	15	3	2	5,6	3	1,2,3	4	3	6
15 Age Discrimination	2,3	1	2	15	3	2	5,6	3	1,2,3	4	3	6
16 Americans with Disabilities Act	16	4	2	15	3	2	5,6	3	1,2,3	4	3	
PART IV — Recruitment												
17 Recruitment	6	4	4	2	5,6	4	8	6	5,6	5	5	9
18 International Recruiting: Replacing the Overseas Manager	6,17	5	4	2	6,7	4	8	6	5,6	5	5,21	9

Human Resource Management In Action

Skill Building Experiences

FIFTH EDITION

PART 1
Managing the Human Resource in Organizations

American managers now face challenges dramatically different from the ones they have had to deal with in the past. In two short decades, our economic pre-eminence has been challenged by competitive forces around the globe. The problem is compounded by drastic changes in the American labor market: white males are exiting the labor force more quickly than any other group, while minorities, females, and immigrants are entering it at a fast rate. The challenge before all managers is to create organizations that fully utilize the potential of every employee. Chapter 1 discusses the impact of corporate culture on the individual's work behavior and suggests ways to identify the many faces of an organization's culture.

Chapter 2 introduces organization climate, a relatively new issue of importance to today's managers. Every organization behaves in ways that reflect its climate. For example, the degree of formality or informality is part of its climate. Whether the organization rewards performance or seniority is also part of the climate. So, too, is the way conflict is resolved and the degree of autonomy individuals have within the organization. Assessing an organization's climate is important since climate affects people's work behaviors. In this chapter, students first review actual data that measures the climate of an existing organization, and then decide what impact the climate has on employees.

The international dimension of human resources management was virtually non-existent a decade ago. Today, however, knowledge of the international dimension is so important that many organizations require an individual to have international experience before being promoted to upper management. Chapter 3 addresses the international dimension by asking students to determine how each HR function is changed vis-à-vis the international dimension.

Chapter 4 introduces the student to another topic that has only recently become part of the modern HR manager's responsibility. This chapter illustrates how human sexuality can lead to situations at work that create sensitive, complicated problems for the manager. Historically, problems which involved sexual relationship between employees were either

1

ignored or the employees were summarily fired. Usually the women involved were seen as the cause of the problem and therefore they received the brunt of whatever disciplinary action the company administered. The modern HR manager must respond in ways that are fair to all concerned whenever sexual problems arise in the workplace.

Substance abuse also is a rather new topic for HR managers. Chapter 5 is about alcoholism in the workplace, a frequent substance-abuse problem. How can the manager best appraise the work performance of an alcoholic? The person must be made aware that the problem is affecting work and that changes must be made or termination will result? Traditionally, alcoholics were automatically terminated. Today, however, management may have a considerable investment in the training and development of the individual and be reluctant to resort to automatic dismissal. Managers often counsel the individual to seek treatment as an alternative to termination.

In summary, Part 1 of this text covers several broad topics which are relatively new to the HR manager's domain. Each of these topics must be effectively managed if the organization is to make optimum use of its human resources.

Chapter 1

Corporate Culture and the Human Resource Function

Learning Objectives—After completion of this exercise, you should be able to:

1. Understand the concept of corporate culture.

2. Identify the concepts of corporate culture you have experienced as an employee in either a present or past organization.

3. Discuss how the corporate culture influences personnel policies, including recruitment, hiring, firing, and rewards.

4. Discuss other aspects of corporate culture including communication patterns, norms, and interaction with the work environment.

Time Suggested: Approximately one hour

Procedures

1. Read the Introduction.

2. Select an organization to be analyzed (this can be a current or past employer).

3. Use the questions at the end of the exercise to analyze the culture of the organization selected.

4. Select a teammate and share your observations, looking for similarities and differences.

This exercise was prepared by Dr. Phillis Werner, School of Nursing, University of Hawaii.

INTRODUCTION

There is much emphasis today on culture, but what is meant by the term? At its simplest, culture identifies what a stranger would need to know to survive in a specific group. At its most complicated, the term encompasses the language, values, beliefs, rituals, and norms of a group of people.

Do organizations have a culture? If one accepts either of the above definitions, then the answer must be yes. There are behaviors that individuals must know in order to survive or prosper. There is not only the language of the organization's industry, but also the language of the individual organization. The company's philosophy and mission statement should be reflected in its beliefs and expressed values. Beliefs and norms, in turn, structure personnel policies, i.e., recruitment, retention, and promotion.

Norms are unwritten laws of behavior that encompass such diverse topics as dress, communication patterns, and roles assigned to different players. If you go to a preemployment interview dressed in very casual clothes and everyone you see is dressed in a coat and tie, you may not get the job. If you insist on going straight to the president with new ideas when there is a definite chain of communication, you may not stay very long. If an unwritten rule is that executives must socialize over drinks at the end of the day (a business practice in Japan) and you go straight home, you may never be promoted to an executive level.

Rites and rituals are those events that have historical significance to the organization. The company Christmas party, awards dinner, and retirement dinners are just a few of the many rites an organization may have. It is important to attend if one is to be viewed favorably by those in power.

It is important for organizational members to understand the organization's culture if they are to be successful. How and in what manner does communication occur? Are there formal channels? Informal channels? What does top management value? Who has to be consulted to make a decision? Does business take place in meetings or on the golf course? These and many more questions must be answered in order to be successful within the organization's culture.

It also is important to assess culture in order to determine the organization's potential for success. If the beliefs and norms of the organization are inconsistent with what is necessary for success, then the corporation may need to change in order to be viable. Determining whether organizational culture is current and not outdated may be the start of initiating successful change.

Organizational culture has significance for the organization as a whole as well as for the individual within the organization. There are many additional aspects of organizational culture that are beyond the scope of this exercise. As a beginning, the purpose of this exercise is to help you identify the aspects of culture that may affect you within the organization.

QUESTIONS

Write a description of the culture exhibited by your current or a recent employer. Some of the following questions may be helpful in your assessment.

1. Is there a written statement of mission and philosophy? If so, what beliefs are reflected in it? Are the expressed beliefs consistent with what is being practiced? If not expressed, what implicit beliefs do you think the organization values?

2. Is there a dress code (written or unwritten)? What is it?

3. How does formal communication take place? Informal communication? How are decisions made? Who must be included?

4. Name at least two rituals or rites.

5. In your department, who is the official supervisor? The unofficial supervisor? How is power obtained? How is power passed on, i.e., is it inherited?

6. Are there any stories or myths that demonstrate characteristics of the organization, i.e., that executives took pay cuts rather than lay anyone off?

7. Identify at least three norms. How do they guide personnel policies, i.e., hiring or promotion, within the company? For instance, is it an unwritten policy that MBAs from Harvard are ranked above others regardless of other factors? Are family connections important?

8. Write a paragraph summarizing how you see the culture within this organization.

SUGGESTED READINGS

Deal, Terrence E., and Allan A. Kennedy. *Corporate Cultures: The Rites and Rituals of Corporate Life*, Reading, MA: Addison-Wesley, 1982, 7.

Duncan, W. Jack. "Organizational Culture: 'Getting a Fix' on an Elusive Concept," *Academy of Management Executive* 3, no. 3 (August 1989): 229–236.

Eisenberger, Robert, Peter Fasolo, and Valerie Davis-LaMastro. "Perceived Organizational Support and Employee Diligence, Commitment, and Innovation," *Journal of Applied Psychology* 75, no. 1 (1990): 51–59.

Gordon, George G. "Industry Determinants of Organizational Culture." *The Academy of Management Review* 16, no. 2 (April 1, 1991): 396.

Huey, John. "Wal-Mart—Will It Take Over the World?" *Fortune* 119, no. 3 (January 30, 1989): 52–61.

Kilmann, Ralph H., Mary J. Saxton, Roy Serpa, and Associates. *Gaining Control of the Corporate Culture*, San Francisco: Jossey-Bass, 1985, 15–16.

Labich, Kenneth. "Hot Company, Warm Culture," *Fortune* 119, no. 5 (February 27, 1989): 74–78.

Likert, Rensis, and Jane Gibson Likert. *New Ways of Managing Conflict*, New York: McGraw Hill, 1976.

Meares, Larry B. "A Model for Changing Organizational Culture," *Personnel* 63, no. 7 (July 1986): 38–46.

Mintzberg, Henry. *The Nature of Managerial Work*, New York: Harper & Row, 1973.

Naisbitt, John, and Patricia Aburdene. *Re-inventing the Corporation*, New York: Warner Books, 1985, 240.

Peters, Tom. *Thriving on Chaos: Handbook for Management Revolution*, New York: Alfred A. Knopf, 1987.

Peters, Thomas J., and Robert H. Waterman, Jr. *In Search of Excellence*, New York: Harper & Row, 1982.

Schein, Edgar H. "Are You Corporate Cultured?" *Personnel Journal* 65, no. 11 (November 1986): 82–96.

Schneider, Benjamin, ed. *Organizational Climate and Culture*, San Francisco: Jossey-Bass, 1990.

Waterman, Jr., Robert H. *The Renewal Factor: How to Best Get and Keep the Competitive Edge*, New York: Bantam Books, 1987.

Chapter 2

Organization Climate

Learning Objectives—After completion of this exercise, you should be able to:

1. Understand the effect of management's leadership behavior on organization climate.
2. Understand how to use one approach to measuring organization climate through the Job Descriptive Index.

Time Suggested: Fifty minutes

Procedures:

1. Read the Introduction.
2. Individually or in groups of three or four, read "Measuring Organizational Climate" and respond to the problems at the end.
3. Carefully study the "Summary of Employee Responses to Organizational Opinion Survey" (Figure 2–1).
4. Answer the questions at the end.

◢ INTRODUCTION

Organization culture is defined as a relatively enduring quality of the internal environment of an organization that (1) is experienced by its members, (2) influences their behavior, and (3) can be described in terms of the values of a particular set of characteristics (or attributes) of the organization.

An organization's culture conveys important assumptions and norms governing values, attitudes, and goals. It tells employees how things are done and what is important. There appears to be disagreement and confusion concerning the appropriate labeling for this construct—whether it should be organizational culture, or organizational climate. The most popular term used to describe an organization's personality is climate.

Each organization has traditions, values, customs, practices, and specializations that endure over relatively long periods of time and that together create a unique organization culture. Military services are a good example: the U.S. Marine Corps has been able to perpetuate cultural values based on an esprit de corps that makes it different from the other services. Loyalty, discipline, dedication, sacrifice, and respect are terms that describe the basis for its personnel practices. The management literature for years has described the cultures of major U.S. corporations sometimes with praise, other times with criticism. For example, see Peters's and Waterman's *In Search of Excellence* and DeLorean's vision of General Motors' culture—*On a Clear Day You Can See General Motors*.

There are five characteristics that researchers have identified as consistently describing an organization's culture:

1. Individual autonomy—includes individual responsibility, independence, and opportunities for exercising individual initiative.

2. Structure—degree of formalization, centralization, and direct supervision.

3. Reward orientation—factors of reward, promotion-achievement orientation, and emphasis on profits and sales.

4. Consideration—warmth and support provided by superiors.

5. Conflict—degree of conflict present in interpersonal relationships between peers, as well as the willingness to be honest and open about interpersonal differences.

An organization's culture is important because it is related to the organization's effectiveness and performance as well as to the satisfaction of its members. The relationship between an organization's culture and performance is complex and is still undefined. The relationship between culture and satisfaction seems clearer. Robbins has proposed that:

> Satisfaction will be highest when there is congruence between individual needs and the culture. For instance an organization whose culture would be described as low in structure, having loose supervision, and which rewards people for high achievement is likely to have more satisfied employees if those employees have a high achievement need and prefer autonomy. Our conclusion, therefore, is that job satisfaction often varies according to the employee's perception of the organization's culture.[1]

The leadership behavior of management at the top and upper levels of an organization has significant impact on the organization's climate. Behavior of top managers is mirrored, and perhaps often magnified, by successively lower levels in the organization. Managers at each successively lower level have less and less ability to exert influence on the organization climate. Organization climate provides a powerful restraint on middle- and lower-level managers in terms of the kind of management they feel free to use.

MEASURING ORGANIZATIONAL CLIMATE

Many organizations use organizational diagnostic instruments to evaluate management practices and to measure the attitudes of their employees. One of the more popular and easy to use is the Job Descriptive Index (JDI). In this exercise, you will use results from a modified version of the JDI to measure the climate within an *actual* organization.

What follows is real data based on a consultant's initial perceptions of an organization before the JDI was administered.

- The organization is in its mature stage, with little growth the last seven years in a competitive industry. It has a reputation for quality and is relatively profitable.

- Jobs are highly structured, requiring little formal education.

- Job cycles are short—the longest being less than three minutes.

- Jobs are highly repetitive, requiring a minimal amount of initiative or judgment.

- Jobs have been highly routinized and specialized.

- Because of the organization's stable growth and stable employment, there is little opportunity for advancement.

- There is no formal job-evaluation scheme. Pay adjustments are arbitrary. There is little difference between the pay of new and experienced workers.

- Communication in the organization is primarily downward, and there are no formal mechanisms to stimulate either lateral or upward communication.

- Fringe benefits are better than those offered in other firms in the industry.

- Employees are allowed to talk to one another during their two 15-minute breaks.

- Employees are encouraged to use the restrooms only during their breaks.

Figure 2–1 shows the results of using a modified version of the JDI to determine how the workers themselves felt about their job and other aspects of their work at the firm under discussion.

FIGURE 2–1   Employee Responses to Opinion Survey

Question	Strongly Agree	Agree	Disagree	Strongly Disagree
1. It lets me be creative.	12%	37%	41%	8%
2. My work is challenging.	9%	57%	31%	2%
3. My job often puts me under pressure to work too fast.	23%	39%	34%	3%
4. The work is endless.	17%	46%	29%	6%
5. I feel I could improve some of the work methods.	19%	54%	22%	3%
6. I enjoy working here.	27%	64%	8%	0%
7. I feel free to make suggestions.	9%	38%	45%	7%
8. If things are not going right I feel free to raise objections and ask why.	6%	57%	24%	9%
9. I am too tied to the assembly line.	3%	26%	61%	8%
10. My job is secure even if I speak out.	7%	50%	34%	7%
11. Management is open to suggestions and criticism.	7%	53%	28%	10%
12. It is fascinating.	13%	50%	32%	4%
13. It is routine.	14%	59%	21%	4%
14. I find it satisfying.	17%	50%	22%	9%
15. It is boring.	1%	30%	51%	16%
16. My supervisor praises good work.	17%	50%	22%	9%
17. My supervisor doesn't supervise enough.	5%	21%	56%	16%
18. My supervisor is hard to please.	8%	13%	59%	19%
19. My supervisor leaves me on my own to do my work.	14%	58%	26%	1%
20. My supervisor is around when needed.	21%	61%	10%	6%

The modified version of the JDI upon which these results were based is too brief to be used by accurate measurement. The JDI is distributed by Bowling Gree State University. Information may be obtained by writing Dr. Patricia Cain Smith, Department of Psychology, Bowling Green State University, Bowling Green, Ohio 43403.

 **PROBLEMS**

1. Based on the consultant's perceptions of the organization, describe what you think the employees' perceptions of this organization climate will be.

2. What would you predict about the effect of this organization's climate on the job satisfaction and work performance of employees?

**QUESTIONS**

1. What are some of the differences between the consultant's observations and the employees' observations as presented in the summary of employee responses in Figure 2–1?

2. How do you explain the differences between (1) the consultant's observations and (2) the employees' responses?

3. How would the climate in an organization in which you have worked compare to the one in this exercise?

4. What are the consequences of having a "poor" organization climate? Explain.

5. How would you explain the effectiveness of this organization, given its climate?

NOTE

1. Robbins, Stephen P. *Organizational Behavior Concepts, Controversies and Applications* (Englewood Cliffs, NJ: Prentice-Hall, 1983), p. 463.

SUGGESTED READINGS

Ansari, M. A., H. Baumgartel, and G. Sullivan. "The Personal Orientation—Organizational Climate Fit and Managerial Success." *Human Relations* 35 (1984): 1159–1178.

Deal, T. R., and A. E. Kennedy. *Corporate Cultures*. Reading, MA: Addison-Wesley, 1982.

Field, R. H. C., and M. A. Abelson. "Climate: A Reconceptualization and Proposed Model." *Human Relations* 35 (1982): 181–201.

Gordon, George G. "Industry Determinants of Organizational Culture." *The Academy of Management Review* 16, no. 2 (April 1, 1991): 396.

Joyce, W. F., and J. W. Slocum. "Climates in Organizations." In *Organizational Behavior*, edited by S. Kerr, 317–333. Columbus, OH: Grid Press, 1979.

Kilmann, Ralph H., et al. "Issues in Understanding and Changing Corporate Culture." *California Management Review* 28 (Winter 1986): 87–94.

O'Toole, James. "Employee Practices at the Best-Managed Companies." *California Management Review* 28 (Fall 1985): 35–66.

Peters, Thomas J., and Nancy K. Austin. *A Passion for Excellence*. New York: Random House, 1985.

Wasmer, D. J., and Gordon C. Bruner. "Using Organizational Culture to Design Internal Marketing Strategies." *Journal of Services Marketing* 5, no. 1 (Winter 1991): 35.

Chapter 3

International Human Resource Management

Learning Objectives—After completion of this exercise, you should be able to:

1. Identify the changes required in human resource functions and activities when an organization internationalizes its operations.

2. Understand the impact of the various external environmental factors on international human resource management.

Time Suggested: Fifty minutes

Procedures:

1. Read the Introduction.

2. Individually answer the questions.

3. In small groups compare your responses and write a group response to the questions.

This exercise was prepared by Dr. Elaine Bailey, College of Business Administration, University of Hawaii.

◢ INTRODUCTION

Today's international business environment requires that human resource management encompass global social and ethical issues as well as the impact of functional activities (recruitment, selection, training and compensation of expatriots) and quality of work life concerns. The international dimensions of these issues will be the focus of this exercise.

The new human resource executive no longer merely runs a staff of personnel specialists on a lower floor of the headquarters building. One of the most dramatic changes in managerial functions since financial executives rose to power in the conglomerate era of the 1960s is that today's human resource manager reports directly to the chief executive officer and plays a crucial role in making strategic business decisions. Human resource managers who deal with the people issues in an organization are rising in power and influence in organizations. The human resource management role is taking on the business-driven attributes of the traditionally more influential sales, marketing, and finance departments. This trend reflects more competitive business environments, the growing complexity of sociopolitical problems, and a change in corporate philosophy from asset management to human resource management, as well as the globalization of business.

International human resources management is becoming recognized as a subject worthy of attention in its own right. It requires a perspective that is broader and more encompassing than domestic human resources management.

All organizations face a difficult and sensitive task in carrying out key personnel decisions, including personnel planning, administration, and control; however, this task is substantially more complex for the international firm, primarily because of the more diverse environments in which international businesses operate. This exercise will deal with an overview of the complexities associated with the internationalization of the human resource management function.

 **QUESTIONS**

1. List three tasks performed by the human resource management department under each functional heading of Figure 3–1.

2. List two major issues in each of the external environments that have an impact on the human resource management function in the matrix worksheet in Figure 3–1.

3. In small groups discuss how the domestic human resource functions, tasks, and activities are altered when an organization "goes international." Summarize your discussion below. Your instructor will lead discussions over the issues.

FIGURE 3–1 External Environmental Factors That Impact International Human Resource Management

HRM Functions	Environments				
	Legal	Economic	Social	Political	Cultural
A. Recruitment and Selection Functions 1. _____ 2. _____ 3. _____					
B. Training and Development Functions 1. _____ 2. _____ 3. _____					
C. Motivation Function 1. _____ 2. _____ 3. _____					
D. Maintenance Function 1. _____ 2. _____ 3. _____					

◢ SUGGESTED READINGS

Brislin, R. *Cross-Cultural Encounters: Face-to-Face Interaction*. Elmsford, NY: Pergamon, 1981.

Brislin, R., K. Cushner, C. Cherrie, and M. Young. *Intercultural Interactions: A Practical Guide*. Beverly Hills, CA: Sage, 1986.

Dowling, P. J., and R. S. Schuler. *International Dimensions of Human Resource Management*. Boston, MA: PWS-Kent Publishing Co., 1990.

Fiedler, F., T. Mitchell, and H. Triandis. "The Culture Assimilator: An Approach to Cross-Cultural Training." *Journal of Applied Psychology* 55 (1971): 95–102.

Hofstede, G. *Culture's Consequences: International Differences in Work-Related Values*. Beverly Hills, CA: Sage, 1980.

Landis, D., and R. Brislin (Eds.). *Handbook of Intercultural Training* (Vols. 1–4). Elmsford, NY: Pergamon, 1983.

Lanier, A. "Selecting and Preparing Personnel for Overseas Transfers." *Personnel Journal* 58, no. 3 (1979): 160–163.

Ramsey, S., and J. Birk. "Preparation of North America for Interaction with Japanese: Considerations of Language and Communication Style." In D. Landis and R. Brislin (Eds.), *Handbook of Intercultural Training: Vol. 3, Area Studies in Intercultural Training*, 227–259. Elmsford, NY: Pergamon, 1983.

Chapter 4

Human Sexuality in the Workplace

Learning Objectives—After completion of this exercise, you should be able to:

1. Understand the complexity of human sexuality as a factor of influence in the workplace.

2. Examine your own values and beliefs about the expression of sexuality in the workplace.

Time Suggested: One and one-half hours

Procedures:

1. Read the Introduction.

2. Divide the class into sexually mixed groups of five members.

3. Read "The Promotion."

4. Answer the questions at the end of the exercise. For question 2, each group is to reach consensus in ranking the five characters in "The Promotion" from (1) "least objectionable" to (5) "most objectionable" and to reach consensus on what Carol should do. Write a rationale for each ranking decision. The rationale should be expressed in terms of the human sexuality concepts described in the first part of the exercise.

5. A spokesperson from each group will report its rankings and associated rationale to the class as a whole.

6. The instructor will lead a discussion based on group reports.

This exercise was authored by Janet Lee Mills, Ph.D., Department of Human Relations, University of Oklahoma. It is used here, in modified form, with the permission of Dr. Mills.

INTRODUCTION

A DEFINITION OF HUMAN SEXUALITY

Human sexuality as a factor of influence in the workplace is a topic that has received relatively little attention in the literature on human resource management. There is a widespread assumption that the expression of human sexuality in the workplace is inappropriate; hence, people tend to deny, excuse, ignore, or moralize those dynamics or issues involving human sexuality. The position taken here is that the expression of human sexuality, as defined by Gochros,[1] is inevitable in organizations, and that an understanding of sexual dynamics is useful in explaining particular aspects of interpersonal and organizational behavior. The assumption that sexuality is something people can put aside at work is challenged by a growing awareness that sexual needs, attractions, intimacy, and continuing identity development are integral and inevitable aspects of interpersonal relations for men and women who work together.

Gochros points out that human sexuality is influenced by anatomical, physiological, psychological, and cultural factors, along with age, health, gender, physical condition, personality, socioeconomic reference groups, and legal restrictions. He stresses that sexual functioning must be viewed relative to the specific social environment in which it exists. Work organizations constitute one such social environment. He defines human sexuality in terms of the following five interrelated aspects: sensuality, intimacy, sexual identity, sexualization and reproduction.

1. *Sensuality* refers to the psychological and physiological enjoyment of one's body, and often a partner's body, and may or may not include genital contact and orgasmic release. Sensuality refers to the need for physical touching and stroking, the need for exchange of physical affection, and the capacity for the enjoyment of the physical senses, particularly as they spark fantasy and memory. Sensuality can be overt, as in the office affair, or covert, as in sexual fantasy or unconscious approach-avoidance behavior.

2. *Intimacy* is defined as the capacity for and expression of openness, closeness, and interdependency with another person. Intimacy tends to reduce feelings of loneliness and anomie and is manifested behaviorally by verbal expressions of liking, appreciation, support, concern, interest, and encouragement. In organizations, intimacy frequently develops between people as a result of proximity and role relatedness. Intimacy often occurs in relationships such as mentor and protégé, boss and secretary, team members who work closely over long periods of time, and partners who venture risks together, especially risks involving interpersonal trust.

3. *Sexual identity* refers to (1) biological sexuality in terms of anatomical and endocrine characteristics, (2) gender identity or sexual self-image in terms of culturally prescribed attitudes and behaviors, and (3) sexual object choice, including heterosexual and homosexual preference possibilities. The issue of gender identity has become increasingly prominent due to the entry of women into many roles traditionally held only by men. For example, the female manager and her male subordinate are in reversed traditional roles; the self-image of either person might

be threatened since both have likely been socialized to think, feel, and behave in the other's role. Further, the concept of *androgyny* is influencing contemporary thought. Androgyny refers to the psychological and behavioral integration of the traditional masculine/feminine polarities into one person, male or female, who exhibits attitudes and behaviors with situational flexibility and without the constraints of narrowly defined femininity or masculinity.

4. *Sexualization* refers to the use of sexual behavior to influence the attitudes, feelings, or behaviors of other persons. Sexual activity has long been offered or withheld to barter, manipulate, dominate, humiliate, or reward a partner. In organizations, people involved in sexual liaisons may exchange important information along with sexual favors, especially when they hold positions in different departments or at different hierarchical levels. Romantic or marital relationships between people in the same department or team can also work to secure power, threaten others' positions, and introduce competitive undertones that reshape the sociometry of the work group.

5. *Reproduction* refers to the attitudes people hold and the behaviors they engage in to conceive and bear children or to prevent the conception or birth of children. Included are self-expectations, sex role expectations, and the sanctions and taboos of religious, legal, and ethnic groups. In organizations, women between the ages of twenty and forty are frequently questioned about the role conflict inherent in combining family and career. Likewise, men who do not marry and have families are frequently regarded with suspicion. Other issues include maternity and paternity leaves, and absenteeism related to child care.

   Each of these five aspects of human sexuality may be used to generate an awareness of the complexity, inevitability, and pervasiveness of human sexuality as a factor of influence in work organizations. Although these aspects of human sexuality are identified separately for conceptual purposes, they are dynamically interrelated in the ongoing lives of individuals.

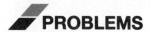 **PROBLEMS**

THE PROMOTION

Carol L. is a bright, ambitious MBA who has set her sights on a managerial career. She is eager to climb the ladder of success and willing to work very hard for her promotions. Carol realizes she works in a highly competitive organization and that she is in a field traditionally dominated by men. She observes that many men and women get stuck on various rungs of the corporate ladder and that only one woman in the company has made it into top management. Carol knows that many tests of her ability and loyalty are to come; she is eager to meet them.

One particular obstacle to Carol's career is her exclusion from some informal networks in the organization. Another obstacle Carol notices is that while many men seem to have special sponsors or mentors who teach them the ropes and provide them inside information, she has no such affiliation. Determined, Carol attends every seminar she can and lunches regularly with her peers, most of whom are men. Over time, Carol has come to trust a coworker named Lynn T.; the two share confidences frequently and provide valuable feedback to each other on work-related matters. Carol values Lynn as a trusted colleague and a friend.

Bob J., Carol's present boss, has his sights set on top management too. In his mid-forties, Bob has made many friends and a few enemies in the corporation. At the upper echelon of middle management, Bob is reexamining his goals and values due to personal crises: His wife is suing him for divorce, claiming he has neglected her and the children in his "workaholic pursuit of a career." Lonely, confused, and seeking comfort for himself, Bob seeks a confidant, someone who will provide a supportive and patient listening ear. He gravitates toward Carol to fill this role. Only a year ago, Bob had felt ambivalent about hiring a woman who would likely "breed and leave." In his current depression, Bob alternately throws himself relentlessly into his work (at which time Carol's loyalty is in evidence by her overtime efforts) or dawdles away his time preoccupied with personal problems and the search for "some values of substance" (at which time Carol and Lynn tend to cover for Bob). On one such occasion when Bob returned from lunch less than sober, Carol volunteered to attend a meeting in his place.

John G., one of the company's several vice-presidents, took an immediate interest in Carol when he met her at the meeting she attended in place of Bob. He saw her as both a capable middle manager and a lovely woman. Their acquaintance grew, and Carol picked up a great deal of informal knowledge about the corporation from John's casual conversations. She learned, among other things, that her boss, Bob J., had locked horns with John G. on an issue some years ago, and that the two were, for all practical purposes, unfriendly. She also learned that Bob's unsteady performance was under close scrutiny and that a parallel transfer to a regional office was imminent; he was about to be farmed out. John's advances to Carol continued and became romantic. No other man was in the picture for Carol, and although she would have preferred to keep her relationship with John a friendly business one, she yielded to her own sexual needs and John's steady pursuit. They became lovers.

Eventually, Carol confided in Lynn, describing both the romance and the wealth of informal knowledge she was gaining. She was not prepared for Lynn's abrupt response: "I don't know what to say. Frankly, I wish it were me." Carol was taken aback, and felt very uneasy around Lynn from then on. As the days passed, a distance seemed to grow between them.

Within a week, Bob J. called Carol into his office and confronted her with the "rumor" he had heard—that she was sleeping with at least one of the company's vice-presidents. He asked her to verify the rumor or deny it. Under pressure, Carol took the stance that her private life was her own. Bob J. said that he understood that as an admission of guilt, and fired Carol with one month's notice. Her appeal to his sense of fairness was of no avail; he answered that her involvement was a serious breach of loyalty that damaged her credibility entirely.

Stunned, Carol sought the support of her lover, John G., who said he was helpless to do anything on her behalf under the circumstances. Nonetheless, he promised continuing emotional support and said he hoped this wouldn't interfere with their relationship. Her former friend and confidante, Lynn, suggested she leave the company quietly and not create a public stir through affirmative action litigation. Her lawyer, although willing to take on the case, advised her similarly: "The best time to find a job is while you have one." Carol's alternatives seemed bleak indeed when Joe W., director of another division in the corporation, heard about the incident and called her to his office.

Joe W. began by briefing Carol on his understanding of recent events, indicating that he was aware of her good work and that he felt her dismissal was unreasonable. He reported that Bob J.'s transfer was now fact and that his replacement—Lynn T.—had been appointed, and added that she, Carol, had been among those considered for the position before her dismissal. Joe shook his head sadly and said he had been an advocate of "free sex" for years. He then told Carol that he was willing to create a position for her in his office in light of her track record, a position equivalent in rank to her present position. He suggested that a couple years of experience in his division would greatly enhance her career.

Carol left Joe W.'s office with mixed feelings. She felt a rapport with Joe and sensed they would get along, but she wasn't sure whether or not to trust his warmth and generosity. She wondered whether or not there was innuendo in his offer, whether or not she was being placated by the organization in some way, whether or not she could discern such, and whether or not it even mattered.

QUESTIONS

1. What would you do if you were Carol? Explain your answer in terms of Gochros's definition of human sexuality.

2. Rank in order the following characters from (1) least objectionable to (5) most objectionable based on their professional behavior. Explain your ranking in terms of Cochros's definition of human sexuality.

    _____ Carol L. (middle manager)

    _____ Lynn T. (colleague and friend)

    _____ Bob J. (Carol and Lynn's boss)

    _____ John G. (vice-president and lover)

    _____ Joe W. (division director)

    a. Rationale for first ranking:

    b. Rationale for second ranking:

c. Rationale for third ranking:

d. Rationale for fourth ranking:

e. Rationale for fifth ranking:

3. Carol was in need of a "mentor." Would it be useful for management to establish a mentoring program for women and minority employees, who are often excluded from the informal mentoring that occurs between white males? Explain your answer.

4. When would "affairs" within an organization be grounds for termination? When wouldn't they be grounds for termination?

Grounds for termination:

No grounds for termination:

NOTE

1. Harvey Gochros, "Human Sexuality," in *Encyclopedia of Social Work*, 17th ed., vol. 1 (New York: National Association of Social Workers, Inc., 1977).

SUGGESTED READINGS

Anderson, Carolyn I., and Phillip L. Hunsaker, "Why There's Romancing at the Office and Why It's Everybody's Problem." *Personnel* 62 (February 1985): 56–63.

Auerbach, S. "How to Deal With Office Affairs." *Computer Decisions* 14 (February 1982): 222–223.

Collins, E. G. "Managers and Lovers." *Harvard Business Review* 61 (May 1983): 71–96.

Estrich, Susan. "Sex at Work." *Stanford Law Review* 43, no. 4 (April 1, 1991): 813.

Halverson, Claire. "Developing Effective Teams to Work on Sex Equity Issues." *Equity & Excellence: The University of Massachusetts* 24, no. 4 (Summer 1990): 51.

Harrison, Ron, and Roger Lee. "Love at Work." *Personnel Management* (January 1986): 20–24.

Josefowitz, Natasha. "Sexual Relationships at Work: Attraction, Transference, Coercion or Strategy." *The Personnel Administrator* 27, no. 3 (March 1982): 91–96.

Obdyke, Louis K. "Employee Intoxication and Employers' Liability." *Personnel Administrator* 31 (February 1986): 109–114.

Rood, Raymond P., and Brenda L. Meneley. "Serious Play at Work." *Personnel Journal* 70, no. 1 (January 1, 1991): 90.

Westhoff, Leslie Aldridge. "What to Do about Corporate Romance." *Management Review* (February 1986): 50–55.

Chapter 5

An Employee Assistance Program: Alcoholism on the Job

Learning Objectives—After completion of this exercise, you should be able to:

1. Describe the impact of alcoholism on job performance.

2. Explore different approaches to handling the delicate alcoholic subordinate reprimand.

Time Suggested: One hour

Procedures:

1. After reading the Introduction, form groups of three to five.

2. Individually, carefully read the four interview approaches (Figure 5–1) and both role descriptions. Without consulting other members of your group, think about how best to deal with this situation.

3. With your group, select one member to play the supervisor role and one person to play the alcoholic subordinate role.

4. The "supervisor" will have fifteen minutes to confront the "subordinate" regarding his drinking problem. The other members will act as observers.

5. With your group, discuss the interview. Answer the questions at the end of the exercise.

INTRODUCTION

ALCOHOLISM ON THE JOB

The popular view of an alcoholic is a male drunk on skid row, but more than 95 percent of all alcoholics are not in this group. Many are employed and have families. Alcoholism has no respect for age, sex, or position.

Alcohol alone drains an estimated $19.6 billion from our economy in lost productivity per year.[1] The National Council on Alcoholism estimates that:

1. One in thirteen Americans are alcoholics.

2. The alcoholic employee is absent two to four times more often than the nonalcoholic.

3. On-the-job accidents for alcoholic employees are two to four times more frequent than for nonalcoholics.

4. Sickness and accident benefits paid to alcoholic employees are three times greater than those paid to nonalcoholic employees.[2]

A five-year General Motors study revealed that alcohol-related problems drain off 70 percent of a company's sickness and accident benefits.

The employee whose alcoholic habit has adversely affected his/her performance in the workplace is no longer considered to have a "personal" problem which must be solved on his/her own. An employee's alcohol problem becomes the problem of the organization and must be dealt with appropriately. Corrective action must be taken to eliminate deficiencies in employee performance by those who are in the best position to do something about them—the supervisor and the troubled subordinate. Currently, about one-third of the largest companies in the United States have alcoholism control programs, while smaller companies send alcoholics to treatment programs and consultants. Drug abuse in the workplace is no less of a problem than alcohol abuse. Estimates are that in 1983 alone drug abuse cost the country $26 billion. Alcoholism costs more than $40 billion annually.

ROLE PLAY

SUPERVISOR (ED ANDERSON)

You have recently arrived to take over as branch manager for a company that bids for large government and commercial contracts. Your evaluation as branch manager is based directly on your success at winning contracts. Two months after taking over, it becomes apparent to you that your highly regarded marketing manager may have an alcohol problem. A recent incident prompts you to call Jim Smith to your office.

SUBORDINATE (JIM SMITH)

You are one of five functional managers reporting to Ed Anderson. After nineteen years with the company, the past ten years as marketing manager of this branch, your consistent performance above quota has resulted in a good companywide reputation and numerous performance awards.

After years of long lunches, late arrivals, and early departures, you find yourself with a new branch manager who appears to be less complacent than his predecessor was about your erratic work habits. Today's interview has been precipitated by the recent loss of a $12 million contract which, according to your sales representatives, was in the bag before going to you for final approval.

> *Note:* It is usually the case that alcoholics refuse to recognize their problem as "alcoholism." Accordingly, they will refuse to acknowledge the problem and may develop facility in attributing the symptoms to some other condition. Alcoholics are typically expert "con artists."

FIGURE 5–1   Cause-and-Effect Relations in Four Types of Appraisal Interviews

Type of Interview:	Tell	Tell and Sell	Tell and Listen	Problem-Solving
Role of Interviewer:	*Judge*	*Judge*	*Judge*	*Helper*
Objective	To communicate evaluation. To persuade employee to improve.	To communicate evaluation. To persuade employee to improve.	To communicate evaluation. To release defensive feelings.	To stimulate growth and development in employee.
Assumptions	Employee does not want to admit problem.	Employee desires to correct weaknesses if he or she knows them.	People will change if defensive feelings are removed.	Growth can occur without correcting faults. Discussing job problems leads to improved performance.
Reactions	Defensive behavior suppressed. Employee feels warned but not reprimanded.	Defensive behavior suppressed. Attempts to to cover	Defensive behavior expressed. Employee feels accepted.	Problem-solving behavior.
Skills	Restraint.	Salesmanship. Patience.	Listening and reflecting feelings. Summarizing.	Listening and reflecting feelings. Reflecting ideas. Using exploratory questions. Summarizing.
Attitude	Discussion is nonproductive.	People profit from criticism and appreciate help.	One can respect the feelings of others if one understands them.	Discussion develops new ideas and mutual interest.

▰▰ **FIGURE 5–1   Cause-and-Effect Relations in Four Types of Appraisal Interviews—(continued)**

Type of Interview:	Tell	Tell and Sell	Tell and Listen	Problem-Solving
Role of Interviewer:	Judge	Judge	Judge	Helper
Motivation	Credit employee as a responsible adult.	Use of positive or negative incentive or both. (Extrinsic in that motivation is added to the job itself.)	Resistance to change reduced. Positive incentive. (Extrinsic and some intrinsic motivation.)	Increased freedom. Increased responsibility. (Intrinsic motivation in that interest is inherent in the task.)
Gains	Identification of *effects* (rather than cause) cannot be denied by employee.	Success most probable when employee respects interviewer.	Develops favorable attitude toward superior, which increases probability of success.	Almost assured of improvement in some respects.
Risk	Employee continues adverse performance.	Loss of loyalty, inhibition of independent judgment. Face-saving problems created.	Need for change may not be developed.	Employee may lack ideas. Change may be other than what superior had in mind.
Values	Opportunity for employee excuses minimized.	Perpetuates existing practices and values.	Permits interviewer to change his/her view in the light of employee's responses. Some upward communication.	Both learn since experience and views are pooled. Change is facilitated.

Source: Reproduced by permission from Norman R. F. Maier, *The Appraisal Interview: Three Basic Approaches*, San Diego, CA: University Associates, Inc., 1976.

QUESTIONS

1. Characterize and evaluate the "supervisor's" approach. What was correctly done? What was incorrectly done?

2. What should a company include in its written policy regarding alcoholism?

3. Should "white collar" alcoholics be treated differently from "blue collar" alcoholics? Why or why not?

4. Will the working relationship between Anderson and Smith be jeopardized by this encounter?

NOTES

1. Earl Selby and Miriam Selby, "Business' Battle against Booze," *Reader's Digest* 119 (September 1981): 107–110.

2. Joseph J. Walker, "Supervising the Alcoholic," *Supervisory Management* 23 (November 1976): 26–32.

SUGGESTED READINGS

Angarola, Robert T. "Drug Testing in the Workplace: Is It Legal?" *Personnel Administrator* 30 (September 1985): 79–89.

Madonia, J. F. "Managerial Responses to Alcohol and Drug Abuse among Employees." *Personnel Administrator* (June 1984): 134–139.

Magnuson, John. "Stress Management/Alcoholism and the Work Place." *Journal of Property Management* 55, no. 3 (May 1, 1990): 24.

Marmo, Michael. "Arbitrators View Alcoholic Employees: Discipline or Rehabilitation?" *Arbitration Journal* 37, no. 1 (March 1982): 17–26.

Masi, Dale A. *Designing Employee Assistance Programs.* Saranac Lake, NY: AMACOM, 1985.

Small, Emma. "Alcoholism: Message in a Bottle." *Social Work Today* 22, no. 31 (April 18, 1991): 19.

Wells, P. A., and M. Amano. "Alcoholism and Drug Abuse in the Workforce." *Management World* 9 (October 1980): 14–16.

PART 2
Job Design

One of the most interesting and fruitful topics for students of human resources management to explore is job design. It is rich with concepts for improving the performance and satisfaction of people at work. Chapter 6, the first exercise in this section, discusses a job design concept that has been used widely since the late 1800s. Work simplification, scientific management, or time and motion study are some of the names used for the concept.

When work simplification was first applied, it led to higher wages for employees and greater profitability for employers. However, as employees became better educated and more affluent, work simplification as a job design strategy became less effective. This exercise exposes the student to the strengths and weaknesses of work simplification.

Chapter 7 introduces the student to one of the most important concepts in human resources management, namely, the job description. A job description is nothing more than a summary of the responsibilities and duties of a job. Yet, this information is used for many other important human resource activities including job design, recruitment, selection, training, performance evaluation, and compensation. From this exercise, students will begin to see the value of job descriptions in human resources management.

In Chapter 8 the student is introduced to several new approaches to job design and ways in which each approach can be applied in the workplace. The important lesson to be learned from this exercise is that managers do have control, however small, over the design of the work done by employees. If the workplace is designed so as to tap the abilities, motivations, and interests of the workers, greater performance and satisfaction are likely to occur.

Human resources managers often have to redesign jobs to meet the expectations and abilities of the people doing those jobs. Chapter 9 covers this activity, which is known as job redesign. In this chapter, students will diagnose a job and then use a job redesign strategy (called the job diagnostic model) to make changes in the job. Because human resources managers are more likely to have old jobs to redesign than new jobs to design, the job diagnostic model is an important tool for human resources managers.

The final exercise in this section, Chapter 10, introduces another approach to designing work—the use of quality circles. Although an individual's job may not be changed substantially by quality circles, the way the person interacts with peers, solves work-related problems, communicates with management, and assumes responsibility for quality of work is affected through the use of quality circles. In this exercise, the student examines the work performed by the group (quality circle) and begins to learn the advantages of group work over individual work when it comes to identifying and solving work-related problems.

In summary, Part 2 introduces the student to important concepts that can be used to help the modern human resources manager to become successful at managing people through the design of work.

Chapter **6**

Work Simplification

Learning Objectives—After completion of this exercise, you should be able to:

1. Apply the principles of work simplification to the design of jobs.

2. Describe the limitations of work simplification for management in the 1990s.

3. Understand the relationship between jobs designed by work simplification and the characteristics of workers suited for those jobs.

Time Suggested: Forty-five minutes

Procedures:

1. Read the Introduction.

2. Complete the Problems and Questions sections.

◢ INTRODUCTION

The division of labor, or work simplification, is an integral part of industrial society. It was first acclaimed by Adam Smith in his *Wealth of Nations*. In fact, the first paragraph of his first chapter reads as follows:

> The greatest improvement in the productive powers of Labour, and the greater part of the skill, dexterity and judgment with which it is anywhere directed, or applied, seems to have been the effects of the division of Labour.[1]

The idea behind the division of labor is to break down a complex job into several simpler jobs. Smith used the manufacture of pins as an example. Instead of one individual making the entire pin, the process is broken down into several tasks—one person draws the wire, one straightens it, one cuts it, one points it, and so on.

Simplifying jobs received even greater popularity at the turn of this century when Frank Gilbreth classified hand motions into seventeen "Therbligs" (Gilbreth spelled backward). Some of these Therbligs are search, select, grasp, transport empty and loaded, hold, release, and position.

Perhaps the most famous of all the advocates of work simplification is Frederick W. Taylor. Writing at about the same time as Gilbreth, Taylor proposed the following general steps for simplifying a job:

1. Study the exact series of elementary operations or motions . . . in doing the work.

2. Study with a stopwatch the time required to make each of these elementary movements and then select the quickest way of doing each element of the work.

3. Eliminate all false movements, slow movements, and useless movements.

4. Collect into one series the quickest and best movements.[2]

Smith, Gilbreth, and Taylor all reflect a school of management thinking known as scientific management. Carefully read each principle that follows, keeping in mind that changing social values and increasing education levels have caused a decline in the popularity these principles held during the times of Smith, Gilbreth, and Taylor. They constitute only a small aspect of managing people at work today.

WORK SIMPLIFICATION PRINCIPLES

I.   *Rules for Minimizing Human Movements.* Never do a job the hard way if there is an easier way.

  1. Don't do jobs by hand if machines can do them.

  2. Use the fewest motions possible. Move as little of the body as is necessary to do the job; in fact, move only the fingers if finger motion will do.

II. *Rules for Making the Best Use of Men.* A whole man produces more than does part of a man.

  3. Use two hands but avoid using hands purely as holding devices. Idle hands do no work. If both are not busy, redistribute the work between them. The man won't do twice as much work as with one hand but he is likely to do half as much more.

  4. Study and analyze all hesitations and short delays within jobs, and eliminate them when possible.

  5. Where unavoidable delays occur, give men other work to let them keep working.

  6. The time an expert takes is a possible time for everyone. Try to get all men to do as well.

III. *Rules for Saving Energy.* Tiring movements waste energy.

  7. Transfer all heavy lifting to mechanical lifting devices.

  8. Assign all work to the body member best suited for it, as in typing; don't do it all with the little fingers.

  9. On fatiguing jobs, allow rest periods. The heavier the task, the more necessary are frequent short rest periods. Many short rest periods are better than a few long rest periods.

  10. On monotonous jobs, provide an occasional break. Monotony and fatigue are related.

IV. *Rules for Placing Men.* Use manpower to its best advantage, considering the jobs to be filled and the men available.

  11. Where there are several workers doing the same job day after day, cut the job up into small tasks and let each worker specialize. Each will acquire greater proficiency and the group will produce more.

  12. Put workers on jobs well suited to them and place only those suited on the job. Put women on jobs where they are better than men; usually light, fast jobs requiring finger dexterity. Put men on men's jobs.

13. Never use high-priced labor on low-priced work even if the lower-priced work is but a small part of a high-priced man's job.[3]

WORK SIMPLIFICATION IN THE 1990S

Is the theory behind work-simplification principles as relevant today as it was at the turn of the century? When it originated, scientific management, along with its central concept, work simplification, was viewed as a revolutionary approach to managing people. When work-simplification principles were applied, productivity soared and employee morale and wages increased dramatically. It was felt that any manager could improve the productivity and economic welfare of his or her employees if scientific management was put into practice.

But what about today? Several events have occurred to make scientific management and work simplification principles outdated. First, workers at the turn of the century had an average educational level of less than junior high school, whereas the average workers of today have more than a high school education. Second, the turn of the century was an economically unstable time with high unemployment rates and low standards of living. People were willing to take any kind of job, even if it was monotonous or repetitive. They needed to work to earn money simply to survive.[4]

Today, however, credit cards and savings accounts can keep us alive for months on end. Having been raised in an affluent society where not hunger but obesity poses a national health problem, the modern worker tends to resent monotonous and repetitive jobs. Unlike our poverty-stricken predecessors, the modern workers of today are less willing to continue for very long in undesirable jobs. Instead, what is expected is a challenging job, one that matches the educational level of the worker. What is expected is responsibility and control over the job rather than having the job duties assigned by a scientific management "efficiency" expert.

PROBLEMS

JOB DESCRIPTION

Keypunch operator (clerical), card-punch operator; printing-card punch operator, printing-punch operator. Operates alphabetic and numeric keypunch machine, similar in operation to electric typewriter, to transcribe data from source material onto punchcards, paper or magnetic tape, or magnetic cards, and to record accounting or statistical data for subsequent processing by automatic or electronic data processing equipment:

- Attaches skip bar to machine and previously punched program card around machine drum to control duplication and spacing of constant data.

- Loads machine with decks of tabulating punchcards, paper or magnetic tape, or magnetic cards.

- Moves switches and presses keys to select automatic or manual duplication and spacing, select alphabetic or numeric punching, and transfer cards or tape through machine stations.

- Presses keys to transcribe new data in prescribed sequence from source material into perforations on card, or as magnetic impulses on specified locations on tape or card.

- Inserts previously processed card into card gauge to verify registration of punches.

- Observes machine to detect faulty feeding, positioning, ejecting, duplicating, skipping, punching, or other mechanical malfunctions and notifies supervisors.

- Removes jammed cards, using prying knife.

- May tend machines that automatically sort, merge, or match punchcards into specified groups.

- May verify accuracy of data by using verifying machine.

- May perform general typing tasks.

ASSESSMENT OF MINIMUM HUMAN TRAIT REQUIREMENTS

Given the job description just presented, which of the following human traits are necessary for completing the job requirements?

Physical Requirements	*Necessary?*	*If "Yes," to What Extent?*
Climbing	Yes _____ No _____	Comments _____ _____
Color discrimination	Yes _____ No _____	Comments _____ _____
Eye-hand coordination	Yes _____ No _____	Comments _____ _____
Finger dexterity	Yes _____ No _____	Comments _____ _____
Hand dexterity	Yes _____ No _____	Comments _____ _____
Kneeling	Yes _____ No _____	Comments _____ _____
Lifting	Yes _____ No _____	Comments _____ _____
Sitting	Yes _____ No _____	Comments _____ _____
Standing	Yes _____ No _____	Comments _____ _____
Stooping	Yes _____ No _____	Comments _____ _____
Walking	Yes _____ No _____	Comments _____ _____

Intelligence Requirements	*Necessary?*	*If "Yes," to What Extent?*
Clerical skills (sorting, classifying, etc.	Yes _____ No _____	Comments _____
Creativity	Yes _____ No _____	Comments _____
Form perception	Yes _____ No _____	Comments _____
Quantitative skills	Yes _____ No _____	Comments _____
Spatial relations	Yes _____ No _____	Comments _____
Verbal skills	Yes _____ No _____	Comments _____

What general educational achievement level will be necessary to do this job?

What special education will be necessary to do this job?

What writing skills will be necessary to do this job?

Temperament Requirements	*Necessary?*	*If "Yes," to What Extent?*
Aggressive	Yes _____ No _____	Comments _____ _____
Ambitious	Yes _____ No _____	Comments _____ _____
Assertive	Yes _____ No _____	Comments _____ _____
Cheerful	Yes _____ No _____	Comments _____ _____
Confident	Yes _____ No _____	Comments _____ _____
Decisive	Yes _____ No _____	Comments _____ _____
Organized	Yes _____ No _____	Comments _____ _____
Patient	Yes _____ No _____	Comments _____ _____
Responsible	Yes _____ No _____	Comments _____ _____
Sociable	Yes _____ No _____	Comments _____ _____
Trustworthy	Yes _____ No _____	Comments _____ _____

 **QUESTIONS**

1. The educational achievement level of U.S. workers reflects a belief in the accessibility of higher education for most individuals. What are the implications of this trend for managers who are responsible for supervising people performing highly simplified jobs? Explain your answer.

2. For work simplification to be successful, human beings must behave according to certain assumptions. Discuss within your group what some of these assumptions might be. Summarize your discussion here.

3. Review Work Simplification Principle no. 12. Discuss within your group the relevance of this principle for today's organizations. Summarize your discussion here.

4. Describe the job specifications for your current job or a previous job you have held.

 **NOTES**

1. Adam Smith, *The Wealth of Nations* (New York: Random House, 1937), 3.

2. Frederick Winslow Taylor. *The Principles of Scientific Management* (New York: Harper and Row, 1947), 117.

3. Franklin Moore. *Production Management*, 6th ed. (Homewood, IL: Richard D. Irwin, 1973), 313–314.

4. *Work in America*, a Report of a Special Task Force to the Secretary of Health, Education, and Welfare (Cambridge, MA: MIT Press, 1973), 18–19.

SUGGESTED READINGS

Hitt, M. A., and D. R. Cash. "Task Technology, Individual Differences, and Job Satisfaction." *Review of Business and Economic Research* 17 (Winter 1982): 28–36.

Levine, E. L., R. A. Ash, H. Hall, and F. Sistrunk. "Evaluation of Job Analysis Methods by Experienced Job Analysts." *Academy of Management Journal* 26, no. 2 (1983): 339–348.

Mount, Michael K. "The Big Five Personality Dimensions and Job Performance: A Meta-Analysis." *Personnel Psychology* 44, no. 1 (Spring 1991): 1.

Taylor, F. W. *The Principles of Scientific Management*. New York: Harper & Row, 1947. Originally published in 1911.

Vasey, Joseph. "Job Analysis: The Composition of SME Samples." *Personnel Psychology* 44, no. 1 (Spring 1991): 27.

Chapter 7

Job Descriptions

Learning Objectives—After completion of this exercise, you should be able to:

1. Understand the development and use of job descriptions.

2. Understand how job descriptions relate to other aspects of human resources management; in particular, recruitment and selection.

3. Understand the linkage between the job description and the organization's culture.

Time Suggested: Forty-five minutes

Procedures:

1. Read the sections "Uses of job descriptions" and "Required Terms."

2. Answer the questions in Project 1.

3. Read Project 2's job description from the Dade Yacht Club and answer the questions pertaining to the manager's job description.

◢ USES OF JOB DESCRIPTIONS

The *job description* is a summary of the duties and responsibilities of a job. Especially in larger organizations where the person responsible for recruiting and selection cannot be familiar with all the organization's jobs, the accuracy and completeness of job descriptions become very important. Even in small organizations, job descriptions are important because they contribute to an understanding of the role of the job in the organization and its relative position.

The uses of a job description include:

1. Evaluation. In defining the duties and responsibilities, it also defines the required competence. The competencies can become standards for employee evaluation.

2. Recruitment. By analyzing the duties and responsibilities, more accurate, valid ads can be created.

3. Selection. The job description provides the information needed by the interviewer to assess the qualifications of applicants. For example, the position might require the understanding and preparation of monthly budgets. The job description should reflect this and the applicants' knowledge of budgets should be ascertained.

4. Promotion and transfer. When considering the qualifications necessary for the vacant positions and a match between other positions in the organization, an analysis and comparison of job descriptions can provide useful information.

5. Workforce planning. An inventory of present job descriptions can be useful information for determining future personnel requirements.

REQUIRED TERMS

- *Job analysis*. The process of gathering information about the duties and responsibilities of a job.

- *Job*. A group of positions that are the same in respect to their major or significant tasks.

- *Task*. A discrete unit of work performed; a logical, necessary step required in a job. The task statement consists of two elements—an action verb and an indication of what is acted on, such as "*prepare* the monthly budget."

- *Job description*. A summary of the job's duties and responsibilities. It often includes the job title, to whom the holder reports, and who reports to the holder. It can serve a number of important uses such as workforce planning, recruiting, selection, training, transfers, promotion, and evaluation. The job description's accuracy and completeness is very important.

- *Job specification*. The job specification defines the minimum human traits required to perform the job, which might include mental (educational, intellect, etc.), physical (standing, sitting, etc.), and behavioral elements.

 **PROJECT 1**

Have your professor bring a recent faculty recruitment ad from her/his department. What does it state? Does it include the duties and responsibilities that you feel are necessary for this position?

How does the ad reflect the values of the organization's culture?

PROJECT 2

You are on the search committee for the Dade Yacht Club and have been given the job description shown in Figure 7–1. You are reviewing the description in order to determine the *job specifications*—the minimum human qualifications necessary to perform the job.

1. Write a job specification given the information in the job description.

2. How does this job description reflect the values of this organization?

FIGURE 7–1   Sample Job Description

DADE YACHT CLUB
Duties and Responsibilities of Club Manager

The DYC Club Manager has full responsibility for the operation and maintenance of the club facilities, working under the direction of the Board of Directors and in cooperation with the Operations Committee of which he is a member. He will report directly to and receive guidance from the Commodore or such other representative of the Board of Directors as may be designated from time to time.

Although the Manager must maintain an operating staff, the Dade Yacht Club is essentially a one-man operation. The Manager is expected to oversee all operations, personally. He should not delegate to the employees his responsibility as host, high-risk security matters, cash control or similar sensitive duties.

Members

- Provide club services as approved by Board of Directors

- Work with standing and special committees to carry out their functions

- Carry out and enforce the spirit of the club, by-laws and house and ground rules

- Receive, evaluate and carry out or report suggestions of the members

- Act as host to the members and their guests

Employees

- Full responsibility, within budgetary limitations, to maintain an adequate, competent and trained staff capable of operating and maintaining the club facilities

Office

- Oversee operation of club office, insuring that records, accounts, billing, member communications, etc. are properly prepared and maintained.

Fiscal

- In cooperation with Treasurer and utilizing services of Office Manager, establish fiscal controls, banking services, accounting and audit procedures

- Oversee all fiscal operations

- Approve and pay bills within established authority

- Maintain and operate adequate petty cash fund

- Provide banks for bar, snack bar, script sales

- Receive and account all receipts

- Ring out all cash registers daily

- Make daily bank deposits

- Review monthly financial statements

- Make recommendations to Treasurer, Board of Directors, etc.

Security

The Club Manager is responsible for the security of the Club, its facilities and equipment. He will take appropriate steps to secure the club premises and members' property stored thereon. Establish and vary procedures

- Guards: night, weekends, happy hour, special

- Alarm service: maintenance, authorized personnel, etc.

- Night lighting appropriate areas

- Daily closing: lock-up, alarms, clear premises, etc.

- Personally maintain security of office safe, liquor supplies and other high risk items

Bar and Galley

Operate club bar and galley with a view to profitability, exemplary service, cash control, and improvement

- Adequate staffing; training

- Appropriate equipment

- Inventory: maintenance, security, procedures

- Decor

- Work with galley concessionaire (if any)

- Establish menus

- Provide cash control

Supplies

The Manager is expected to maintain adequate inventories of the supplies and materials required to operate and maintain the club premises, bar, galley, office, etc. He will select suppliers, order and receive goods, approve invoices for payment and exercise cost controls.

- Bar: liquor, mix, glasses, snacks, utensils, etc.

- Galley: food, beverages, utensils, crockery, etc.

- Office: forms, stationery, office supplies, etc.
- Locker rooms: soap, paper towels, tissue, etc.
- Grounds: tools and equipment, fertilizer, etc.
- Maintenance materials
- Monthly inventory

Maintenance

All club facilities, equipment and grounds must be maintained in good order and appearance. (Employees, Work parties, Contractors)

- Buildings
- Bar and galley equipment
- Grounds
- Piers
- Hoists
- Tennis Court
- Parking areas
- Garbage disposal
- Janitorial services and housekeeping
- Regular inspections

Improvements

The Club Manager is expected to recognize the functions, facilities, procedures, and equipment of the club which can be improved or upgraded. Within the limits of his authority, he is expected to initiate such improvements or make recommendations to the Board of Directors, Operations Committee, House and Grounds Committee, etc.

Special Functions

From time to time, DYC sponsors special events, i.e. parties, regattas, tournaments, etc. These events are normally planned and directed by a committee of members. The Club Manager is expected to provide support services and often detailed planning in some phases. Procurement of special supplies and equipment for these functions is usually his responsibility.

In addition, club members will request the use of the Club's facilities for private parties. The Club Manager will book such functions (not to conflict with regular club activities) and provide such support, planning, catering, etc. as the host member may request, all within the established club policy for such functions.

Deckhands

The DYC Womens Auxiliary, the Deckhands, is an autonomous organization. It lends support to club activities and sponsors functions of its own. Cooperation between the Club Manager and the Deckhands is essential to the harmonious operations.

SUGGESTED READINGS

Bomis, Stephan E., Ann Holt Delenky, and Dee Ann Soder. *Job Analysis: An Effective Management Tool*. Washington: DC: The Bureau of National Affairs, Inc., 1983, 225.

Cazzell, Michael R., Frank E. Kuzmits, and Norbert F. Elbert. *Personnel: Human Resources Management*. Columbus, OH: Merrill Publishing Co., 1989.

Jones, Mark A. "Job Descriptions Made Easy." *Personnel Journal* 63, no. 5 (May 1984), 31–34.

Levine, Edward L. *Everything You Always Wanted to Know About Job Analysis*. Tampa, FL: Mariner Publishing Co., Inc., 1983, 4.

Sherman Jr., A. W., George W. Bolander, and Herbert J. Cruden. *Managing Human Resources*, 8th ed. Cincinnati, OH: South Western Publishing Co., 1990.

U.S. Department of Labor. *Dictionary of Occupational Titles*, 4th ed. Washington, DC: U.S. Government Printing Office, 1977, xiv.

Chapter 8

Job
Design

Learning Objectives—After completion of this exercise, you should be able to:

1. Describe the major differences between work simplification, job enrichment, job enlargement, and autonomous work groups.

2. Identify recent changes in job design and how they might affect worker satisfaction and productivity.

Time Suggested: One hour

Procedures:

1. Read the Introduction.

2. In groups, read and answer the questions in Parts A and B of the Problems section.

# INTRODUCTION

TAYLORISM

The concept of *job design* is not new. It dates back to the beginning of the industrial era when Charles Babbage wrote on rationalized jobs.[1] Perhaps the best-known theorist on job design is Frederick Taylor, who wrote *The Principles of Scientific Management*.[2] He proposed using motion studies to analyze and break down jobs into *simplified* tasks. Job design defines and delineates the tasks, duties, and responsibilities of a job. This information is then used to write job descriptions. With this tool, the personnel manager can assess the skills and knowledge required for job candidates.

Although Taylor stressed that productivity resulted from the least time and motion wasted, in recent years we have realized that productivity is closely linked to motivation and morale as well. The purpose of job design is to increase worker efficiency and satisfaction and to stimulate motivation by improving the nature of work itself.

JOB ENLARGEMENT

The reverse of Taylor's work-simplification theory is *job enlargement*. This involves enlarging a job by horizontally increasing the number of tasks or activities required. The rationale behind the theory is that an enlarged job will increase job satisfaction and productivity. For example, in a plastic container fabricating plant, an experienced die cutter might, under the job simplification process, cut one shape, a circle, from one color of plastic. In a job enlargement program, this single task would be enlarged to include cutting a multitude of shapes from a variety of colors. Perhaps the die cutter would cut all circles from six colors first, then all triangles from the six colors, and so on. Or perhaps the cutter would alternate colors and shapes. In this way there would be a variety of activities to keep the employee involved. The process of job enlargement is relatively simple and can be applied in numerous situations.

Theoretically, job enlargement will motivate employees. Since change is a stimulation in and of itself, the relief from boredom provides the motivation. Furthermore, employees will enjoy a greater feeling of responsibility and competence since additional abilities are utilized. The major criticism of the approach is that little is actually achieved by adding more of the same tasks to a dull job.

JOB ENRICHMENT

An alternative approach to the horizontal enlarging of a job is the vertical process termed *job enrichment*. Pioneered in the 1960s by Frederick Herzberg, job enrichment stresses job content and structure as the critical issues in job design. Similar to enlargement, job enrichment increases the tasks and duties of a job, but it includes more responsibility for decision making, planning, and/or control. It entails more self-monitoring and more planning and controlling decisions. The traditional information-feedback loop between superior and subordinate is altered in job enrichment. A single employee may follow the project from beginning to end. Because the decision maker and planner and operator are the same person, quick feedback and necessary alterations are possible if standards are not met.

Job enrichment can best be explained by an example. During an annual fund drive for a national cancer research foundation, individual volunteers could decide how to raise funds as opposed to being told how. The volunteers could choose the best approach of soliciting in their neighborhood, plan their course of action, and compose their own letters or personal contact messages. District supervisors, rather than managing by directive, would review the results and help those who needed it. The volunteers would watch the entire cycle, from the planning stage through the collection stage.

The motivation effect of job enrichment is alleged to be greater and more powerful than that of job enlargement. Like enlargement, enrichment lessens boredom and allows workers to feel more responsible and competent. But in addition, it requires more creativity and judgment, the recognition of alternatives, and review and control procedures. Herein lies a problem with enrichment: Some people are not willing (or able) to take on the responsibility. Furthermore, not all jobs can or should be enriched.

AUTONOMOUS WORK GROUPS

The last behavioral approach to job design to be discussed, *autonomous work groups*, is an expansion of the first two approaches. The autonomous work group uses the principles of both job enlargement and job enrichment, but rather than concentrating on a single job it involves a project worked on by a group of people. This concept allows the workers to control the project from beginning to end. What will make up each individual's job, how the work will be laid out, how it will be inspected and by whom are all factors addressed within the autonomous work group. Whereas job enrichment can result in more "individual" accomplishments, autonomous work groups tap "group" accomplishments, thus enlarging the number of tasks performed while also enriching the job by adding the planning and controlling processes. As the concept broadens, autonomous work groups can choose their own pace and work breaks. This approach was used in the production of automobile bodies at a Volvo plant in Sweden. In this case, the group of workers followed the body down the assembly line.

The motivation effect of this job design approach encompasses and takes advantage of all the effects of job enlargement and enrichment, and adds to them. The greater variety of tasks and the greater responsibility make the job more meaningful. Also, workers are more satisfied because there is more social contact. The success of this approach depends, of course, on the cooperation of the group and the ability to achieve goals in virtually leaderless groups.

Job enlargement, job enrichment, and autonomous work groups are primarily behavioral approaches to the design of jobs. Each has been shown to increase production in some cases and to actually decrease production in others. Therefore, no generalizations can be made concerning effects on production. One generalization, however, can be made: All three approaches have made important contributions to job satisfaction and work quality.

**PROBLEMS**

PART A

PERSONAL SECRETARY

Imagine the position of personal secretary in a large firm. This is a job filled with lots of tasks—answering the phone, typing, taking dictation, filing, opening the mail, making copies, and so on. However, in all of these duties the secretary is carrying out someone else's orders, making only such decisions as how dark the copies should be—lots of tasks, but many of them dull and unchallenging. In this firm, salary, fringe benefits, and vacation time are all fixed. As the secretary's boss you would like to enrich the job. How could this be done?

Why would you want to enrich your secretary's job? What would be some of the expected benefits?

PART B

AUTOMOBILE MECHANIC

Bobby Turner has just been approached by his friend, Ray Williams, who is opening an automobile tune-up shop, Ace Tune-Up, Inc. Ray does not have a background in business administration. After high school, he attended an automobile mechanics course. His new shop will specialize in tune-ups—replacing spark plugs, ignition points, rotors, distributor caps, gas and air filters, and fuel pumps, and rebuilding carburetors. He feels it is very important to organize the work properly. Ray told Bobby that the way to be successful is to have a good company and satisfied mechanics. "Satisfied mechanics make good mechanics," Ray stated as his basic human resources management philosophy. "If they aren't happy, they do sloppy work, and I just can't afford to have customers complaining about poor work. You know, word-of-mouth is the most important advertising we have. Commercial ads will draw attention to your business, but word-of-mouth gets you business right now. The mechanics just have to do quality work." The reason Ray approached Bobby was to get advice on designing the jobs in his shop. The shop expects to service about eighty cars per day. The standard tune-up takes about fifty-five minutes. It involves replacing points (if nonelectrical), rotor, distributor cap, and plugs; setting the ignition timing and dwell; and adjusting the carburetor. The shop foreman has estimated the time breakdown as follows:

- Replacing four spark plugs   15 minutes
- Replacing points, rotor, and distributor cap   20 minutes
- Adjusting timing, dwell, and carburetor   20 minutes

QUESTIONS

1. What would be the main jobs if your design of the tune-up work was based on work simplification?

	Job	*Job Requirements*
a.	_____	_____
		_____
b.	_____	_____
		_____
c.	_____	_____
		_____
d.	_____	_____
		_____

2. Design a mechanic's position based on the job-enrichment approach.

   Job Description

3. If the tune-up work was designed according to autonomous work groups, jobs in the shop might be as follows:

   Job Description

4. What might the manager of this repair shop expect the advantages and disadvantages to be if an autonomous work group approach was implemented instead of a work simplification method?

◢ NOTES

1. Charles Babbage, *On the Economy of Machinery and Manufacturers* (Charles Knight, 4th ed., 1835; *Reprints of Economic Classics*, New York: Augustus M. Kelly, 1965).

2. Frederick W. Taylor, *The Principles of Scientific Management* (Harper & Row, 1911).

◢ SUGGESTED READINGS

Campion, Michael A., and Chris J. Berger. "Conceptual Integration and Empirical Test of Job Design and Compensation Relationships." *Personnel Psychology* 43, no. 3 (Fall 1990); 525.

Hensy, Melville. "Organizational Design: Some Helpful Notions." *Journal of Management in Engineering* 6, no. 3 (July 1, 1990): 262.

Herzberg, F. "One More Time: How Do You Motivate Employees?" *Harvard Business Review* (January–February 1968).

Mackenzie, Kenneth D. "The Organizational Audit and Analysis Technology for Organizational Design." *Human Systems Management* 5 (Spring 1985): 46–55.

Martyniak, Zbigniew. "On the Organizational Design." *Design Methods and Theories* 24, no. 4 (October 1, 1990): 1317.

Taylor, F. W. *The Principles of Scientific Management*. New York: Norton, 1967. Originally published in 1911.

Weisbord, Marvin R. "Participative Work Design: A Personal Odyssey." *Organizational Dynamics* (Spring 1985): 4–20.

Chapter 9

Job Redesign

Learning Objectives—After completion of this exercise, you should be able to:

1. Diagnose jobs in terms of core job dimensions.
2. Apply job enrichment concepts to jobs.

Time Suggested: Fifty minutes

Procedures:

1. The instructor will review the job-redesign model in Figures 9–1 and 9–2.
2. Read "A New Strategy for Job Enrichment" and answer the questions at the end.
3. Form groups of three or four. With your group, discuss the core job dimensions that were assessed to be "low" or "medium" and then recommend ways to add these dimensions to the job. Recommendations are to be written in the form entitled "Student Job-Redesign Recommendations."
4. Individually, read the "Consultant's Report." As a group, compare the group's recommendations with those of the consultant's. Combine the best recommendations from both reports. Appoint a spokesperson to present the group's final recommendations.

INTRODUCTION

A NEW STRATEGY FOR JOB ENRICHMENT

The work group chosen for job enrichment was a keypunching operation in Travelers Insurance Company. The group's function was to transfer information from printed or written documents onto punched cards for computer input. The work group consisted of ninety-eight keypunch operators and verifiers (both in the same job classification), plus seven assignment clerks. All reported to a supervisor who, in turn, reported to the assistant manager and manager of the data-input division.

The size of individual punching orders varied considerably, from a few cards to as many as 2,500. Some work came to the work group with a specified delivery date, while other orders were to be given routine service on a predetermined schedule.

Assignment clerks received the jobs from the user departments. After reviewing the work for obvious errors, omissions, and legibility problems, the assignment clerk parceled out the work in batches expected to take about one hour. If the clerk found the work not suitable for punching it went to the supervisor, who either returned the work to the user department or cleared up problems by phone. When work went to operators for punching, it was with the instruction, "Punch only what you see. Don't correct errors, no matter how obvious they look."

Because of the high cost of computer time, keypunched work was 100 percent verified—a task that consumed nearly as many work hours as the punching itself. Then the cards went to the supervisor, who screened the jobs for due dates before sending them to the computer. Errors detected in verification were assigned to various operators at random to be corrected.

The computer output from the cards was sent to the originating department, accompanied by a printout of errors. Eventually the printout went back to the supervisor for final correction.

A great many phenomena indicated that the problems being experienced in the work group might be the result of poor motivation. As the only person performing supervisory functions of any kind, the supervisor spent most of his time responding to crisis situations, which recurred continually. He also had to deal almost daily with employees' salary grievances or other complaints. Employees frequently showed apathy or outright hostility toward their jobs.

Rates of work output, by accepted work measurement standards, were inadequate. Error rates were high. Due dates and schedules frequently were missed. Absenteeism was higher than average, especially before and after weekends and holidays.

The single, rather unusual exception was turnover. It was lower than the companywide average for similar jobs. The company has attributed this fact to a poor job market in the base period just before the project began, and to an older, relatively more settled work force—made up, incidentally, entirely of women.

QUESTIONS

On a scale of 1 to 5, where 1 indicates small and 5 indicates large, how would you rate:

	Small		*Medium*		*Large*
1. The variety of skills needed to perform this job satisfactorily?	1	2	3	4	5
2. The degree to which an employee identifies with this job?	1	2	3	4	5
3. The degree of significance the employee gives to this work?	1	2	3	4	5
4. The amount of independent decision making allowed?	1	2	3	4	5
5. The amount of feedback the employee receives?	1	2	3	4	5

From Hackman, J. R., G. R. Oldham, R. Janson, and K. Purdy, "A New Strategy for Job Enrichment," *California Management Review* 17, no. 4 (Summer 1975): 57–72.

STUDENT JOB-REDESIGN RECOMMENDATIONS

FIGURE 9–1   Job-Redesign Model

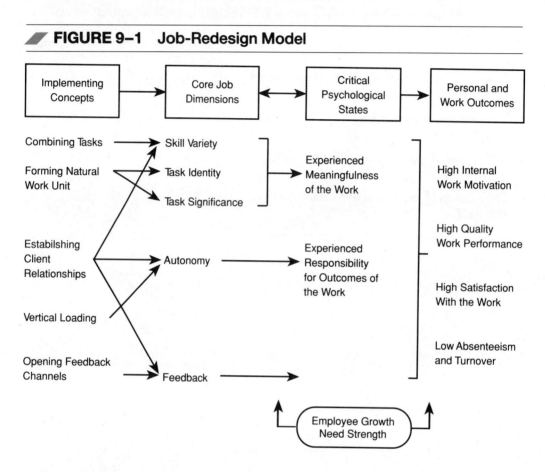

1. Recommendations for adding skill variety:

2. Recommendations for adding task identity:

3. Recommendations for adding task significance:

4. Recommendations for adding autonomy:

5. Recommendations for increasing feedback to the job:

CONSULTANT'S REPORT

THE DIAGNOSIS

A consulting team concluded that the keypunch operator's job exhibited the following serious weaknesses in terms of the core dimensions.

- Skill variety: there was none. Only a single skill was involved—the ability to punch adequately the data on the batch of documents.

- Task identity: virtually nonexistent. Batches were assembled to provide an even workload, but not whole identifiable jobs.

- Task significance: not apparent. The keypunching operation was a necessary step in providing service to the company's customers. The individual operator was isolated by an assignment clerk and a supervisor from any knowledge of what the operation meant to the using department, let alone its meaning to the ultimate customer.

- Autonomy: none. The operators had no freedom to arrange their daily tasks to meet schedules, to resolve problems with the using department, or even to correct, in punching, information that was obviously wrong.

- Feedback: none. Once a batch was out of the operator's hands, she had no assured chance of seeing evidence of its quality or inadequacy.

Design of the Experimental Trial.   Since the diagnosis indicated that the motivating potential of the job was extremely low, it was decided to attempt to improve the motivation and productivity of the work group through job enrichment. Moreover, it was possible to design an experimental test of the effects of the changes to be introduced. The results of changes made in the target work group were to be compared with trends in a control work group of similar size and demographic make-up. Since the control group was located more than a mile away, there appeared to be little risk of communication between members of the two groups.

A base period was defined before the start of the experimental trial period, and appropriate data were gathered on the productivity, absenteeism, and work attitudes of members of both groups. Data also were available on turnover; but since turnover was already below average in the target group, prospective changes in this measure were deemed insignificant.

An educational session was conducted with supervisors, at which they were given the theory and implementing concepts and actually helped to design the job changes themselves. Out of this session came an active plan consisting of about twenty-five change items that would significantly affect the design of the target jobs.

From Hackman, J. R., G. R. Oldham, R. Janson, and K. Purdy, "A New Strategy for Job Enrichment," *California Management Review* 17, no. 4 (Summer 1975): 57–72.

The Implementing Concepts and the Changes. Because the job as it existed was rather uniformly low on the core job dimensions, all five of the implementing concepts were used in enriching it.

- Natural units of work. The random batch assignment of work was replaced by assigning to each operator continuing responsibility for certain accounts—either particular departments or particular recurring jobs. Any work for those accounts now always goes to the same operator.

- Task combination. Some planning and controlling functions were combined with the central task of keypunching. In this case, however, these additions can be more suitably discussed under the remaining three implementing concepts.

- Client relationships. Each operator was given several channels of direct contact with clients. The operators, not their assignment clerks, now inspect their documents for correctness and legibility. When problems arise, the operator, not the supervisor, takes them up with the client.

- Feedback. In addition to feedback from client contact, the operators were provided with a number of additional sources of data about their performance. The computer department now returns incorrect cards to the operators who punched them, and operators correct their own errors. Each operator also keeps her own file of copies of her errors. These can be reviewed to determine trends in error frequency and types of errors. Each operator receives weekly a computer printout of her errors and productivity, which is sent to her directly, rather than given to her by the supervisor.

- Vertical loading. Besides consulting directly with clients about work questions, operators now have the authority to correct obvious coding errors on their own. Operators may set their own schedules and plan their daily work, as long as they meet schedules. Some competent operators have been given the option of not verifying their work and making their own program changes.

Results of the Trial. The results were dramatic. The number of operators declined from ninety-eight to sixty. This occurred partly through attrition and partly through transfer to other departments. Some of the operators were promoted to higher-paying jobs in departments whose cards they had been handling—something that had never occurred before. Some details of the results are given below.

- Quantity of work. The control group, with no job changes made, showed an increase in productivity of 8.1 percent during the trial period. The experimental group showed an increase of 39.6 percent.

- Error rates. To assess work quality, error rates were recorded for about forty operators in the experimental group. All were experienced, and all had been in their jobs before the job enrichment program began. For two months before the study, these operators had a collective error rate of 1.53 percent. For two months toward the end of the study, the collective error rate was 0.99 percent. By the end of the study the number of operators with poor performance had dropped from 11.1 percent to 5.5 percent.

- Absenteeism. The experimental group registered a 24.1 percent decline in absences. The control group, by contrast, showed a 29 percent *increase*.

- Attitudes toward the job. An attitude survey given at the start of the project showed that the two groups scored about average, and nearly identically, in nine different areas of work satisfaction. At the end of the project the survey was repeated. The control group showed an insignificant 0.5 percent improvement, while the experimental group's overall satisfaction score rose 16.5 percent.

- Selective elimination of controls. Demonstrated improvements in operator proficiency permitted them to work with fewer controls. Travelers Insurance Company estimates that the reduction of controls had the same effect as adding seven operators—a saving even beyond the effects of improved productivity and lowered absenteeism.

- Role of the supervisor. One of the most significant findings in the Travelers experiment was the effect of the changes on the supervisor's job, and thus on the rest of the organization. The operators took on many responsibilities that had been reserved at least to the unit leaders and sometimes to the supervisor. The unit leaders, in turn, assumed some of the day-to-day supervisory functions that had plagued the supervisor. Instead of spending his days supervising the behavior of subordinates and dealing with crises, he was able to devote time to developing feedback systems, setting up work modules and spearheading the enrichment effort—in other words, managing. It should be noted, however, that helping supervisors change their own work activities when their subordinates' jobs have been enriched is itself a challenging task. And if appropriate attention and help are not given to supervisors in such cases, they rapidly can become disaffected—and a job enrichment "backlash" can result.

Summary. By applying work measurement standards to the changes wrought by job enrichment—attitude and quality, absenteeism, and selective administration of controls—Travelers was able to estimate the total dollar impact of the project. Actual savings in salaries and machine rental charges during the first year totaled $64,305. Potential savings by further application of the changes were put at $91,937 annually. Thus, by almost any measure used—from the work attitudes of individual employees to dollar savings for the company as a whole—The Travelers test of the job-enrichment strategy proved a success.

▰ **FIGURE 9–2   The Moderating Effect of Employee Growth-Need Strength**

SUGGESTED READINGS

Cunningham, J. Barto. "A Guide to Job Enrichment and Redesign." *Personnel* 67, no. 2 (February 1, 1990): 56.

Hackman, J. R., and G. R. Oldham. "Motivation through the Design of Work: Test of a Theory." *Organizational Behavior and Human Performance* 16 (1976): 251–279.

———. *Work Redesign*. Reading, MA: Addison-Wesley, 1980.

Herriot, Peter. " 'Candidate-Friendly' Selection for the 1990's." *Personnel Management* 22, no. 2 (February 1, 1990): 32.

Orphen, W. "The Effects of Job Enrichment on Employee Satisfaction, Motivation, Involvement, and Performance: A Field Experiment." *Human Relations* 32 (1979): 189–217.

Roberts, K., and W. Glick. "The Job Characteristics Approach to Task Design: A Critical Review." *Journal of Applied Psychology* 66 (1981): 193–217.

Chapter **10**

Quality Circles

Learning Objectives—After completion of this exercise, you should be able to:

1. Describe the characteristics of quality circles and why they can lead to improved organizational performance.
2. Describe the major components of the problem-solving process used by quality circle members.
3. Recognize and write problem *definitions* on organizational issues that are clearly worded, that deal with causes as opposed to symptoms, and that do not contain restrictive solutions.

Time Suggested: One hour

Procedures:

1. Read the Introduction, Operating Perceptions, and Training sections.
2. Read and complete the Exercise section.
3. Answer all questions in the Exercise section.

◢ INTRODUCTION

Quality circles are small groups of employees with common work responsibilities who volunteer to meet regularly on company time in an effort to find solutions to work-related problems. The basic philosophy is that no one understands problems better than the workers themselves. Management supports quality circles by giving circle leaders and members time for training and meetings, providing facilities and materials, and responding promptly to proposals. Quality circles are meant to improve quality and productivity; however, they also may lead to higher worker morale and open lines of communication. Quality circles encourage employees to participate in decisions that in the past were made only at higher levels. Figure 10–1 shows the quality circle process.

◢ FIGURE 10–1　The Quality Circle Process

OPERATING PERCEPTIONS

Quality circles are controversial. Criticisms of the concept are based on several factors, such as lack of measurement of results, little change in management behavior, excessive operational costs, and rapid decay of initial worker enthusiasm. These criticisms are usually unfounded. Often they are made after observing a quality circle program that is poorly operated. For example, many organizations initiate quality circle programs without providing training to prepare workers for participation. In such instances, it is not surprising that efforts fail.

One of the most prevalent criticisms of quality circles is that the problems and the solutions chosen for analysis are of little consequence. The following is a list of erroneous perceptions held by some detractors of quality circles, accompanied by a more realistic appraisal of situations in organizations, which suggests that what the circles do is significant.

Erroneous Perceptions	*Reality*
Inefficiency is rare.	Inefficiencies of all types occur daily even in well-run operations.
Inefficiencies that do occur are of little consequence.	Inefficiencies cost money in excess labor, material, and/or lost revenue.
Inefficiencies are always effectively handled so as not to reappear.	Inefficiencies continually recur, diminishing the capacity of organizations.

The reason(s) for such inaccurate perceptions in organizations are understandable. Management typically does not report inefficiencies. They are seldom "costed." Applicable costs are not known, and are almost always higher than management believed. Managers in many organizations are receptive to quality circles as being valuable extensions of their own efforts. Many companies in the United States, primarily those in the high-technology industry where there is a great need for creativity, have pioneered the initiation of quality circles. The Minnesota Mining and Manufacturing Company, for example, has hundreds of circles.

◢ TRAINING

The one crucial factor necessary to make quality circles effective is training. The members are taught group dynamics, idea-generation methods, circle operations and history, management-presentation techniques, and problem-solving methodology. Although the problem-solving techniques vary, there is a common sequence taught to circles, as follows:

1. Define the problem. Circles are taught to differentiate between symptom and cause, to identify and separately solve important subproblems, and to avoid building restrictive solutions into problem statements.

2. Establish the impact. In this step, circles determine what organizational pain the problem is causing. If it is insignificant, a different problem is selected.

3. Vision of future. This step requires a little dreaming. Circles try to describe what the future will look like if the problem is successfully solved. This provides a target.

4. Blocks. In this step, circles generate information about what might prevent them from reaching their target. If solutions provided fail to cope with these blocks, the solutions are inadequate.

5. Potential solutions. This is a free-wheeling, brainstorming step listing actions that might help reduce or eliminate a problem.

6. Final solutions. Working from the items provided in step 5, circles select the solutions they actually want to implement. Solutions must include specific provisions for implementation; for example, determining who will complete an action, when it will be completed, and whether or not a review (compliance) element is necessary.

 **EXERCISE**

When the definition of an organization problem includes a solution, people working on the problem are prevented from generating additional solutions that may be even better than the one listed. This happens with poorly defined problems, where people are forced into providing the *stated solution* rather than eliminating or lessening the problem. For example, a problem statement such as "because of being overweight, I need to reduce my caloric intake" is unnecessarily restrictive, since the phrase "I need to reduce my caloric intake" leads to solutions that pertain only to reducing caloric ingestion. Other possibilities, such as exercising to burn off unwanted calories, may be overlooked. Therefore, a better problem definition would likely be "what are the methods I may use to reduce my weight?" Such a solution-free problem definition allows a wider array of options.

Exercise process:

A. As individuals, read the four problem statements that follow. Mark with an *S* those that contain a solution.

B. Form discussion groups of five or six people. Reach a group consensus on which of the problem statements contain solutions. Mark such items with an *S* in the group discussion column.

C. As a group, find a better way to reword designated items so that they no longer contain solutions. Rewrite the items in the space provided.

PROBLEM STATEMENTS

Individual	*Group Discussion*	
_____	_____	**1.** Our problem is that we need to have more meetings in order to improve communication in our company.
_____	_____	**2.** Our problem is that we have no uses for scrap lumber available after a construction project is completed.
_____	_____	**3.** Our problem is that it takes us too long to complete engine repairs on malfunctioning equipment.
_____	_____	**4.** Our problem is that we need to have more people in our shop to handle our huge backlog of work.

Rewrite Space

Problem Statement 1.

Problem Statement 2.

Problem Statement 3.

Problem Statement 4.

Another major factor in effective problem solving is ensuring that problem definitions include causes, not symptoms. The medical profession provides excellent illustrations of this concept. For example, a physician would likely suggest an external treatment of the symptom to provide immediate relief from a severe skin irritation, but would also probably conduct blood tests and/or other diagnoses to determine whether a malfunctioning of an internal organ was causing the problem. Similarly, regarding organizational issues, fundamental causes must be identified in order to truly eliminate problems. When an organization's problem definition contains a "symptom" instead of a "cause," the problem is not likely to totally disappear. In fact, a proposed solution that deals only with symptoms often makes the problem worse. For example, without clear goals and objectives, teaching time management might make managers more efficient at doing the wrong thing.

Exercise process:

A. As individuals, read the four problem statements that follow. Mark with an *S* those that deal with symptoms.

B. Form discussion groups with five or six individuals in each. Reach a group consensus on which of the problem statements deal with symptoms. Mark such items with an *S* in the group discussion column.

C. As a group, find a better way to reword designated items so that they describe causes, not symptoms. Rewrite the items in the space provided.

PROBLEM STATEMENTS

Individual	Group Discussion	
_____	_____	1. Our problem is that our workforce has low morale.
_____	_____	2. Our problem is that excessive time is required to write research reports.
_____	_____	3. My problem is the excessive consumption of soft drinks and sweets, and the inadequate brushing of my teeth, which is resulting in massive tooth decay.
_____	_____	4. Our problem is that workers operating milling machines are refusing to wear safety goggles.

Rewrite Space

Problem Statement 1.

Problem Statement 2.

Problem Statement 3.

Problem Statement 4.

 **QUESTIONS**

1. In your group, discuss the underlying characteristics of quality circles that make them so attractive to employees. Summarize your discussion.

2. Why is member training important to the success of quality circles? Discuss this issue within your group and write a group response.

3. Why are quality circles considered to be "people building?" Discuss this idea within your group and write a group response.

◢ SUGGESTED READINGS

Cairns, Donald V. "Staff Development Through Quality Circles." *The Clearing House* 64, no. 2 (November 1, 1990): 87.

Cole, Robert E., and Philippe Byosiere. "Managerial Objectives for Introducing Quality Circles: A U.S.-Japan Comparison." *Quality Progress* 19, no. 3 (March 1986): 25–30.

Ebiahimpour, Maling. "An Examination of Quality Management in Japan: Implications for Management in the United States." *Journal of Operations Management* 5, no. 4 (August 1985): 419–431.

Frayer, V. C. M., and B. G. Dale. "UK Quality Circle Failures—The Latest Picture." *Omega* 14 (January 1986): 23–33.

Lawler, Edward E., III, and Susan A. Mohrman. "Quality Circles after the Fad." *Harvard Business Review* 63, no. 1 (January–February 1985): 64–71.

Meyer, Gordon W., and Stott, Randall G. "Quality Circles: Panacea or Pandora's Box?" *Organizational Dynamics* (Spring 1985): 34–50.

Mohrman, Susan A., and E. Gerald, Jr. "The Design and Use of Effective Employee Participation Groups: Implications for Human Resource Management." *Human Resources Management* 24, no. 4 (Winter 1985): 413–428.

"Putting Quality Circles to Work." *Electrical World* 204, no. 8 (August 1, 1990): 27.

Richardson, Peter A. "Courting Greater Employee Involvement through Participative Management." *Sloan Management Review* 26, no. 2 (Winter 1985): 33–44.

Saito, Mamoru. "Nippon Steel's Use of UK Activities." *International Studies of Management and Organization* 15, no. 3/4 (Fall–Winter 1985–1986): 126–143.

Strier, Franklin. "Quality Circles in the United States: Fad or Fixture?" *Business Forum* 9, no. 3 (Summer 1984): 19–23.

Wood, Robert, et al. "Evaluating Quality Circles: The American Application." *California Management Review* 26 (Fall 1983): 37–53.

PART 3
Fair Employment Practices in the Workplace

The implementation of Title VII of the Civil Rights Act of 1964, revised in 1972, is probably the most important event affecting the human resources manager since the passage of labor legislation in the first part of this century. Today, fair employment issues affect every aspect of an organization's human resources activities. This section of the book begins with Chapter 11, which discusses several landmark cases under Title VII. After completing the activities of this chapter, students will know which criteria traditionally used in employment decisions are likely to be viewed as unlawful.

Chapter 12 addresses the job relatedness of certain traditional selection criteria. Using job advertisements found in newspapers, students are to decide whether or not asking only men or only women to apply for certain jobs is job-related and therefore lawful. Because the management practices in this country often have included sex-based criteria in making employment decisions, it is important to understand that Title VII made such practices unlawful unless they could be shown to be bona fide occupational qualifications.

One of the most common sources of employment information is the application blank. In Chapter 13 students are required to analyze a traditional job application form to determine whether parts of it are lawful or unlawful. It has been common practice for organizations to use the same application form year after year without carefully examining it for compliance with Title VII. Students will discover that the information requested on many forms has little or no connection to the job in question, and is therefore unlawful.

In Chapter 14 the important issue of sexual harassment at work is addressed. Students will learn about the law and sexual harassment and then respond to several important issues stemming from the law. Discussing these issues in sexually mixed groups is an effective way to discover how men and women often differ in their perceptions regarding what is and is not harassment.

Age discrimination is covered in Chapter 15. In this exercise, students will study landmark age discrimination cases, become aware of the effects of age on performance, and learn how age differences among people at work can lead to problems for managers. As the population in the United States ages, knowing about this topic becomes more and more important for the modern human resource manager.

The Americans with Disabilities Act (ADA) was passed in 1990 to protect those qualified, disabled individuals from discrimination in employment. In Chapter 16 students will learn to identify individuals who qualify for handicapped status under ADA and to identify those organizations that are covered under the Act.

Fair employment issues are an ever-present part of the modern human resource manager's job. Effectively dealing with these issues keeps the organization out of court, protects the organization's public image, and creates a climate of fairness and concern for how well a person performs rather than whether or not the person has certain non-job-related characteristics.

Chapter 11

Landmark Cases of Title VII

Learning Objectives—After completion of this exercise, you should be able to:

1. Understand the types of employment situations that lead to important legal interpretations of Title VII of the Civil Rights Act of 1964.

2. Understand the courts' positions on selection criteria, customer preferences, and traditional sex roles in terms of their interpretation of Title VII of the Civil Rights Act.

3. Identify employment situations that are likely to be discriminatory under Title VII.

Time Suggested: One and one-half hours

Procedures:

1. Read the Introduction.

2. Read the three cases: *Griggs* v. *Duke, Diaz* v. *Pan American*, and *Rosenfeld* v. *Southern Pacific*, taking note of the most important points and decisions.

3. Form groups of four or five, and answer the questions at the end of each case brief.

4. The instructor will lead a discussion based upon the group answers and the courts' findings.

 **INTRODUCTION**

FACTS ABOUT TITLE VII OF THE CIVIL RIGHTS ACT OF 1964 AS AMENDED BY THE EQUAL OPPORTUNITY ACT OF 1972

Who Is Covered?	All institutions with fifteen or more employees who work twenty or more calendar weeks.
What Is Prohibited?	Discrimination in employment (including hiring, upgrading, salaries, fringe benefits, training, and other conditions of employment) on the basis of race, color, religion, national origin, or sex.
Exemptions from Coverage	Religious (corporations, associations, or educational) institutions are exempt with respect to employment of individuals of a particular religion or religious order.
Who Enforces the Provisions?	Equal Employment Opportunity Commission (EEOC). (Sec. 705(a))
Record-Keeping Requirements and Government Access to Records	Institutions must keep and preserve specified records relevant to the determination of whether violations have occurred. Government is empowered to review all relevant records. (Sec. 709(c))
Enforcement Power and Sanctions	If attempts at conciliation fail, EEOC or the U.S. Attorney General may file suit. Aggrieved individuals may also initiate suits. Court may enjoin respondent from engaging in unlawful behavior, order appropriate affirmative action, order reinstatement, and award back pay. (Sec. 706(f))
Affirmative Action Requirements	Affirmative action is not required unless charges have been filed, in which case it may be included in the conciliation agreement or be ordered by court.
Coverage of Labor Organizations and Employment Agencies	Both are covered by the same requirements and sanctions as employers.
Is Harassment Prohibited?	Institutions are prohibited from discharging or discriminating against any employee or applicant for employment because she/he has made a complaint, assisted with an investigation, or instituted proceedings.

CASE STUDIES

Griggs v. Duke Power Company
United States Court of Appeals
420 F.2d 1225 (4th Cir. 1970)

Thirteen black employees of the Duke Power Company brought a class action suit against their employer on the ground that company employment practices violated the Civil Rights Act of 1964. The United States District Court of North Carolina dismissed the case, and the plaintiffs appealed.

PLAINTIFF'S POSITION:

Prior to 1965, blacks were relegated to the Labor Department and deprived of access to other departments due to the racial discrimination practiced by the company. Maximum wage in the Labor Department was $1.57 per hour, which was less than the minimum paid to any other Duke Power Company employee. Maximum wages paid to employees in other departments ranged from $3.18 to $3.65 per hour.

Admitting that at present Duke has apparently abandoned its policy of restricting all blacks to the Labor Department, the plaintiffs complain that the education and testing requirements preserve and continue the effects of Duke's past racial discrimination, thereby violating the Civil Rights Act of 1964.

DEFENDANT'S POSITION:

Duke is a corporation engaged in the generation, transmission, and distribution of electrical power in North and South Carolina. The work at the Dan River Station is divided into five departments—the lowest paying of which is the Labor Department, which has general custodial duties. In 1955, Duke initiated the policy of requiring a high school diploma or its equivalent for employment in all departments except the Labor Department. The company claims that this policy was instituted due to the increasingly more complicated work requirements. Within each department, promotions are generally given to the senior man in the classification below the department vacancy. Transfers into another department are made, depending on the qualifications of the employee.

An amendment to the promotion and transfer policy was made in 1965. All employees hired prior to September 1965 who did not have a high school education or its equivalent could become eligible for transfer or promotion by passing the Wonderlic

General Intelligence Test and the Bennett Mechanical AA General Mechanical Test with scores equivalent to those achieved by an average high school graduate.

Prior to 1966, no black had ever held a position at Dan River in any department other than the Labor Department. Since then, the only three blacks with high school educations were promoted into higher-classified departments.

 **QUESTIONS**

1. Would a high school diploma be a valid prerequisite for employment at Duke Power Company? Justify your answer.

2. Job requirements determine what qualifications applicants need. Could promotion potential also be a qualification in hiring decisions:

   Yes _____   No _____   Why?

3. List the points in support of the plaintiff's argument.

   a.

   b.

   c.

   d.

4. List the points in support of the defendant's argument.

   a.

   b.

   c.

   d.

5. Is your group's prediction of the court finding in favor of Griggs or Duke? Briefly state the rationale for your decision.

CASE STUDIES

Diaz v. Pan American World Airways, Inc.
United States Court of Appeals
442 F.2d 385 (5th Cir. 1971)

In this class action suit, the plaintiff alleged that Pan American World Airways had refused to employ him on the basis of his sex, thus violating the 1964 Civil Rights Act. Plaintiff sought the position of flight cabin attendant. Judgment in the U.S. District Court for the Southern District of Florida was in favor of Pan Am, and the plaintiff appealed.

PLAINTIFF'S POSITION:

Celio Diaz applied for a job as flight attendant with Pan American World Airways in 1967. He was rejected because Pan Am had a policy of restricting its hiring for that position to females. Diaz filed charges with the Equal Employment Opportunity Commission, and although the Commission found probable cause to believe his charge, they were unable to resolve the matter through reconciliation with Pan Am. Next, a class action suit was filed, in which Diaz sought an injunction and damages.

DEFENTANT'S POSITION:

Pan Am admitted that it had a policy of restricting its hiring for cabin attendants to females. However, it held that being a female is a bona fide occupational qualification necessary for normal operation of Pan American's business. This was based on its history of the use of flight attendants, passenger preference, basic psychological reasons for the preference, and the actualities of the hiring process. Pan Am based its hiring policy on its experience with both male and female cabin attendants. The performance of female attendants was better in the sense that they were superior in such nonmechanical aspects of the job as providing reassurance to anxious passengers, giving courteous personalized service and, in general, making flights as pleasurable as possible. The defendant contended that an air carrier is required to take account of the special psychological needs of its passengers, and argued that these needs are better attended to by females.

 **QUESTIONS**

1. List the points favoring of the plaintiff's argument.

   a.

   b.

   c.

   d.

2. List the points favoring of the defendant's argument.

   a.

   b.

   c.

   d.

3. Why would an airline want female flight attendants? Are the reasons you have identified job-related? Explain.

4. What is your group's prediction of the court finding—in favor of Diaz or Pan American? Briefly state the rationale for your decision.

CASE STUDIES

Rosenfeld v. Southern Pacific Company
United States Court of Appeals
442 F.2d 1219 (9th Cir. 1971)

In this case the plaintiff, an employee of Southern Pacific Company, alleged that her employer had discriminated against her solely on the basis of her sex by assigning a position to a junior male employee. The United States District Court for the Central District of California entered judgment, and appeal was taken.

PLAINTIFF'S POSITION:

Leah Rosenfeld, an employee at Southern Pacific Company, brought this action against her employer. Plaintiff alleged that in filling the position of agent-telegrapher at Thermal, California, in March 1966, Southern Pacific discriminated against her solely because of her sex. Originally asking for injunctive relief and damages specifically related to the Thermal incident, plaintiff expanded the pleadings. Circumstances of the incident were held to represent the company's general labor policies regarding the employment of women. Some of these policies were in accordance with the state labor laws of California. As such, the state of California was permitted to intervene to defend the validity of the state's labor laws regarding capabilities of women.

DEFENDANT'S POSITION:

Southern Pacific argued that it was the company's policy to exclude women from certain positions. The company restricted these job opportunities to men for two basic reasons: (1) the arduous nature of the work-related activity rendered women physically unsuited for the jobs, and (2) appointing a woman to any such position would result in a violation of California labor laws and regulations which limited hours of work for women and restricted the weight they were permitted to lift. The position of agent-tele-grapher at Thermal was illustrative of this kind of job. During certain times in the year, the position required work in excess of ten hours a day and eighty hours a week. The position required lifting various objects of more than twenty-five pounds, and in some instances over fifty pounds. Hiring a woman for this position would have been in defiance of the California state labor laws.

   While the case was pending in the district court, Southern Pacific closed its agency at Thermal. Although the issue of mootness was argued by Southern Pacific and the state of California, the district court found that the case was not a moot issue. This was due to the expanded pleading by the plaintiff to include general declaratory and injunctive relief not limited to the Thermal agency. The findings and conclusions extend beyond Thermal.

◢ QUESTIONS

1. List the points in defense of Southern Pacific's practice.

   a.

   b.

   c.

   d.

2. List the points in support of the plaintiff.

   a.

   b.

   c.

   d.

3. Do you think that Southern Pacific's actions were justifiable? Why?

◢ SUGGESTED READINGS

Belohlav, James A., and Eugene Ayton. "Equal Opportunity Laws: Some Common Problems." *Personnel Journal* 61, no. 4 (April 1982): 282–285.

Brown, Abby. "Employment Tests: Issues without Clear Answers." *Personnel Administrator* 30 (September 1985): 43–56.

Capers, I. Bennett. "Sexual Orientation and Title VII." *Columbia Law Review* 91, no. 5 (June 1, 1991): 1158.

Jablin, Frederic M. "Use of Discriminatory Questions in Screening Interviews." *The Personnel Administrator* 27, no. 3 (March 1982): 41–46.

Judd, Kenni F. "Burdens of Proof Under Title VII in the 90's: Wards." *Nova Law Review* 15, no. 1 (Winter 1991): 67.

Ledvinka, J. *Federal Regulation of Personnel and Human Resource Management*. Belmont, CA: Kent Publishing Company, 1982, 19–69.

Lookatch, Richard P. "Alternatives to Formal Employment Testing." *Personnel Administrator* 29 (September 1984): 111–116.

Mathews, Susan M. "Title VII and Sexual Harassment: Beyond Damages Control." *Yale Journal of Law and Feminism* 3, no. 2 (Spring 1991): 299.

Peterson, D. J. "The Impact of Duke Power on Testing." *Personnel* 51, no. 2 (March–April 1974): 30–37.

Pingpank, J. C. "Preventing and Defending EEO Charges." *The Personnel Administrator* (February 1983): 35–40.

Portwood, J. D., and S. M. Schmidt. "Beyond *Griggs* v. *Duke Power Company*: Title VII after *Washington* v. *Davis*." *Labor Law Journal* (March 1977): 174–181.

Scalise, David G., and Daniel J. Smith. "Legal Update: When Are Job Requirements Discriminatory?" *Personnel* 63 (March 1986): 41–48.

Chapter 12

Bona Fide Occupational Qualifications

Learning Objectives—After completion of this exercise, you should be able to:

1. Understand the characteristics of bona fide occupational qualifications (BFOQs).
2. Evaluate particular jobs in terms of their BFOQs.
3. Experience the views of others in terms of their sex-stereotyping of specific jobs.

Time Suggested: Forty-five minutes

Procedures:

1. Individually, read the Introduction.
2. Form mixed groups of four or five to assess the employment ads. (*Note:* Classified ads numbers 1–4 are for female applicants, and numbers 5–8 are for male applicants.)
3. Establish by consensus whether or not BFOQs are present in each ad, then prepare a rationale to support each decision.

 **INTRODUCTION**

DISCRIMINATION AND BONA FIDE
OCCUPATIONAL QUALIFICATIONS

Title VII of the Civil Rights Act prohibits discrimination in employment in terms of race, color, sex, religion, or national origin. Its interpretive guidelines, Title VII itself, and related cases have established exceptions that allow for discrimination on the basis of the terms listed above. These exceptions are called bona fide occupational qualifications (BFOQs). Faced with charges of discrimination, employers have used such defenses as BFOQ, bona fide seniority system, business necessity, and customer services. Although some of these defenses have been successful, others have not.

The bona fide occupational qualifications allow the employer to discriminate, but it must be proven that there is factual basis for believing that all or substantially all of the group (for instance, women) would be unable to perform the work in a safe and efficient manner. "Distasteful" and "unromantic" job duties have not been found to be BFOQs. Working in poolrooms or bars, jobs requiring strenuous physical effort, working long hours, and jobs requiring "masculine" traits have not been deemed proper grounds for BFOQS. Authenticity and genuineness can be prerequisites for a BFOQ—an example would be requiring that an actress play the part of a female in a theatrical production.

The bona fide seniority or merit system was written into the act, and only allows systems that do not discriminate. For example, systems that assign jobs only to men having seniority have been held to be in violation of Title VII.

Business necessity is another defense available to the employer under Title VII. In order to justify a policy that disproportionately rejects or affects members of a minority group under Title VII, the employer must prove this to be a business necessity. This means that there is no acceptable alternative to the practice under question. An additional defense that has been attempted is customer preference. Customer preference as a defense to Title VII actions has been rejected. As discussed in the last chapter, the *Diaz* v. *Pan American World Airways* case was concerned with a male applicant for a flight attendant position. A survey showed that Pan Am's customers preferred females as flight attendants, but the Supreme Court's findings were not sympathetic to that argument. Other examples of court decisions concerning BFOQs:

1. A railroad discriminated against females for a particular job that required heavy physical effort and a work week that could be in excess of eighty hours. The court stated that the applicant must be given the opportunity to demonstrate the personal qualifications specified; strenuous physical demands are not a BFOQ. According to the Civil Rights Act, women can be excluded as individuals (not because they are women) upon showing individual incapacity.

This section is based on Jeri D. Gilbreath, "Sex Discrimination and Title VII of the Civil Rights Act," *Personnel Journal* (January 1977): 23–28.

2. A firm discriminated against women who had children under school age. The court concluded that there could be discrimination against mothers who had children under school age if there was also discrimination against fathers with children under school age.

EMPLOYMENT ADS

BFOQs

The following classified advertisements are examples of ads found in newspapers. You are required to decide whether sex is a bona fide occupational qualification for each position. Write a justification for your answer in the space provided.

HELP WANTED: FEMALE

1. Experienced cocktail waitress wanted for evening shift. Must wear costume provided and high heels. Apply 9 to 4 at Lovejoy Lounge.

   BFOQ   Yes _____   No _____

   Justification

2. Energetic, vivacious lady wanted to instruct aerobic classes and assist manager at prestigious women's health center. Send resume and salary history to P.O. Box 469.

   BFOQ   Yes _____   No _____

   Justification

3. Part-time gal Friday for growing law firm. Must file, answer phones, type 65 wpm and run errands. Will become full-time within one year. Call 949-2000, ext. 127 for appointment.

   BFOQ   Yes _____   No _____

   Justification

4. Live-in help for handicapped lady. Room, board and salary. Duties include preparing meals, cleaning, some driving and administering medicine. Send resume and 3 references to Box 1452.

   BFOQ   Yes _____   No _____

   Justification

HELP WANTED: MALE

5. Private golf club desires experienced male bartender for men's grill. Work 10 to 4, Wednesday thru Sunday. Apply in person on Monday, 9 to 11, Maui Golf Center.

   BFOQ   Yes _____   No _____

   Justification

6. Needed immediately: cook for offshore oil rig platform. On 21 days—off 7. Call (202) 321-1415 for application.

   BFOQ   Yes _____   No _____

   Justification

7. Welder trainee. High school grads. Wage $7.00 to start. Apply in person Monday, 9 to 5. Eagle Construction Company.

   BFOQ   Yes _____   No _____

   Justification

8. Male Polynesian fire dancer needed. Join our terrific dinner show and travel the coast with us. Experience not necessary, will train the right person. Tavannah's Tahitian Show, P.O. Box 343.

   BFOQ   Yes _____   No _____

   Justification

◢ SUGGESTED READINGS

Dalton, Dan R., and William D. Tador. "Gender and Workplace Justice: A Field Assessment." *Personnel Psychology* 38 (January 1985): 133–152.

Gilbreath, Jeri D. "Sex Discrimination and Title VII of the Civil Rights Act." *Personnel Journal* (January 1977): 23–28.

"Labor and Employment Law Notes: OTJAG Labor and Employment Law Office." *The Army Lawyer* (June 1, 1990): 61.

Millenson, D. A. "Title VII Class Actions after Falcon." *Employment Relations Law Journal* 8 (Winter 1982–1983): 526–539.

Scalise, David G., and Daniel J. Smith. "Legal Update: When Are Job Requirements Discriminatory?" *Personnel* 63 (March 1986): 41–48.

Sculnick, M. W. "Settlement of Discrimination Cases." *EEO Today* 9 (Summer 1982): 109–119.

Williams, Jim. "Employment Law Developments." *Clearinghouse Review* 23, no. 9 (January 1, 1990): 1116.

Chapter **13**

Application Blank

Learning Objectives—After completion of this exercise, you should be able to:

1. Identify the lawfulness/unlawfulness of items on an application blank.

2. Design a legal application blank.

Time Suggested: Thirty minutes

Procedures:

1. Break into groups of four or five.

2. As a group, evaluate the lawfulness/unlawfulness of the application blank (Figure 13–1) that follows. Use the Pre-Employment Inquiry Guide (Figure 13–2).

3. Answer the questions at the end of the exercise.

◢ FIGURE 13–1   Application Blank

		DATE
	PERSONNEL OFFICE	POSITION APPLYING FOR:
ATTACH RECENT PHOTOGRAPH HERE	Telephone 646-2805	FULL-TIME ☐ PART-TIME ☐
	APPLICATION FOR EMPLOYMENT	MINIMUM SALARY REQUIREMENTS PER MONTH (DO NOT LEAVE BLANK)
		WHEN WILL YOU BE AVAILABLE FOR EMPLOYMENT?

PRINT NAME	LAST	FIRST	MIDDLE	MAIDEN	SOCIAL SECURITY NUMBER

PRESENT ADDRESS	STREET & NUMBER	CITY	STATE	TELEPHONE NUMBER

PREVIOUSLY EMPLOYED HERE DEPARTMENT AND DATES   YES ☐   NO ☐   **HOW LONG DO YOU PLAN TO WORK HERE?**

AGE LAST BIRTHDAY	HEIGHT	MALE ☐	SINGLE ☐	WIDOW ☐	DIVORCED ☐
DATE OF BIRTH	WEIGHT	FEMALE ☐	MARRIED ☐	WIDOWER ☐	SEPARATED ☐

NAME OF HUSBAND OR WIFE   **OCCUPATION OF HUSBAND OR WIFE (IF STUDENT, GIVE CLASSIFICATION)**

NUMBER OF DEPENDENTS   **NUMBER OF CHILDREN AND AGES OF CHILDREN**

ARE YOU A CITIZEN OF THE UNITED STATES?   YES ☐ NO ☐   **ARE YOU PREGNANT?**   YES ☐ NO ☐

PHYSICAL LIMITATIONS, IF ANY _____

HAVE YOU EVER HAD A WORKMEN'S COMPENSATION INSURANCE INJURY?   YES ☐   NO ☐

DETAILS _____

HAVE YOU EVER BEEN CONVICTED FOR VIOLATION OF ANY LAW, OTHER THAN A MINOR TRAFFIC VIOLATION?   YES ☐   NO ☐

IF YES, GIVE DETAILS _____

MILITARY SERVICE (BRANCH)	FROM TO	HIGHEST RANK	TYPE OF DISCHRAGE	RES. OBLIGATION	DRAFT STATUS

ARE YOU NOW A LICENSED OR CERTIFIED MEMBER OF ANY PROFESSION OR TRADE?   YES ☐ NO ☐   **GIVE KIND OF LICENSE AND STATE LICENSE OR CERTIFICATE NUMBER AND YEAR:**

EDUCATION—CIRCLE HIGHEST GRADE COMPLETED   **GIVE NAME AND ADDRESS OF LAST HIGH SCHOOL ATTENDED**

1 2 3 4 5 6 7 8 9 10 11 12

NAME AND LOCATION OF COLLEGE	DATES ATTENDED FROM	TO	YEARS COMPLETED	DEGREES AWARDED TITLE	DATE

COLLEGE MAJOR   **COLLEGE MINOR**

Other schools or training *(for example, trade, vocational, armed forces, or business)*. Give for each the name and location *(city, State, and ZIP Code if known)* of school, dates attended, subjects studied, certificates, and any other pertinent data.

AN EQUAL OPPORTUNITY EMPLOYER

◢ FIGURE 13–1   Application Blank—(continued)

EXPERIENCE–START WITH YOUR PRESENT OR LAST POSITION AND WORK BACK. IF YOU WERE EVER EMPLOYED IN ANY POSITION UNDER A DIFFERENT NAME, GIVE THE NAME USED.

NAME OF FIRM OR ORGANIZATION	FROM		TO		MONTHLY SALARY
	MONTH	YEAR	MONTH	YEAR	STARTING $ _____
STREET ADDRESS					FINAL $ _____
CITY AND STATE	TITLE _____				
NAME & TITLE OF IMMEDIATE SUPERVISOR	JOB DUTIES _____				
REASON FOR LEAVING					

NAME OF FIRM OR ORGANIZATION	FROM		TO		MONTHLY SALARY
	MONTH	YEAR	MONTH	YEAR	STARTING $ _____
STREET ADDRESS					FINAL $ _____
CITY AND STATE	TITLE _____				
NAME & TITLE OF IMMEDIATE SUPERVISOR	JOB DUTIES _____				
REASON FOR LEAVING					

NAME OF FIRM OR ORGANIZATION	FROM		TO		MONTHLY SALARY
	MONTH	YEAR	MONTH	YEAR	STARTING $ _____
STREET ADDRESS					FINAL $ _____
CITY AND STATE	TITLE _____				
NAME & TITLE OF IMMEDIATE SUPERVISOR	JOB DUTIES _____				
REASON FOR LEAVING					

MAY WE CONTACT YOUR PRESENT EMPLOYER?   YES ☐   NO ☐

PERSONAL REFERENCES–LIST THREE PERSONS WHO ARE NOT RELATED TO YOU, AND WHO CAN FURNISH INFORMATION ABOUT YOU. DO NOT REPEAT NAMES OF SUPERVISORS FURNISHED IN YOUR EMPLOYMENT RECORD.

FULL NAME	BUSINESS OR HOME ADDRESS	OCCUPATION
1.		
2.		
3.		

THE REMAINING PART OF THIS APPLICATION IS FOR YOUR CONVENIENCE IN FURNISHING ADDITIONAL INFORMATION

CONCERNING ANY JOBS, SPECIAL TRAINING, ACCOMPLISHMENTS, OR WORK EXPERIENCE YOU HAVE HAD. _____

I CERTIFY THAT THE STATEMENTS MADE BY ME IN THIS APPLICATION ARE TRUE, COMPLETE AND CORRECT TO THE BEST OF MY KNOWLEDGE AND BELIEF AND ARE MADE IN GOOD FAITH. I UNDERSTAND THAT ANY FALSE STATEMENTS MADE HEREIN WILL VOID THIS APPLICATION AND ANY ACTIONS BASED ON IT.

DATE _____ SIGNATURE OF APPLICANT _____

FOR PERSONNEL OFFICE USE ONLY

TEST SCORES: TYPING _____   SHORTHAND _____   ADDING MACHINE _____

FIGURE 13–2   Pre-Employment Inquiry Guide

Subject	Lawful Inquiries	Unlawful Inquiries
1. Name		Inquiries about the name which would indicate applicant's lineage, ancestry, marital status, national origin, or descent. Inquiry into previous names of applicant where it has been changed by court order or otherwise. Mr., Mrs., Miss, or Ms.
2. Address or Duration of Residence	Applicant's address Inquiry into place and length of current and previous addresses. "How long a resident of this state or city?"	Specific inquiry into foreign addresses which would indicate national origin.
3. Birthplace	"Can you after employment submit a birth certificate or other proof of of U.S. citizenship?''	Birthplace of applicant. Birthplace of applicant's parents, spouse, or other relatives. Requirement that applicant submit proof of birth document prior to hiring.
4. Age	If a minor, require proof of age in form of a work permit or a certificate of age. Require proof of age by birth certificate after being hired. Inquire whether or not the applicant meets the minimum age requirement set by law.	Requirement that applicant state age or date of birth. Requirement that applicant produce proof of age in the form of a birth certificate or baptismal record.
5. Religion	An applicant may be advised concerning normal hours and days of work.	Applicant's religious denomination or affiliation, church, parish, pastor, or religious holidays observed. "Do you attend religious services or a house of worship?" Applicants may not be told "This is a Catholic/Protestant/Jewish/atheist/etc., organization." Applicants may not be told that employees are required to work on religious holidays which are observed as days of

◢◢ **FIGURE 13–2   Pre-Employment Inquiry Guide—(continued)**

Subject	Lawful Inquiries	Unlawful Inquiries
5. Religion— Continued		of prayer by members of their specific faith. Any inquiry to indicate or identify religious denomination or customs.
6. Race or Color		Applicant's race. Color of applicant's skin, eyes, hair, etc., or other questions directly or indirectly indicating race or color. Applicant's height.
7. Photograph	May be required after hiring for identification.	Request photograph before hiring.
8. Citizenship	"Are you a citizen of the United States?" "If you are not a U.S. citizen, have you the legal right to remain permanently in the U.S.? Do you intend to remain permanently in the U.S.?"	"Of what country are you a citizen?" Whether applicant or his parents or spouse are naturalized or native-born U.S. citizens. Date when applicant or parents or spouse acquired U.S. citizenship. Requirement that applicant produce his or her naturalization papers or first papers.
9. Ancestry or National Origin	Languages applicant reads, speaks, or writes fluently.	Applicant's nationality, lineage, ancestry, national origin, descent, or parentage. Nationality of applicant's parents or spouse; maiden name of applicant's wife or mother. Language commonly used by applicant. "What is your mother tongue?" How applicant acquired ability to read, write, or speak a foreign language.
10. Education	Applicant's academic, vocational, professional education, or school attended.	Any inquiry asking specifically the nationality, racial, or religious affiliation of a school. Dates of attendance and/or graduation from school.
11. Experience	Applicant's work experience. Other countries visited.	

FIGURE 13–2   Pre-Employment Inquiry Guide—(continued)

Subject	Lawful Inquiries	Unlawful Inquiries
12. Conviction, Arrest, and Court Record		Ask or check into person's arrest, court, or conviction record if not substantially related to functions and responsibilities of the prospective employment.
13. Relatives	Name of applicant's relatives already employed by this company. "Do you live with your parents?" Names and addresses of guardian of minor applicant.	Name or address of any relative of adult applicant.
14. Notice in Case of Emergency	Name and address of person to be notified in case of accident or emergency.	Relationship of person to be notified in case of emergencies.
15. References	"By whom were you referred for a position here?" Names of persons willing to provide professional and/or character references for applicant.	Require the submission of a religious reference.
16. Organization	Inquiry into membership in organizations providing the name or character of the organization does not reveal the race, religion, color, physical handicap, marital status, or ancestry of the applicant. What offices are held, if any.	The names of organizations to which the applicant belongs if such information would indicate through character or name the race, religion, color, or ancestry of the membership.
17. Sex	Only if required by business necessity.	Sex of the applicant. "Are you expecting?" or "Are you pregnant?" Applicant's weight.
18. Physical Handicap	Any illnesses that may interfere with your job duties.	Whether applicant has a physical handicap or defect. "Have you collected workers' compensation for a previous illness or injury?"
19. Marital Status		Whether single, married, divorced, widowed, separated, etc.

FIGURE 13–2   Pre-Employment Inquiry Guide—(continued)

Subject	Lawful Inquiries	Unlawful Inquiries
19. Marital Status— Continued		Names and ages of spouse and children. Spouse's place of employment.
20. Miscellaneous	Notice to applicants that any misstatements or omissions of material facts in the application may be cause for dismissal.	Require resume containing unlawful information.

ANY INQUIRY IS FORBIDDEN WHICH, ALTHOUGH NOT SPECIFICALLY LISTED AMONG THE ABOVE, IS DESIGNED TO ELICIT INFORMATION AS TO RACE, COLOR, ANCESTRY, AGE, SEX, RELIGION, PHYSICAL HANDICAP, MARITAL STATUS, OR ARREST AND COURT RECORD UNLESS BASED ON A BONA FIDE OCCUPATIONAL QUALIFICATION.

Compiled from *EEOC Compliance Manual* (Washington, D.C.: The Bureau of National Affairs, Inc., October 28, 1975), and from *A Guide for Application Forms and Interviews Under the Employment Practices Law* (Department of Labor and Industrial Relations, State of Hawaii, January 1977). Used with permission from the State of Hawaii.

QUESTIONS

1. In what ways are the items on the application blank (Figure 13–1) unlawful? Explain in the spaces provided here.

    a.

    b.

    c.

    d.

    e.

    f.

    g.

    h.

    i.

    j.

    k.

2. Is the information from an application blank useful for selecting "cooperative and productive" employees? Discuss this question within your group and write a group response here.

3. Discuss within your group the major job-related predictors that can be found on an application blank, then discuss their corresponding work behaviors. (For example, achievement behavior is best predicted by a work history with many successes.) List the important predictors and their corresponding work behaviors.

Major Predictors   *Work Behaviors*

a.

b.

c.

d.

e.

f.

g.

4. As a group, prepare an application blank that will meet the conditions of lawfulness yet still be useful to management. Use the space here to draft your application blank.

SUGGESTED READINGS

Dennis, Donn L. "Evaluating Corporate Recruitment Efforts." *Personnel Administration* 30 (January 1985): 21–26.

Edwards, Cathy. "Aggressive Recruitment: The Lessons of High-Tech Hiring." *Personnel Journal* 65 (January 1986): 40–48.

Keenan, Tony. "Where Application Forms Mislead." *Personnel Management* 15, no. 2 (February 1983): 40–43.

Lauderdale, Chris. "Extraterritorial Application of the Age Discrimination in Employment Act . . ." *Georgia Journal of International and Comparative Law* 20, no. 1 (1990): 207.

Lawrence, D. G., D. L. Salsburg, J. G. Dawson, and Z. D. Fasman. "Design and Use of Weighted Application Blanks." *The Personnel Administrator* 2, no. 3 (March 1982): 47–54.

Mondy, R. Wayne, et al. "What the Staffing Function Entails." *Personnel* 63 (April 1986): 55–58.

Powell, G. N. "Effects of Job Attributes and Recruiting Practices on Applicant Decisions: A Comparison." *Personnel Psychology* 37 (April 1984): 721–732.

Taylor, John W. "Strategic Military Employment Options: Theory and Application." *Comparative Strategy* 10, no. 2 (April 1, 1991): 155.

Chapter 14

Sexual Harassment

Learning Objectives—After completion of this exercise, you should be able to:

1. Recognize sexual harassment behaviors when they occur.
2. Describe important issues related to sexual harassment.
3. Describe management's responsibility for preventing and responding to sexual harassment.

Time Suggested: One and one-half hours

Procedures:

1. Break into mixed groups of males and females. Have at least two males and two females in each group. Groups should not be larger than six members.
2. Individually read the Introduction.
3. Read and follow the instructions for the Sexual Harassment Survey.
4. Answer the questions at the end of the exercise.
5. The instructor will lead the class in a discussion of the exercise.

 **INTRODUCTION**

TITLE VII SEXUAL HARASSMENT GUIDELINES

On November 10, 1980, the Equal Employment Opportunity Commission (EEOC) issued guidelines on sexual harassment in the workplace. These were interpretive guidelines under Title VII of the Civil Rights Act of 1964 which state that:

- Title VII prohibits sexual harassment of employees.
- Employers are responsible for the actions of their agents and supervisors.
- Employers are responsible for the actions of all other employees if the employer knew or should have known about the sexual harassment.[1]

WHY WERE THE GUIDELINES ISSUED?

Sexual harassment in the workplace is a continuing and widespread problem. The EEOC has stated, "Sexual harassment like harassment on the basis of color, race, religion, or national origin has long been recognized by the EEOC as a violation of . . . Title VII of the Civil Rights Act of 1964 . . . However, despite the position taken by the Commission, sexual harassment continues to be especially widespread. . . ."

An example of the breadth of this problem is shown by a 1975 study conducted by Working Women's Institute in which 70 percent of the respondents reported that they had experienced sexual harassment on the job. In another study, conducted by *Redbook Magazine* (November 1976), almost one-half of employed women surveyed said that they—or a woman they knew—had quit a position or been fired because of sexual harassment on the job.[2]

DO THE GUIDELINES HAVE THE FORCE OF LAW?

Strictly speaking, no. The guidelines are advisory and courts take them into account. Moreover, the guidelines closely parallel already existing court decisions in which the courts have held that sexual harassment violates Title VII and that employers are responsible for the actions of their employees. Thus, the guidelines are consistent with current case law.

DO THE GUIDELINES PROHIBIT PERSONAL RELATIONSHIPS BETWEEN EMPLOYEES?

No. The guidelines address themselves to unwelcome conduct and clearly distinguish sexual harassment from a "particular action or incident (which is) a purely personal, social relationship without a discriminating employment effect."[3] In determining whether conduct constitutes sexual harassment, the commission "will look at the record as a whole and at the totality of the circumstances, such as the nature of the sexual advances and the context in which the alleged incidents occurred. The determination of the legality of a particular action will be made from the facts, on a case by case basis."[4]

WHAT IS SEXUAL HARASSMENT?

The guidelines define sexual harassment as unwelcome sexual advances, requests for sexual favors, and other verbal or physical conduct of a nature that constitutes harassment when:

- Submission to the conduct is either explicitly or implicitly a term or condition of an individual's employment.

- Submission to or rejection of such conduct by an individual is used as the basis for employment decisions affecting that individual.

- Such conduct has the purpose or effect of unreasonably interfering with an individual's work performance or creating an intimidating, hostile, or offensive working environment.[5]

DO THE GUIDELINES GIVE SPECIFIC EXAMPLES OF ACTIVITIES THAT CONSTITUTE SEXUAL HARASSMENT?

No. The guidelines simply offer a flexible and very broad definition of sexual harassment with no specific examples.

Specific examples, however, that may constitute sexual harassment under the guidelines are:

- Subtle pressure for sexual activity.
- Unnecessary patting or pinching.
- Constant brushing against another employee's body.
- "Friendly" arms around the shoulder.
- "Accidental" brushes or touches.
- Deliberate assaults or molestations.
- Demanding sexual favors accompanied by implied threats concerning an individual's employment status.
- Demanding sexual favors accompanied by implied or overt promises of preferential treatment with regard to an individual's employment status.
- Explicit offers of money for sex.[6]

ARE SEXUAL JOKES, SLURS, AND INSULTS DIRECTED
AT MEMBERS OF ONE SEX PROHIBITED BY THE GUIDELINES?

The answer to this question is unclear. Though the guidelines state that sexual harassment can be "physical" or "verbal," the guidelines also state that the conduct must be "of a sexual nature." Thus, it is unclear whether derogatory and degrading comments or jokes directed at members of one sex constitute sexual harassment.

The Circuit Court of the District of Columbia, howwever, has found that activity need not have a sexual content in order to constitute sexual harassment. Though the cases involved activity that was sexual in content, the court said that the content of the activity was "immaterial." The activity need only be directed at members of one sex.

> . . . (R)etention of her job was conditioned upon submission to sexual relations—an extraction which the supervisor would not have sought from any male.
> . . . The vitiating sex factor thus stemmed not from the fact that [what] appellant's supervisor demanded was sexual activity—which of itself is immaterial—but from the fact that he imposed upon her tenure in her then position a condition which he would not have fastened upon a male employee. (*Williams* v. *Saxbe*, 413 F.Supp. 654 (D.D.C.1972)).

WHAT MUST EMPLOYERS DO TO COMPLY WITH THE GUIDELINES?

The guidelines state that an employer should take all necessary steps to prevent sexual harassment, such as:

- Affirmatively raising the subject.

- Expressing strong disapproval.

- Developing appropriate sanctions.

- Informing employees of their rights to raise and how to raise the issue of harassment under Title VII.

- Developing methods to sensitize all concerned.[7]

IS AN EMPLOYER RESPONSIBLE FOR THE
ACTIONS OF ITS AGENTS AND SUPERVISORS?

Yes. The guidelines hold an employer fully responsible for the actions of its agents and supervisors "regardless of whether the specific acts complained of were authorized or even forbidden by the employer and regardless of whether the employer knew or should have known of their occurrence."[8]

IS AN INSTITUTION RESPONSIBLE
FOR THE ACTIONS OF ITS EMPLOYEES?

Yes. The guidelines, however, impose a less strict standard by which to measure the employer's responsibility if the harasser is simply an employee and not an agent or a supervisory employee. The employer is responsible for the actions of such employees only if the employer (or its agents or supervisory employees) "knows or should have known of the conduct and fails to take immediate and appropriate corrective action."[9]

In addition, an employer may also be responsible for the actions of nonemployees who sexually harass employees in the workplace where the employer (or its agents or supervisory employees) "knows or should have known of the conduct and fails to take immediate and appropriate corrective action."[10]

WHY SHOULD INSTITUTIONS BE INTERESTED IN PROHIBITING SEXUAL HARASSMENT?

As a booklet published by AFSCME[11] argues, "Probably the majority of offenders are supervisors, so sexual harassment should be considered a problem for management to resolve. Work environments in which sexual harassment is sanctioned are not the most productive, and personnel decisions may be made without regard to the job performance."[12] The booklet notes "sexual harassment undermines the integrity of the workplace,"[13] and therefore, "it is good management practice to have a strong policy against sexual harassment."[14]

In addition, employers will also want to avoid charges of sexual harassment. In such cases, the EEOC can ask for an award of front pay, back pay, reinstatement, promotion, or any other type of relief that will rectify the situation. Both the EEOC and the courts have wide discretion in correcting situations where sexual harassment has been or is occurring. If an employer refuses to settle a complaint through the conciliation process, the EEOC can file suit and ask a federal judge for relief.

WILL INSTITUTIONS BE INFORMED IF A SEXUAL HARASSMENT COMPLAINT IS FILED AGAINST THEM?

Yes. The EEOC notifies institutions of complaints within ten days.

WHO CAN FILE A COMPLAINT AGAINST AN INSTITUTION?

Individuals and/or organizations on behalf of aggrieved employee(s) or applicant(s). Organizations also may file class or pattern complaints without identification of individuals. Members of the commission may also file charges.

IS THERE A TIME LIMIT FOR FILING COMPLAINTS?

Yes. A complaint must be filed within 180 days of the alleged incident.

HOW IS A COMPLAINT MADE?

By a sworn complaint form, obtainable from the Equal Employment Opportunity Commission, 2401 E Street, NW, Washington, DC 20508, or the district area EEOC office.

ARE THE NAMES OF COMPLAINANTS KEPT CONFIDENTIAL?

The complainant's name is divulged to the institution when an investigation is made. Charges, however, are not made public by the EEOC, nor can any of its efforts during the conciliation process be made public by the EEOC or its employees. The aggrieved party, however, and the respondent are not bound by the confidentiality requirement. If court action becomes necessary, the identity of the parties becomes a matter of public record.

DO THE GUIDELINES APPLY TO LABOR ORGANIZATIONS?

Yes. Labor organizations are subject to the same requirements and sanctions as employers.

IS RETALIATION FOR FILING COMPLAINTS ILLEGAL?

Yes. Employers are prohibited from discharging or discriminating against any employee or applicant for employment because he or she has made a complaint, assisted with an investigation, or instituted proceedings.

WHAT CAN AN INSTITUTION DO?

An institution can make people more aware about the problem of sexual harassment by the following activities:

- Developing a specific policy against sexual harassment.
- Disseminating the policy in memos, posters, flyers, radio spots, etc.
- Developing a procedure to inform new employees.
- Surveying the workplace to find out the extent of the problem at the institution.
- Developing and disseminating information about grievance procedures to handle sexual harassment complaints. (Sexual harassment complaints are often initially handled more appropriately by informal procedures followed by more formal procedures if the complaint is not resolved. Individuals who wish to pursue a grievance are likely to go to court if the institution has no procedure for them to use.)

- Developing a union grievance procedure, where appropriate.
- Developing a code of conduct for all employees.

These guidelines add strength to the growing commitment of management that sexual harassment will no longer be tolerated.

SEXUAL HARASSMENT SURVEY

Now that each member of your group has read the information in the Introduction, use what you have learned to analyze each of the following six situations. Discuss each situation within your group and make a group decision as to whether you think sexual harassment has occurred. Limit yourselves to *five* minutes per situation. Appoint a timekeeper to control the time spent on each situation.

After the discussion, if your group thinks sexual harassment has occurred, check "Yes." Indicate the degree of severity. If your group thinks no sexual harassment has occurred, simply check "No."

Once your group has finished all six situations, individually answer the questions at the end of the chapter.

SEXUAL HARASSMENT SURVEY

Determine whether you think SEXUAL HARASSMENT occurred in each of the following scenarios. If yes, rank on the appropriate scale.

1. Jackie thinks Bob is very well built. She often stares at his body when she thinks he isn't looking. Although he hasn't told her, Bob has noticed Jackie looking and, frankly, it makes him uncomfortable.

   No _____   Yes _____

   If yes, rank on following scale:

   Severe _____

   Moderate _____

   Subtle/Ambiguous _____

2. Barbara is attending a party; her boss is present and has been drinking. He tells her how beautiful she is and that she understands him better than his wife. He says he intends to make an obvious token of his appreciation of her and her work. Then he asks to drive her home.

   No _____   Yes _____

   If yes, rank on following scale:

   Severe _____

   Moderate _____

   Subtle/Ambiguous _____

3. Sylvia hates the days when she has to work with Jeremy, a co-worker with whom she once had a stormy and romantic relationship. Jeremy hasn't gotten over Sylvia and persistently *asks her* to come back to him. Sylvia tells her manager about the situation. The manager suggests that they should try to work it out, reasoning that it is best for her to stay out of Sylvia's personal business.

   No _____   Yes _____

   If yes, rank on following scale:

   Severe _____

   Moderate _____

   Subtle/Ambiguous _____

4. A new clerical support person in your area of responsibility tells you that she feels uncomfortable during breaks. She says the men who are in the designated break area tell crude jokes and pass girlie magazines while she is present.

   No ____   Yes ____

   If yes, rank on following scale:

   Severe _____

   Moderate _____

   Subtle/Ambiguous _____

5. Your manager and one of your colleagues are having an affair. Since the affair started, your colleague has received better and easier work assignments, a bigger raise and a recent promotion. Until the relationship began, you had been the star of the department.

   No ____   Yes ____

   If yes, rank on following scale:

   Severe _____

   Moderate _____

   Subtle/Ambiguous _____

6. The institute director, a male, walks up behind a subordinate and touches her in the ribs to scare her. She reacts by saying "Don't do that!" He apologizes.

   No ____   Yes ____

   If yes, rank on following scale:

   Severe _____

   Moderate _____

   Subtle/Ambiguous _____

7. The manager of the office takes pictures of the office staff. He brings back the developed photographs and tells one of the females that in the photo she looks like "a lady of the night."

   No ____   Yes ____

   If yes, rank on following scale:

   Severe _____

   Moderate _____

   Subtle/Ambiguous _____

8. The institute director has a forty-one-foot sloop and is an active sailor. He normally has 6–10 guest/crew members on his boat for Sunday afternoon sails. He invites one of his female subordinates to go on a Sunday afternoon sail. Several other workers of the institute have been on the Sunday afternoon sails.

   No ____   Yes ____

   If yes, rank on following scale:

   Severe   _____

   Moderate   _____

   Subtle/Ambiguous   _____

9. A male supervisor asks a female staff member out on a date. Although she refuses, he continues to ask her.

   No ____   Yes ____

   If yes, rank on following scale:

   Severe   _____

   Moderate   _____

   Subtle/Ambiguous   _____

10. A manager is having an affair with her boss but wants to break up. He says that she will not get the promotion she's been expecting if she does so.

    No ____   Yes ____

    If yes, rank on following scale:

    Severe   _____

    Moderate   _____

    Subtle/Ambiguous   _____

11. Two men and a woman enter an elevator. The men make comments about the woman's anatomy.

    No ____   Yes ____

    If yes, rank on following scale:

    Severe   _____

    Moderate   _____

    Subtle/Ambiguous   _____

12. A group of men paste photos from "Playboy" onto biographies of new women employees that the company includes in its newsletter.

    No _____   Yes _____

    If yes, rank on following scale:

    Severe _____

    Moderate _____

    Subtle/Ambiguous _____

13. A female worker is repeatedly patted on the behind by a male co-worker.

    No _____   Yes _____

    If yes, rank on following scale:

    Severe _____

    Moderate _____

    Subtle/Ambiguous _____

14. At staff meetings, a manager frequently sits next to an employee. He occasionally touches her arm and rubs her neck.

    No _____   Yes _____

    If yes, rank on following scale:

    Severe _____

    Moderate _____

    Subtle/Ambiguous _____

15. Company administrators show the X-rated movie "Deep Throat" at a company sales meeting after telling employees they would show an educational film.

    No _____   Yes _____

    If yes, rank on following scale:

    Severe _____

    Moderate _____

    Subtle/Ambiguous _____

16. A manager tells a lot of off-color jokes in a female employee's presence. He finds the employee's embarrassment amusing.

No _____   Yes _____

If yes, rank on following scale:

Severe _____

Moderate _____

Subtle/Ambiguous _____

QUESTIONS

1. Describe below the differences in perceptions and feelings between the males and the females in your group.

2. Summarize below what you believe are the key aspects of the sexual harassment guidelines that specifically relate to the manager's job.

3. In addition to following the guidelines, what other actions can the manager take to prevent sexual harassment from occurring?

4. Should managers do more than follow the guidelines? Why? Write your answer below.

 **NOTES**

1. 29 *C.F.R.*, Section 1604.11, 45 *Federal Register 1980*, pp. 74676–74677.

2. *Redbook Magazine*, November 1976.

3. Memo to public interest groups from Eleanor Holmes Norton, Chair, EEOC, March 11, 1980.

4. 29 *C.F.R.*, Section 1604.11(b).

5. Ibid., Section 1604.11(a).

6. *Sexual Harassment on the Job: What the Union Can Do.* Pamphlet available from American Federation of State, County, and Municipal Employees (AFSCME), Research Department, 1625 L Street, NW, Washington, DC 20036.

7. 29 *C.F.R.*, Section 1604.11(f).

8. Ibid., Section 1604.11(c).

9. Ibid., Section 1604.11(d).

10. Ibid., Section 1604.11(e).

11. AFSCME, *Sexual Harassment on the Job.*

12. Ibid., 11.

13. Ibid., 32.

14. Ibid., 11.

◢ SUGGESTED READINGS

Brandon, Billie, and Robert A. Snyder. "ADEA Update: Case Law and 'Cost' as a Defense." *Personnel Administrator* 30 (February 1985): 116–119.

Ford, Robert C. "Sexual Harassment at Work: What is the Problem?" *Akron Business and Economic Review* 20, no. 4 (Winter 1990): 79.

Greenbaum, Marcia L., and Bruce Fraser. "Sexual Harassment in the Workplace." *Arbitration Journal* 36, no. 4 (December 1981): 30–41.

Hopkins, C. H., and D. A. Johnson. "Sexual Harassment in the Workplace." *Journal of College Placement* 42, no. 3 (Spring 1982): 30–35.

James, Jennifer. "Sexual Harassment." *Public Personnel Management* 10, no. 4 (Winter 1981): 402–407.

Lewis, Kathryn E., and Pamela R. Johnson. "Preventing Sexual Harassment Complaints Based on Hostile Work Environments." *SAM Advanced Management Journal* 56, no. 2 (Spring 1991): 21.

Linenberger, Patricia, and Timothy J. Keaveny. "Sexual Harassment: The Employer's Legal Obligations." *Personnel* 58, no. 6 (November–December 1981): 60–68.

Miller, J., and M. Miller. "Hands Off." *Perspectives: The Civil Rights Quarterly* (Spring 1982): 31–33.

Oswald, Sharon L., and William L. Woerner. "Sexual Harassment in the Workplace: A View Through the Eyes of the Courts." *Labor Law Journal* 41, no. 11 (November 1, 1990): 786.

Peterson, D. J., and D. Massengill. "Sexual Harassment—A Growing Problem in the Workplace." *The Personnel Administrator* (October 1982): 79–89.

Rubenstein, Michael. "Devising a Sexual Harassment Policy." *Personnel Management* 23, no. 2 (February 1, 1991): 34.

"Sexual Harassment: The Views From the Top." *Redbook Magazine*, March 1981, 46–51.

Strayer, Jacqueline F., and Sandra E. Rapoport. "Sexual Harassment, 2: Limiting Corporate Liability." *Personnel* 63 (April 1986): 26–33.

Thornton, B. Terry. "Sexual Harassment, 1: Discouraging It in the Workplace." *Personnel* 63 (April 1986): 18–25.

Chapter 15

Age Discrimination

Learning Objectives—After completion of this exercise, you should be able to:

1. Understand the key aspects of the Age Discrimination in Employment Act of 1967 and its amendments in 1978 and 1986.

2. Identify common age discrimination situations.

3. Identify your own age biases.

Time Suggested: One hour

Procedures:

1. Read the Introduction.

2. Read the case studies and answer the questions.

3. Take the age discrimination awareness quiz.

4. The instructor will lead a class discussion regarding each case and the age discrimination awareness quiz.

5. Form groups of four. Three members are to role play and one is to observe.

   a. Everyone should read the background to the role-playing situation.

   b. Each role player is to read his or her role. One is the personnel director, one is a younger applicant, one is an older applicant.

   c. The personnel director is to interview each applicant separately, in any order, for ten minutes each.

   d. Anyone may ask for another interview.

   e. The observer is to take constructive notes on the proceedings.

   f. The personnel director must decide which applicant gets the job and tell the winner and loser.

   g. The observer reports observations.

INTRODUCTION

The Age Discrimination in Employment Act (ADEA) was passed in 1967 and amended in 1978 and 1986. The purpose of the ADEA is to eliminate age discrimination for persons over forty years of age with regard to hiring, promotion, compensation, termination, or any related privilege of employment. The ADEA covers employers who have twenty or more employees who work a minimum of twenty weeks annually; employment agencies, including the United States Employment Service; and labor organizations.

Originally only employees between ages forty and sixty-five were covered by the ADEA. In 1978, an amendment was passed stating that individuals could not be forced to retire on the basis of age until age seventy, except for certain executives in major policy decision positions who have a guaranteed pension of at least $44,000 annually and have been in the policy decision position for at least two years. The 1986 amendment removed the age seventy cap for most private sector employees.

The ADEA includes a bona fide occupational qualification (BFOQ) clause that allows employers to discriminate based on age if job safety can be shown to be at risk due to age-related diminished capacity. For certain job categories such as police officers, the courts have upheld maximum hiring ages and mandatory retirement ages when issues of public safety and employee fitness are BFOQs.

ADEA is the only antidiscrimination law that allows for jury trial. Two factors are important to remember about ADEA jury trials. First, employees win over 50 percent of litigated cases. Second, in cases where employers are found to be abusive, large monetary awards (punitive damages) have been given to the employee even though the ADEA law does not specifically include punitive damages.

The Equal Employment Opportunity Commission (EEOC) is the government agency responsible for enforcement and regulation of the ADEA.

CASE STUDIES

Houghton v. McDonnell Douglas Corp.
413 F.Supp. 1230 (E.D.Mo.1976)

McDonnell Douglas Corporation transferred a 52-year-old employee from the position of chief-production test pilot to another position in 1971 and subsequently discharged him for nonproductivity. Plaintiff Houghton's removal from flying status was made upon defendant McDonnell's good-faith determination that his continued employment as a test pilot would be an increased safety risk due to plaintiff Houghton's age.

PLAINTIFF'S POSITION:

Houghton's complaint alleged that defendant McDonnell Douglas Corporation had violated the Age Discrimination in Employment Act by removing him from flight status and terminating his employment, thus entitling him to injunctive and monetary relief. The plaintiff also alleged that defendant McDonnell limited, segregated, or classified him in a way that deprived, or tended to deprive, him of employment opportunities and otherwise adversely affected his status as an employee, because of his age.

DEFENDANT'S POSITION:

Defendant McDonnell admitted removing plaintiff Houghton from flight status because of his age but contended that this action was taken because age is a bona fide occupational qualification (herein BFOQ) reasonably necessary to the normal operation of defendant's business [see Chapter 12 for a definition of BFOQ]. Defendant also admitted terminating Houghton's employment, but contended that this action was not taken because of his age but was based on reasonable factors other than age and was "for good cause."

FINDINGS:

A production test pilot must perform his duties under conditions of psychological and physiological stress. Aging is a loss of function, a loss of ability at a particular time to meet the particular demands of a person's environment. These changes occur and increase in the forties to the point that anyone over the age of fifty is showing signs of aging, and in general those over the age of sixty can be said to have aged. Pilots, like all other people, are subject to this process, and plaintiff Houghton has experienced it.

Dr. Earl T. Carter determined that plaintiff was not physically capable at age fifty-three of safely and effectively performing the duties of a production test pilot at McDonnell. Dr. Carter described the age range in the lower fifties as a "gray area" where it becomes increasingly easy to demonstrate the advantages of youth below fifty and increasingly easy to demonstrate the impact of aging above fifty.

RULING:

In accordance with the Mandate of the United States Court of Appeals for the Eighth Circuit, this Court finds that plaintiff Houghton became physically unable to safely and effectively perform the duties of chief production test pilot at some time prior to his removal from flight status. Plaintiff Houghton's damages must therefore be fixed as non-existent since his removal from flight status and subsequent dismissal were not in violation of the ADEA.

 **QUESTION**

1. Do you agree with the court's ruling in the *Houghton* case? Explain.

CASE STUDIES

McMahon v. Barclay
510 F.Supp. 1114 (S.D.N.Y.1981)

In this case, two individuals challenged the validity of the New York statute prohibiting employment of persons over age 29 as police officers. Section 58(1)(a) provides:

". . . no person shall be eligible for provisional or permanent employment in the competitive class of the civil service as a police officer of the capital police force of the state office of general services after July 1, 1976 . . . unless he shall satisfy the following basic requirements:

(a) he is not less than twenty nor more than twenty-nine years of age, provided however that the time spent on military duty or on terminal leave, not exceeding a total of six years, shall be subtracted from the age of any applicant who has passed his twenty-ninth birthday. . . ."

PLAINTIFF'S POSITION:

Plaintiffs seek a declaration that Section 58(1)(a) is invalid as being arbitrary, unreasonable, and bearing no rational relationship to any legitimate state purposes and thus deprives such persons of equal protection of the laws. Plaintiffs point to the fact that the New York State Department of Civil Service prepared and recommended introduction and passage of legislation to repeal the age requirements. This legislation was not enacted, apparently never reaching the floor of the legislature.

In its Memorandum to the legislature, the Department wrote:

This amendment would remove a requirement founded on tradition rather than on any demonstrable physical or operational need. This age requirement has proven to be a barrier to employment of otherwise well-qualified applicants, often to the detriment of the appointing authority concerned. In addition, the age limit is not uniformly applied under the present statute as it may be extended under certain conditions and up to six years is required to be subtracted from the age of those applicants who have spent time on military duty.

DEFENDANT'S POSITION:

Defendants advance the contention that the statute is a legal exception to the Civil Rights Act which allows for discrimination. The justification offered for this contention is:

Reprinted by permission from Fair Employment Practices Service, Copyright © 1980 by The Bureau of National Affairs, Inc., Washington, D.C.

(1) that younger police can serve for a longer period of time after being trained than older recruits and (2) younger recruits will remain physically fit for longer periods of time.

Defendants rely heavily on *Mass. Bd. of Retirement* v. *Murgia*, upholding a mandatory retirement age for all uniformed state police upon reaching age fifty. Defendants urge that both mandatory retirement age and the maximum hiring age ensure that police ranks will be filled by relatively young men at the police officer level.

RULING:

The argument that the investment in training younger recruits is more likely to be recouped than that in the training of older persons would negate the entire concept of protection against age discrimination. The physical fitness contention overlooks requirement that recruits must satisfy physical fitness requirements, fact that statute has numerous exceptions to maximum age requirement, and fact that there is no state-wide mandatory retirement age.

The court disagreed with the applicability of the Murgia case. Section 58 totally precludes persons age 29 from entering certain police forces. Murgia deals with persons who have had the opportunity to serve as police officers. Section 58 deprives relatively young and physically fit persons from pursuing a career for many years as police officers without a showing of the need for such a blanket disqualification.

We find that Section 58 bears no relational relationship to any legitimate state purpose and is violative of the equal protection of the law.

Plaintiffs' motion is granted.

 **QUESTION**

1. Do you agree with the ruling? Explain.

 **PROBLEMS**

This quiz is designed to help you recognize any age biases you may have.

AGE-DISCRIMINATION AWARENESS QUIZ

Agree	Disagree	
_____	_____	1. Everything equal, younger workers should be promoted before older workers.
_____	_____	2. Older high-technology workers are not as up-to-date as recent graduates.
_____	_____	3. Advertising a position only in a college newspaper is discriminatory.
_____	_____	4. During a business recession, when staff reductions are necessary, workers closest to retirement should be laid off first.
_____	_____	5. In choosing between a 40-year-old and a 28-year-old for a bus driver position, I would choose the 28-year-old.
_____	_____	6. Giving a 60-year-old employee a three-year training program is not cost-efficient.
_____	_____	7. In the above case I would counsel the employee on a career change.
_____	_____	8. Employees who stay on after normal retirement age should continue to accrue full benefits.
_____	_____	9. A tenured university professor, age 65, should be retired.
_____	_____	10. A person over 70 should not be president of the United States.
_____	_____	11. An airline pilot should be retired at age 55.
_____	_____	12. An older worker on an assembly line is slowing down the process; he or she should be retired.
_____	_____	13. A worker's pension should commence even if he or she works beyond the normal retirement age.
_____	_____	14. Younger workers are healthier and therefore they have less absenteeism than older workers.
_____	_____	15. A woman returning to the workforce at age 45 is as productive as a 30-year-old.

Agree   ***Disagree***

_____   _____   16. A woman at age 35 probably has children at home and thus cannot be as productive as a younger man.

_____   _____   17. An employee working past normal retirement age should contribute to the added expense borne by the company for life insurance benefits.

_____   _____   18. An employee disabled on the job should receive disability pay only until the normal retirement age of 65.

_____   _____   19. Forty years old is too old to begin training as a police officer.

_____   _____   20. Old fogies should move over and give younger people a chance.

ROLE-PLAYING

BACKGROUND

A large real estate management company has an opening for an account manager. This is a salaried middle-management position that entails quite a lot of overtime and responsibilities. The company policy is to promote from within. The personnel director has narrowed the field down to two equally qualified resident managers and must select one of them.

The available position calls for someone to manage five medium-size middle-income-level apartment condominiums, each of which has a resident manager. The account manager will prepare operating budgets, contract major maintenance work, supervise the resident managers, and attend and report at all board of directors meetings and annual homeowners' meetings. Often these meetings are in the evening or on weekends.

The resident managers work closely with the account manager and thus are familiar with the demands and duties of the position. In the past the personnel director has found they adapt quite easily to the account manager's position—more so than "outsiders" who are not aware of the company policies and condominium bylaws.

THE PERSONNEL DIRECTOR: FRANCES MARSHALL

You have been with the company for eight years and have done a good job. Your selections for positions have been successful. Now you're feeling quite a lot of pressure in this selection. You know the work and habits as well as the strong and weak points of both applicants, and you feel that either could do a good job. However, some things you have to consider are:

1. The overtime takes the account manager away from home on evenings and weekends. Chris has two children and a spouse at home. Dale's spouse died a couple of years ago and the children are grown and gone.

2. The manager must deal with complaints from the condo owners, some of whom are nasty and discriminatory.

3. The manager must report to the owners and command their respect, and must not miss a meeting.

    Chris's appearance is sometimes quite trendy whereas Dale maintains a "mature, conservative" look. Both are careful workers, but Chris is absent on occasion.

4. The position is a career steppingstone from resident manager to management. Chris feels ready to move upward and probably will look elsewhere if this position is filled by someone else. On the other hand, Dale is near retirement and will stay as resident manager if not promoted.

5. The cost to the company will be different depending on the person you select. If it is Chris, vacation will still be two weeks, sick leave will be ten days, and profit sharing will start in two more years. For Dale, however, vacation is four weeks, sick leave is twenty days, and profit sharing begins immediately, because of his time with the company; also, as of age sixty-five, Dale will be paid some retirement money even if he continues to work.

CHRIS TREVOR—YOUNGER APPLICANT

At twenty-eight you feel an urge to get going on your career. You began with the company four years ago when you were finishing your business degree at night school. You have been resident manager for two years now. The position has been good, and you have enjoyed being around and seeing your two babies growing up and having all your meals at home with your family. Some of the condominium owners call and bug you at strange hours or on your days off, but generally you get along with them, although many of them are old enough to be your grandparents, you think.

This new position will take you to the downtown office every day, so you will not see your family as much. You feel that if you do not get the promotion it will be time to look for a new position. Either way, it will entail moving and resettling. You have a slight case of asthma and so you miss a couple of days of work when the seasons change. Being with the company only four years has entitled you to two weeks of vacation and ten sick days a year, and in two years you will be able to qualify for the profit sharing fund, if you're an account manager.

DALE BURGESS—OLDER APPLICANT

You only have four years until you can retire at the normal retirement age. However, the company, by law, will let you stay on for an additional five and you expect to stay if you receive the promotion. If you are not promoted you will retire at 65, because you have worked as resident manager for thirty years and are rather bored with it. You realize the new position will demand more of your time, but since your spouse has died and your children have grown you enjoy working to fill your days.

You have known many of the owners for years, and you get along well with them. When they call at odd hours, you understand. You have enjoyed good health and have not missed work for a year.

Once concern you have is, if you work past retirement age, what is the policy on benefits?

OBSERVER'S FORM

1. Did it make a difference in which order the personnel director interviewed the applicants?

2. Who seemed to lead the interview?

3. Were proper questions asked?

4. Was anyone's age referred to? Was it a legal reference?

SUGGESTED READINGS

Beohmer, Robert G. "The Age Discrimination in Employment Act—Reductions in Force as America Grays." *American Business Law Journal* 28, no. 3 (Fall 1990): 379.

Bompey, Stuart H. "Cases and Issues in Age Discrimination." *Employee Relations Law Journal* 3, no. 3 (Winter 1978): 382.

Burstein, James A. "The Arbitrability of Age Discrimination Claims: A Split in the Circuits." *Employee Relations Law Journal* 16, no. 2 (Fall 1990): 139.

Coleman, John J., III. "Age-Conscious Remarks: What You Say Can Be Used against You." *Personnel* 62 (September 1985): 22–29.

Cuddy, Robert W. "Age Discrimination Amendments and Their Impact on Personnel." *Employee Relations Law Journal* no. 3 (Winter 1978): 339.

Dalton, Dan R., and William D. Tador. "Gender and Workplace Justice: A Field Assessment." *Personnel Psychology* 38 (January 1985): 133–152.

Gertzog, Gary. "The 1978 Amendments to the Age Discrimination Act and Their Impact on Personnel Administration." *Industrial and Labor Relations Forum* (June 1980): 83.

Greenlaw, Paul S., and John P. Kohl. "Age Discrimination in Employment Guidelines." *Personnel Journal* 61, no. 3 (March 1982): 224–228.

Livingston, Donald R. "The Age Discrimination in Employment Act After Betts." *Journal of Intergroup Relations* 17, no. 2 (Summer 1990): 3.

Moens, Gabriel. "Age Discrimination." *Quadrant* 34, no. 10 (October 1, 1990): 70.

Rosenblum, Marc, and George Biles. "The Aging of Age Discrimination—Evolving ADEA Interpretations and Employee Relations Policies." *Employee Relations Law Journal* 8, no. 1 (Summer 1982): 22.

Stone, Julia E. "Age Discrimination in Employment Act: A Review of Recent Changes." *Monthly Labor Review* (March 1980): 32.

Chapter 16

Americans with Disabilities Act

Learning Objectives—After completion of this exercise, you should be able to:

1. Identify individuals who have qualifying handicaps under ADA.

2. Identify organizations that are covered under ADA.

Time Suggested: Forty-five minutes

Procedures:

1. Individually read the Introduction and "The Case of the Paraplegic."

2. The class should be divided into three groups representing the applicant, the employer, and the investigating agency.

3. Complete the group requirements in the exercise.

INTRODUCTION

The Americans with Disabilities Act (ADA) was passed in 1990 to protect qualified individuals with a disability and otherwise qualified handicapped individuals from discrimination in employment, public accommodations, transportation, and telecommunications. The ADA supersedes the Vocational Rehabilitation Act (VRA) of 1973.

A qualified individual with a disability has a physical or mental impairment that limits one or more normal life activities, including work. An "otherwise qualified handicapped individual" is one who can perform a job in spite of the handicap or can meet the performance requirements if reasonable accommodations are made. Reasonable accommodations include such activities as making facilities accessible to employees with disabilities, restructuring jobs, modifying work schedules, modifying equipment, and providing qualified readers or interpreters. As with all groups protected under Title VII of the Civil Rights Act, the qualified individual with a disability is protected from having the disability used as the only reason for making employment decisions such as selection, level of compensation, promotion, job training, or discharge.

The ADA covers any business that employs fifteen or more employees. However, for two years following the July 1992 enforcement date, only employers with twenty-five or more employees will be required to comply.

One of the most important protections offered by the ADA is the limiting of potentially discriminatory preselection medical examinations. The employer may require a medical examination only if it is deemed a "business necessity" or if the exam is necessary to assess how well the applicant can perform the job.

Current users of illegal drugs cannot qualify as disabled under ADA. However, an individual who has completed a drug rehabilitation program and no longer uses illegal substances may be covered by ADA. The ADA specifically excludes gender orientation and identity disorders, compulsive gambling, kleptomania, and pyromania.

The Equal Employment Opportunity Commission enforces Title I of the Americans with Disabilities Act, which covers fair employment practices.

THE CASE OF THE PARAPLEGIC

A paraplegic applicant for a computer data entry operator position has indicated an interest in XYZ Company's current opening. The disabled applicant meets minimum qualifications and is one of the three top applicants to be considered for the job. The workstation and the entry to the office complex are not built to allow wheelchair access. Although the data entry supervisor would like to hire this applicant, she is concerned about the cost of making the workplace accessible to the wheelchair. The work involved would include reconstruction of one doorway (approximately $500) and purchase of a new, wider computer workstation (approximately $400). The supervisor meets with her vice president and discusses the needed renovations. The vice president advises her that the company has not planned for physical renovations in this year's budget so her requests would either be delayed until next year or denied. The supervisor decides to offer the job to one of the other applicants. The disabled applicant sues the company for illegal hiring practices under ADA.

   Divide the class into three groups and complete the assignments below. If possible, have class presentations from the applicant and the employer groups. The investigating agency group may present findings based on the law at the next meeting.

1. One-third of the group will represent the applicant. List reasons below to substantiate the reasons for hiring.

   a.

   b.

   c.

   d.

   e.

2. One-third of the group will represent the supervisor. List reasons below for not hiring the disabled applicant.

   a.

   b.

   c.

   d.

   e.

3. One-third of the group will represent an investigating agency. After listening to presentations by the first two groups, this group will make a decision for the applicant or the employer based on ADA law.

   Decision:

◢ SUGGESTED READINGS

Creasman, R. L., and P. G. Butler. "Will the Americans with Disabilities Act Disable Employers?" *Labor Law Journal* 42, no. 1 (1991): 52–56.

Geber, B. "The Disabled: Ready, Willing and Able." *Training* 27, no. 12 (1990): 29–36.

Hunsicker, Jr., J. F. "Ready or Not: the ADA." *Personnel Journal* 60, no. 8 (1990): 81–86.

Jay, L. "The Americans with Disabilities Act: Feel Good Legislation?" *Management Review* (September 1990): 22–24.

Kelly, E. P., and R. J. Aalberts. "Americans with Disabilities Act: Undue Hardships for Private Sector Employers?" *Labor Law Journal* 41, no. 10 (1990): 675–684.

Murphy, B. S., W. E. Barlow, and D. D. Hatch. "ADA Signed into Law." *Personnel Journal* 69, no. 9 (1990); 18, 20.

Shultz, J. D. "The Americans with Disabilities Act." *Safety & Health* 142, no. 5 (1990): 63–65.

PART 4
Recruitment

The process of attracting people to seek employment with an organization is known as recruitment. At first glance one might think that this activity is unimportant and doesn't require the attention of the human resources manager. Perhaps this assumption was true during the early part of this century when most jobs could be done by virtually anyone. However, over time jobs have become more complex and thus require individuals with special skills and knowledge to perform them. Management must carefully decide what type of recruits it wants and where they are to be found, and then design a recruiting strategy to attract them. Chapter 17 requires students to brainstorm the many sources of recruits, and then to identify the advantages and disadvantages of each source.

Chapter 18 introduces students to the complex issues associated with international human resources management. In this exercise students will begin to see the relationship between job analysis and successful selection, and learn how international assignments create new problems for the human resources manager. Students also will analyze their own cross-cultural sensitivity as a way of gauging their ability to work internationally.

Chapter 17

Recruitment

Learning Objectives—After completion of this exercise, you should be able to:

1. Identify at least four sources of recruits and the strengths and weaknesses associated with each.
2. Identify at least four sources of information about recruits.

Time Suggested: Thirty minutes

Procedures:

1. Break into groups of four or five.
2. Read the Introduction. Read and complete "Design of Recruitment Systems." Answer the questions at the end.
3. Read and complete "Sources of Information about Recruits." Answer the questions at the end.

 **INTRODUCTION**

Efforts designed to attract potential employees to fill job vacancies are referred to as recruitment activities. Recruitment can be as simple as having applicants walk in off the street, or as complex and expensive as hiring full-time professional recruiters. Usually recruiting efforts intensify as the importance of the vacancy to be filled increases.

DESIGN OF RECRUITMENT SYSTEMS

The objective of this part of the exercise is to recruit potential employees who you feel will turn out to be cooperative and productive work-group members. Your group is to list four to six sources of recruits, and the advantages and disadvantages of each. The following is an example:

- *Source:* Private employment agency.
- *Advantages:* Some prescreening is done by the agency.
- *Disadvantages:* The organization is charged a fee for the services of the agency.

1. *Source:* _____
   Advantages: _____
   Disadvantages: _____
2. *Source:* _____
   Advantages: _____
   Disadvantages:

3. *Source:* _____
   Advantages: _____
   Disadvantages: _____
4. *Source:* _____
   Advantages: _____
   Disadvantages: _____
5. *Source:* _____
   Advantages: _____
   Disadvantages: _____
6. *Source:* _____
   Advantages: _____
   Disadvantages: _____

 QUESTIONS

1. Did your group identify at least one source of *minority* recruits? Does this type of recruiting pose any special problems for management? Discuss within your group and write a group response here.

2. At the request of your instructor, a spokesperson from one group is to read aloud all the sources identified by the group. The instructor will write the sources on the board. A member of another group will read aloud only those sources not identified by the first group. The instructor will write the additional sources on the board. Continue the process until all groups have been polled.

   List those sources your group did not identify but which were identified by other groups. Discuss within your group the various advantages and disadvantages associated with each source.

   - *New Source:* _____
   - *Advantages:* _____
   - *Disadvantages:* _____

   - *New Source:* _____
   - *Advantages:* _____
   - *Disadvantages:* _____

   - *New Source:* _____
   - *Advantages:* _____
   - *Disadvantages:* _____

   - *New Source:* _____
   - *Advantages:* _____
   - *Disadvantages:* _____

   - *New Source:* _____
   - *Advantages:* _____
   - *Disadvantages:* _____

SOURCES OF INFORMATION ABOUT RECRUITS

You need to know certain personal information about recruits before you can select those who will be cooperative and productive. Figure 17–1 lists the kinds of information needed. Within your group, read and discuss each characteristic and then decide which are appropriate means of assessing the information desired. Indicate your group's choice with a checkmark. More than one source can be checked for each characteristic.

FIGURE 17–1   Assessment of Information about Recruits

Information Required: Desirable Characteristics	References	Application Blank	Interview	Test	Other (Specify)
1. Work experience					
2. Educational attainment					
3. Medical history					
4. Ability to get along with others					
5. Intelligence					
6. Career plans					
7. Reasons for applying for the job					
8. Dependability					

QUESTIONS

1. References are often used to obtain certain information about a recruit. Discuss within your group some of the weaknesses in using references for this purpose and list them here.

2. If you are recruiting to fill the job vacancy of an electrician, which (if any) types of information listed in Figure 17–1 would not be of value? Why? Discuss the question within your group and write a group response here.

3. Are there equal employment opportunity issues associated with recruiting? Discuss within your group and write a group response below.

◢ SUGGESTED READINGS

Deckhard, N. S., and K. W. Lessey. "A Model for Understanding Management Manpower, Forecasting, and Planning." *Personnel Journal* (March 1975): 171–175.

"Ethical Recruitment." *The Engineer* 271, no. 7012/7013 (August 16, 1990): 27.

Gore, Jane. "Innovative Recruitment Strategies: How to Woo and Win Applicants." *Clinical Laboratory Science* 3, no. 4 (July 1, 1990): 231.

Hodes, Bernard S. "Planning for Recruitment Advertising: Part I." *Personnel Journal* 62, no. 5 (May 1983): 380–384.

Hughes, L. "Help Wanted: Prresent Employees Please Apply." *Personnel* (July–August 1974): 39–45.

"Let Job Demands Dictate Questions." *Recruitment Today* 3, no. 5 (Fall 1990): 45.

Schofield, Philip. "Getting the Best From Recruitment Agencies." *Personnel Management* 13, no. 8 (August 1981): 40–43.

Chapter 18

International Recruitment: Replacing the International Manager

Learning Objectives—After completion of this exercise, you should be able to:

1. Understand the relationship between job analysis and successful selection.

2. Be sensitive to the increased personnel requirements of international assignments.

3. Understand feedback concerning your cultural sensitivity.

Time Suggested: One and one-half hours

Procedures:

1. Break into groups of four or five.

2. Read the Introduction and "Replacing Pete Dufman."

3. Take and score the cultural sensitivity test. Your instructor will provide the interpretations for the various subscores.

4. Complete the "Job Specifications for International Assignment" exercise.

5. Answer the questions at the end.

◢ INTRODUCTION

It is difficult today to define a business that in some way is not affected by or is not involved in international business. The free trade pact with Canada and the proposed trade agreement with Mexico will intensify our international business involvement. U.S. firms will operate without national border restrictions from the North Pole to Central America. Some international experts estimate that there are over 6,000 U.S. firms with overseas operations. Business schools across the U.S.—and those in other countries—are internationalizing their curriculum in response to this changing business environment.

International work assignments introduce a host of changes, which often results in work ineffectiveness. Research by Laruer in 1979 found that approximately one-third of all personnel transferred abroad returned prematurely. Brislin (1987) reports that as many as 70 percent of those who have not had specialized training prior to their departure may return early. Brislin states, "The ability of a company to operate efficiently overseas, as well as the strengthening of international relations, personal satisfaction, and economic performance of the firm can all be influenced by the degree of adjustment of the employee." Thus the selection of individuals who will adapt and function well in other cultures is a serious problem for human resource departments.

The usual human resource functions become more, not less critical to the firm in terms of its international operations because turnover and early returns are more expensive.

REPLACING PETE DUFMAN

Able Company has been represented in Korea for the last fifteen years by Pete Dufman. He plans to retire next year so the company is planning now for his replacement.

Pete has been very successful selling his company's product line to Korea garment manufacturers. Able Company has a highly trained service team in Pete's office that prides itself on quick, prompt reaction time. The company's line of machines is considered to be highly competitive in terms of price and quality but other manufacturers from the U.S., Japan, Germany, and Italy have very aggressive marketing programs.

Pete calls on approximately 170 customers during the year of which 130 are established customers. His contacts in a typical firm are the individuals responsible for plant engineering and the purchasing agent. Most often the purchasing agent gets the production specifications and the product recommendation from the engineer and then contacts Pete or one of his competitors to supply the machines.

Business dealings in Korea are a little different from those in the U.S. As in Japan, businesses like to establish longterm relationships by dealing with the same firms and the same individuals for long periods of time. Pete's customers will often pay higher prices for his product because they know that he will stand behind its quality and provide them quick, prompt service. Pete has been known to expedite express shipments and help install equipment at night so that the production lines are operational the next morning. Pete is knowledgeable about his product line and the latest advances in the industry.

During the week, Pete entertains existing and potential customers on two or three nights. On a typical night they have dinner at a quality restaurant and then drinks and entertainment at a "room salon." These establishments, which are very popular in Korea, offer separate rooms that contain sofas, a low serving table, and a small space for dancing. The "room salon" is often managed by a woman who oversees the entertainment and there is a hostess for each guest. During the evening, music is provided by a guitarist backed up by an electric rhythm machine. Singing is very popular in Korea and each person is expected to sing accompanied by the guitarist. A good voice is highly respected and admired in this culture. It is also expected that each person in turn will exchange glasses and pour the drinks, usually an expensive Scotch (about $100 on the market and about $400 per bottle at "room salons"). Custom dictates using two hands in pouring to show respect. Older or higher status individuals can pour with one hand. Koreans also love to dance and it is not unusual for dancing couples to be of the same sex.

Another practice expected in Korea is gift-giving. The larger buyers will receive the largest gifts, such as sets of golf clubs and golf bags.

INVENTORY OF CROSS CULTURAL SENSITIVITY

The following questionnaire asks you to rate your agreement or disagreement with a series of statements. The directions read as follows:

Please circle the number that best corresponds to your level of agreement with each statement below.

   1 = Strongly Disagree   7 = Strongly Agree

For example, imagine the following statement:

I like chocolate ice cream   1 2 3 4 5 6 7

If chocolate ice cream was your absolute favorite flavor and you never or rarely ate any other flavor, your response would probably be like this:

I like chocolate ice cream   1 2 3 4 5 6 ⑦

      or

I like chocolate ice cream   1 2 3 4 5 ⑥ 7

If you absolutely could not stand the taste of chocolate ice cream and never or rarely ate it, your response would probably be like this:

I like chocolate ice cream   ① 2 3 4 5 6 7

      or

I like chocolate ice cream   1 ② 3 4 5 6 7

If you enjoyed chocolate ice cream as much as some other flavors, your response would probably be somewhere near the middle as the following show:

I like chocolate ice cream   1 2 ③ 4 5 6 7

      or

I like chocolate ice cream   1 2 3 ④ 5 6 7

      or

I like chocolate ice cream   1 2 3 4 ⑤ 6 7

Now, please continue with the following statements.

Please circle the number that best corresponds to your level of agreement with each statement below.

1 = Strongly Disagree   7 = Strongly Agree

1. I speak only one language

    1 2 3 4 5 6 7

2. The way other people express them-
    selves is very interesting to me.

    1 2 3 4 5 6 7

3. I enjoy being with people from other
    cultures.

    1 2 3 4 5 6 7

4. Foreign influence in our country
    threatens our national identity.

    1 2 3 4 5 6 7

5. Others' feelings rarely influence
    decisions I make.

    1 2 3 4 5 6 7

6. I cannot eat with chopsticks.

    1 2 3 4 5 6 7

7. I avoid people who are different from
    me.

    1 2 3 4 5 6 7

8. It is better that people from other
    cultures avoid one another.

    1 2 3 4 5 6 7

9. Culturally mixed marriages are wrong.

    1 2 3 4 5 6 7

10. I think people are basically alike.

    1 2 3 4 5 6 7

11. I have never lived outside my own
    culture for any great length of time.

    1 2 3 4 5 6 7

12. I have foreigners to my home on a
    regular basis.

    1 2 3 4 5 6 7

13. It makes me nervous to talk to people
    who are different from me.

    1 2 3 4 5 6 7

14. I enjoy studying about people from
    other cultures.

    1 2 3 4 5 6 7

15. People from other cultures do
    things differently because they do not
    know any other way.

    1 2 3 4 5 6 7

16. There is usually more than one good
    way to get things done.

    1 2 3 4 5 6 7

17. I listen to music from another culture
    on a regular basis.

    1 2 3 4 5 6 7

18. I decorate my home or room with
    artifacts from other countries.

    1 2 3 4 5 6 7

19. I feel uncomfortable when in a crowd
    of people.

    1 2 3 4 5 6 7

20. The very existence of humanity depends upon our knowledge about other people.

    1 2 3 4 5 6 7

21. Residential neighborhoods should be culturally separated.

    1 2 3 4 5 6 7

22. I have many friends.

    1 2 3 4 5 6 7

23. I dislike eating foods from other cultures.

    1 2 3 4 5 6 7

24. I think about living within another culture in the future.

    1 2 3 4 5 6 7

25. Moving into another culture would be easy.

    1 2 3 4 5 6 7

26. I like to discuss issues with people from other cultures.

    1 2 3 4 5 6 7

27. There should be tighter controls on the number of immigrants allowed into my country.

    1 2 3 4 5 6 7

28. The more I know about people, the more I dislike them.

    1 2 3 4 5 6 7

29. I read more national news than international news in the daily newspaper.

    1 2 3 4 5 6 7

30. Crowds of foreigners frighten me.

    1 2 3 4 5 6 7

31. When something newsworthy happens I seek out someone from that part of the world to discuss the issue with.

    1 2 3 4 5 6 7

32. I eat ethnic foods at least twice a week.

    1 2 3 4 5 6 7

SCORING THE ICCS

The ICCS can be scored by subscales. Simply insert the number circled on the test form in the spaces provided under each subscale heading. Reverse the values for the items marked with an asterisk (*). For instance, reverse scoring results in:

7 = 1, 6 = 2, 5 = 3, 4 = 4, 3 = 5, 2 = 6, 1 = 7

Then, add the values in each column for the subscale score. A total ICCS score is obtained by adding the various subscale scores together. At the present time, individuals can be ranked relative to others in a particular group. Further studies to expand the 32 items and to assess the predictive ability of the instrument are currently underway.

ICCS Scoring Guide   Subject ID _____

C Scale		B Scale		I Scale		A Scale		E Scale	
item	score	item	score	item	score	item	score	item	score
1*		2		3		4*		5*	
6*		7*		8*		9*		10	
11*		13*		14		15*		16	
12		19*		20		21*		22	
17		25*		26		27*		28*	
18		30		31					
23*									
24									
29*									
32									

Totals

C Scale = _____

B Scale = _____

I Scale = _____

A Scale = _____

E Scale = _____

Total ICCS Score = _____

*Reverse score all items marked with * as these are negatively worded scores.

How do your scores compare to others in your group? Discuss the importance of each subscale as it relates to recruiting the international manager. Answer below.

JOB SPECIFICATIONS FOR
INTERNATIONAL ASSIGNMENT EXERCISE

INSTRUCTIONS

1. Your team is to brainstorm a list of the qualifications needed for a manager to be successful on international assignment. Continue this process until ten to fifteen qualifications are identified. List your characteristics below.

a. _____

b. _____

c. _____

d. _____

e. _____

f. _____

g. _____

h. _____

i. _____

j. _____

k. _____

l. _____

m. _____

n. _____

o. _____

2. Now, discuss within your group and rank order (1 = high, 5 = low) the five most important. Be prepared to justify your ranking to the class.

Qualifications	*Justifications*
1. _____	_____
	_____
	_____
	_____
2. _____	_____
	_____
	_____
	_____
3. _____	_____
	_____
	_____
	_____
4. _____	_____
	_____
	_____
	_____
5. _____	_____
	_____
	_____
	_____

 QUESTIONS

1. In what important ways do Korean business practices differ from U.S. business practices? Base your answer in part on the material in the first part of the exercise.

2. Design a recruitment program for hiring U.S. managers to work in Asia. Specify the key components of your program. Be prepared to justify/explain your program to the class.

3. Should companies have different human resource policies for different countries? Explain.

◢ SUGGESTED READINGS

Brislin, R. *Cross-Cultural Encounters: Face-to-Face Interaction.* Elmsford, NY: Pergamon, 1981.

Brislin, R., K. Cushner, C. Cherrie, and M. Yong. *Intercultural Interactions: A Practical Guide.* Beverly Hills, CA: Sage, 1986.

Fiedler, F., T. Mitchell, and H. Triandis. "The Culture Assimilator: An Approach to Cross-Cultural Training." *Journal of Applied Psychology* 55 (1971), 95–102.

Landis, D., and R. Brislin (Eds.). *Handbook of Intercultural Training*, Vols. 1–4. Elmsford, NY: Pergamon, 1983.

Lanier, A. "Selecting and Preparing Personnel for Overseas Transfers." *Personnel Journal* 58, no. 3 (1979), 160–163.

Ramsey, S., and J. Birk. "Preparation of North Americans for Interaction with Japanese: Considerations of Language and Communication Style." In D. Landis and R. Brislin (Eds.), *Handbook of Intercultural Training: Area Studies in Intercultural Training*, Vol. 3, pp. 227–259. Elmsford, NY: Pergamon.

PART 5
Selection

The most important decisions human resources managers make today are in selecting new employees. Employees who are either unable or unwilling to perform their jobs pose difficult and costly problems. If a person is selected who can't do the work, then management must provide the training necessary to bring the person up to an acceptable level of performance. If the person selected is unwilling to work, another set of expensive problems is created. The employee has to be either terminated or counseled. In both cases, expenses are unnecessarily incurred because of a poor selection decision.

In Chapter 19, students conduct a selection interview by using accepted principles of interviewing. Through role play, students learn how to conduct interviews that produce the information necessary for making an accurate selection decision—one that is likely to result in a productive, satisfied employee.

Using employment tests to aid in the selection decision is the focus of Chapter 20. Many jobs today require skills and abilities that cannot be directly measured through interviews or application blanks. Employment tests can provide this additional information. For example, aptitudes are commonly measured through aptitude tests, many physical skills such as dexterity are measured through dexterity tests, and intelligence is measured through I.Q. tests. Because any test provides only indirect measures of human characteristics, more errors occur in testing than in measuring the trait directly. This source of error can lead to wrong selection decisions, and just as importantly, to violations of Title VII of the Civil Rights Act. Students analyze important court cases to discover some of the basic issues regarding the legality of employment tests.

The final exercise in Part 5, Chapter 21, requires that students conduct a correlation analysis to determine whether or not a test measures what it purports to measure. In addition, the degree to which various groups of people score differently on a test is examined to determine whether the use of the test will result in the hiring of more individuals from one group than from another. This problem is commonly referred to as adverse impact and it is an important legal issue for the human resource manager to understand.

In summary, if selection decisions are not made on the basis of accurate information, the organization incurs unnecessary expenses in correcting the problem. But additional expenses are only part of the possible problems created. Tests that discriminate against one group more than other groups can land the organization in court and thus cause undue expenses, create an unfavorable public image, and lead to low employee morale. Therefore, test validation is an important topic for the student of human resources.

Chapter 19

Selection Interview

Learning Objectives—After completion of this exercise, you should be able to:

1. Identify the characteristics of an effective interview.

2. Describe the principles of interviewing.

3. Differentiate between different types of interviews.

Time Suggested: 2 hours

Procedures:

1. Before class:

   a. Read "How to Conduct a Selection Interview."

   b. Complete the open-ended exercise.

   c. Do the "Search for Limitations" exercise.

   d. Complete the "Press for Specifics" exercise.

   e. Do the "Follow-up Techniques" exercise.

   f. Do the "Active Listening" exercise.

   g. Complete the paraphrasing exercise.

2. In class, form into groups of three. Assign one individual to serve as the interviewer, a second person to serve as the interviewee, and a third to function as an observer.

The interview will last for thirty minutes and should be started after all parties becomes familiar with their requirements in the interview.

a. Interviewer role. Read "Company Background." You will function as the company interviewer.

b. Interviewee role. Read "Company Background." *You* are applying for a position. You will be interviewed.

c. Observer role. Complete "Observer's Guide" *during* the interview.

3. The instructor will lead the class in a discussion of observer findings.

INTRODUCTION

HOW TO CONDUCT A SELECTION INTERVIEW

The basic objective of any selection procedure is to find out as much as possible about an applicant in order to make a judgment about the applicant's qualifications against the demands of the job. The selection interview serves certain special purposes: (1) it is helpful for determining the face-to-face effectiveness of the applicant, and (2) it allows the gathering of further detail about information provided in the resumé or application blank.

The interview is not a simple conversation, but a purposeful interaction based on words, manner, voice, expression, and responsiveness. The basic objective of the interviewer is to stimulate interaction with the applicant in order to produce significant behaviors so that the interviewer can evaluate how the applicant measures up to the demands of the job. This can be achieved by following these interviewing principles:

1. Establish rapport by engaging in brief casual conversation and describing what will happen during the interview.

2. Ask about education, work history, and job-relevant knowledge.

3. Ask questions dealing with personal qualities as they relate to the job.

4. Explore the applicant's perception of the job and its requirements.

5. Explain the primary duties and responsibilities of the job.

6. Ask the applicant if he or she has any questions and answer them after you understand why they were asked.

7. Close the interview and immediately evaluate the applicant's responses against the demands of the job.

The applicant is entitled to normal business courtesy and pleasantness on the part of the interviewer. The whole procedure should be cordial, but directed toward achieving the business objective of evaluating the applicant's qualifications for the job.

Selection interviews can range from being open-ended or unstructured on one hand, to closed and structured on the other.

The objective of unstructured interviewing is far more ambitious than simply obtaining additional facts. The purpose of the unstructured interview is to gain a better understanding of the applicant by letting him or her do most of the talking. The interviewer tries to create a supportive environment that encourages the interviewee to talk about his or her objectives, feelings, and attitudes. In order to do this the interviewer must be open and nonjudgmental. Criticism, either verbal or nonverbal, is inhibiting. Attentive, empathetic, and responsible listening is required.

There are no steps, outlines, or plans (other than creating a supportive environment) for the unstructured interview. To get the applicant to talk, the interview team should use open-ended questions such as "What are your short-run and long-run career goals?" and should ask the applicant to elaborate on responses by asking "Why is that important to you?" and "How do you feel about that?"

In its purest form, a structured interview occurs when the interviewer brings to the interview a list of predetermined questions to ask the interviewee. The interviewer in a structured interview usually does most of the talking and controls the direction of the interview. Structured interviews do not allow the interviewee to discuss a topic of his or her choice.

You have ten minutes to conduct the interview. When the interview is finished, you must make a decision to hire or not hire the interviewee. Do not tell the other two interviewers of your decision.

OPEN-ENDED QUESTIONS

As a general rule, an effective interviewer asks as few questions as possible. If you have to ask too many questions it probably means you are asking closed-ended questions that can be answered with one-word responses, such as *yes, no,* or *uh-huh.* Questions that elicit yes/no responses should rarely be used.

The alternative is the open-ended question. The open-ended question solicits views, opinions, thoughts, and feelings; the closed-ended question usually demands cold facts only. The former also helps to open the door to good rapport; the latter usually keeps it shut. The open-ended question is phrased in a way that makes the applicant give a more extensive response. Open-ended questions can begin with words like *how, why, tell me, describe, in what way.* They cannot be answered with a yes or no. Instead, they stimulate the applicant to talk in some detail.

Turn the following closed-ended questions into open-ended questions.

1. Did you enjoy your last job?

2. Do you really want to work on your own for long periods of time?

3. Do you mind working overtime?

4. Would your previous supervisor give you a good reference?

5. Do you think you'll have any problem doing any part of this job?

6. Do you get along well with others?

7. Can you type?

SEARCH FOR LIMITATIONS

Usually it is much easier to discover the positive or strong points of the applicant than reasons the applicant is not the "right" person for the job. A prime objective of the interview is to discover the applicant's weaknesses in relation to the job. Search for negatives throughout the interview. When weaknesses or limitations are discovered, determine whether they apply to the type of work for which the applicant is being considered. If they do apply, decide whether they are the types of limitations that can be developed or improved within the context of the job and resources that are available.

Write a question that would help determine problems in each of the following areas:

1. Resumé indicated four jobs in one and a half years.

2. Reactions to supervision.

3. Distasteful areas of previous job.

4. Transferred to another college after one year.

5. Degree to which applicant understands the job.

PRESS FOR SPECIFICS

During a medical examination, a physician assesses the applicant's physical suitability for the job. Specifics, such as blood pressure, X-rays, and pulse, are checked. Just as the physician focuses on specifics rather than on a general state of health, so must the interviewer. After responses to a large number of specific indicators have been generated, a general statement can be made.

Often interviewers base their judgments on general statements made by the applicant, not realizing that the applicant's remarks are subject to a variety of interpretations, which are usually influenced by the interviewer's biases. The effective interviewer quickly recognizes a general statement and is able to press for specifics.

The following applicant responses are generalities and are difficult to assess. Create follow-up questions that press for specifics.

1. Well, the real reason for leaving my job was that my boss was on my back a lot more than he should have been.

   Press for Specifics:

2. One of the reasons I'm applying for a job with this company is that you're a growing organization where I could move ahead rapidly.

   Press for Specifics:

3. One thing I would really dislike about a job is constant pressure.

   Press for Specifics:

4. I guess you could say being a perfectionist is one of my limitations.

   Press for Specifics:

5. Well, it just seemed to me that I was in a job with no future.

   Press for Specifics:

6. I left the college after two years because I felt like I was wasting my time.

   Press for Specifics:

FOLLOW-UP TECHNIQUES

Certain techniques are more effective than others when attempting to: (1) probe and (2) keep the flow of information going. Many types of responses call for follow-up. When the answer is not specific, or when the interviewer is unclear about the meaning of what has been said, there should be a follow-up.

There are times when straightforward probes are most appropriate. Such probes can be brief.

Example:

- How so?
- In what way?
- Tell me more about it.
- Go on.
- And then what happened?

Example:

> I didn't quite understand what led you to change your job. It would be helpful if you would tell me a bit about that.

There are also times when you may want to phrase a question in a way that will help the interviewee clarify or explore a thought or feeling that has been expressed. The intent is to keep the interviewee on his or her course and not to terminate or divert the response.

Example:

> I wonder how you felt when you found out that Joe got the promotion instead of you.

Each of the following applicant responses needs to be followed up or probed for more information. Write an appropriate probe or follow-up for each statement.

1. I didn't like my last job.

   Probe or Follow-up:

2. I really thought I was going to be promoted.

   Probe or Follow-up:

3. Management made many changes in my old job.

   Probe or Follow-up:

4. I was transferred to another state without being told beforehand.

   Probe or Follow-up:

ACTIVE LISTENING

Still another method of encouraging the applicant to explore a thought or feeling is active listening. When using active listening, the interviewer is displaying empathy and thereby strengthening rapport by picking up, defining, and responding to the feelings expressed by the applicant. This type of response often motivates the applicant to further express feelings and ideas and to rely less on defensive behavior.

In active listening, the interviewer tries to understand what the interviewee is feeling and why. The interviewer then reflects an understanding of the message by rephrasing it for the interviewee. The feedback does not include the interviewer's opinions or advice.

Example:

- Interviewee: In my last job nobody seemed to care what the employees had to say.
- Active-Listening Response: It was discouraging for you not to be consulted.

For each interviewee statement, write an active-listening response, one that reflects back to the interviewee what the interviewee is feeling and why.

1. Interviewee: In that job everybody was your boss, and it was impossible to keep them all happy at the same time.

   Active-Listening Response:

2. Interviewee: If they had kept their promises, I'd be on that job today.

   Active-Listening Response:

3. Interviewee: I gave top priority to being the leader of my class and to maintaining top grades.

   Active-Listening Response:

PARAPHRASING

Paraphrasing is summarizing or repeating in other words what the applicant has said. Used when the applicant has tried to convey something complex, paraphrasing shows the applicant that you have understood what was meant, and encourages the applicant to continue. Paraphrasing also enables the interviewer to find out whether he or she has properly understood the applicant. In paraphrasing, the interviewer is careful to neither approve or disapprove of what the applicant has said.

Example:

- Interviewer: So the reason you liked that job so much was the large variety of activities you were involved in.

    After each applicant's statement, write a response that paraphrases or restates what the applicant has said.

1. I don't know, first one new guy came, then another, then another; it became clear to me that it was time to move on.

2. That school just didn't offer the courses I wanted. I was studying to be an engineer, but I also wanted to be a whole person . . . I had interest in literature, philosophy, etc. . . . . they just didn't offer those things.

COMPANY BACKGROUND

A bank manager at a busy branch called you this morning. The branch's assistant manager is being transferred to the head office, so a replacement is needed.

The branch bank provides full service for its customers. The branch manager is responsible for the overall operation of the branch and also functions as a loan officer. The assistant manager is responsible for the operation of the branch during the frequent absences of the manager, balancing the daily transactions, acting as a loan officer, and supervising the tellers.

The branch has been very successful. Besides the traditional banking services, the bank provides traveler's checks, a notary public, income tax preparation, and automatic payment of insurance premiums and utility bills. The branch also supports community activities, such as the sale of tickets to high school football games and plays.

With the help of the branch manager, you have prepared the job description for the position and have recruited a number of applicants. You have their applications and resumés. You are about to begin an interview with one of the applicants whose resumé and application form suggest that she or he is qualified for the position.

OBSERVER'S GUIDE

Directions: You will be determining the manager's effectiveness by observing whether the six-step interviewing model is followed. Note examples of each step in the spaces provided. Also note examples of the various questioning techniques listed on the next page.

INTERVIEWING MODEL

1. Establish rapport by engaging in brief casual conversation and describing what will happen during the interview.

2. Ask about education, work history, and job-relevant knowledge.

3. Ask questions dealing with personal qualities as they relate to the job.

4. Explain the primary duties and responsibilities of the job.

5. Ask for and answer any questions the applicant may have.

6. Close the interview and immediately evaluate the applicant's responses against the demands of the job.

QUESTIONING TECHNIQUES

1. Examples of searching for limitations:

2. Examples of open-ended questions:

3. Examples of pressing for specifics:

4. Examples of follow-up questions and/or techniques:

5. Was the interviewer evaluative in responses?   ____ yes   ____ no
    Examples:

◢ SUGGESTED READINGS

Arthur, Diane. "Preparing for the Interview." *Personnel* 63 (February 1986): 37–49.

Casey, Thomas F. "Making the Most of a Selection Interview." *Personnel* 67, no. 9 (September 1, 1990): 41.

McDonald, Tracy, and Milton D. Hakel. "Effects of Applicant Race, Sex, Suitability, and Answers on Interviewer's Questioning Strategy and Ratings." *Personnel Psychology* 38 (February 1985): 321–334.

Parsons, Charles K., and Robert C. Linden. "Interviewer Perception of Applicant Qualifications: A Multivariate Field Study of Demographic Characteristics and Non-Verbal Cues." *Journal of Applied Psychology* 69 (1984): 557–568.

Singer, M. S., and Christine Sewell. "Applicant Age and Selection Interview Decisions: Effect of Information Exposure on Age Discrimination in Personnel Selection." *Personnel Psychology* 42, no. 1 (Spring 1989): 135.

Chapter **20**

Legal Aspects of Test Validation

Learning Objectives—After completion of this exercise, you should be able to:

1. Gain insight into the position of the courts on the validation of employment testing.

2. Describe the test validation process requirements for the Civil Rights Act.

Time Suggested: Thirty minutes

Procedures:

1. Read the Introduction. Afterward your instructor will briefly describe criterion-related validity and why it is important.

2. In teams of four or five, assess the arguments of the plaintiff and defendant in two cases: *U.S.* v. *State of North Carolina* and *Dozier* v. *Chupka*. Then predict the finding of the court and assess the court's rationale using the information presented in the Introduction and in each case.

 INTRODUCTION

GUIDELINES FOR REPORTING CRITERION-RELATED VALIDITY STUDIES

Reports of validity should contain the following information. Previously written company reports are acceptable if they are complete in regard to this information.

1. *Firm or organization and location(s) and dates of study.*

2. *Problem and setting*—Explicit definition of purpose and brief discussion of the situation in which the study was conducted.

3. *Job analysis or review of job information*—A description of the procedure used to analyze the job or to review the job information should be provided.

4. *Job title and code*—Job title used in company plus corresponding job title and code from United States Employment Services' *Dictionary of Occupational Titles (Third Edition)* Volumes I, II, United States Government Printing Office, 1965. Where appropriate D.O.T. codes and titles are not available, a notation to that effect should be made.

5. *Criteria*—The bases for the selection of the criteria measures should be provided, together with references to the evidence considered in making the selection of criterion measures. Description of criteria and means by which they were observed, recorded, evaluated, and quantified.

6. *Sample*—Description of race, ethnic, and sex composition of the sample should be provided. Description of educational levels, experience levels, length of service, and age is desirable.

7. *Description of selection procedures*—Any measure, combination of measures, or procedures studied should be completely and explicitly described.

8. *Techniques and results*—Methods used in evaluating data must be described. Measures of central tendency (e.g., means) and measures of dispersion (e.g., standard deviations) for all selection procedures and all criteria should be reported for each race, sex, and ethnic group which constitutes a significant factor in the relevant labor markets.

9. *Alternative procedures investigated*—The selection procedures investigated and available evidence of their impact should be identified.

10. *Uses and applications*—The methods considered for use of the selection procedure (e.g., as a screening device with a cutoff score, for grouping or ranking, or combined with other procedures in a battery) and available evidence of their impact should be described.

Adapted from the *Federal Register*, vol. 43, no. 166, August 25, 1978.

11. *Source data*—Each user should maintain records showing all pertinent information about individual sample members and raters where they are used, in studies involving the validation of selection procedures.

12. *Contact person*—The name, mailing address, and telephone number of the person who may be contacted for further information about the validity of the study should be provided.

13. *Accuracy and completeness*—The report should describe the steps taken to assure the accuracy and completeness of the collection, analysis, and report of data and results.

CASE STUDIES

U.S. v. State of North Carolina
U.S. District Court
400 F.Supp. 343 (E.D.N.C.1975)

This case deals with a North Carolina statute forbidding certification of prospective teachers who score below 950 on the National Teachers Examination (NTE). The North Carolina laws of 1881 established that certification of teachers was to be based on a proficiency test. However, the practice was abandoned from 1921 through 1959, and the state adopted a method of automatic licensing upon completion of a specified course and hour sequence in an accredited institution in North Carolina. From 1960 to 1964, the state returned to testing with the administration of the NTE. During this time, however, applicants were not required to attain a minimum score on the NTE as a prerequisite for certification.

The state adopted minimum score requirements for the first time on January 9, 1964. On March 7, 1968, a minimum score of 950 on the NTE was established for state certification of teachers.

PLAINTIFF'S POSITION:

Relatively little integration was achieved in North Carolina until the 1960s, and we view it as more than coincidental that written testing of teacher applicants coincided with the movement of black teachers into previously all-white schools. Resolution 73 of the General Assembly in 1959 reflected the legislative awareness that no longer could the incompetency of black training schools and black teachers be viewed with indifference, because the day could be coming when some of those teachers would be teaching white pupils.

At the time of the bill to reinstate the NTE, cutoff score requirement figures showed that although 31.08 percent of the black candidates for certification scored below the 950 cutoff, only 1.36 percent of white candidates fell below that score.

DEFENDANT'S POSITION:

There are 32 teaching training institutions accredited by the state of North Carolina. Their quality varies from institutions of the highest academic standards to those that admit any applicant, regardless of high school record. The president of one institution concedes that they sometimes admit functional illiterates, and even graduate some of them. The state, therefore, cannot rely on all its teacher institutions to produce graduates and candidates for certification who possess minimal academic capabilities.

**QUESTION**

1. The court's finding was in favor of _____ .

   The rationale was:

CASE STUDIES

Dozier v. Chupka
U.S. District Court
395 F.Supp. 836 (S.D.Ohio 1975)

PLAINTIFF'S POSITION:

The plaintiffs, six black men, allege that the defendant, the Safety Director of the City of Columbus, has been discriminating and is continuing to discriminate racially when hiring firefighters for the Columbus Fire Department. Most of the members of the Fire Department are white. At the time of the trial, there were 821 firefighters. Only 2.31 percent of the force was black.

In addition to other requirements for qualification (being tested by the court separately within this case), applicants must pass an aptitude test which has a discriminatory impact on blacks. The test in question is the Public Personnel Association test 20(b) (PPA). It is a pencil-and-paper multiple-choice exam with 120 questions. Sixty-nine percent of all applicants taking the PPA passed. Eighty-four percent of the whites passed, while only twenty-seven percent of the blacks passed.

The plaintiffs allege that the PPA is not a predictor of success on the job, even though the test has been validated relative to performance of recruits in the Fire Department's training academy.

DEFENDANT'S POSITION:

In prior years, after trainees in the Fire Department had been selected by the Safety Director, they would take ten weeks' training at the academy. The ten-week training period was used primarily to introduce the trainees to situations they could expect to confront in their careers, and to introduce the trainees to the materials needed to master these situations.

Trainees were graded at the academy. The composite, or final, grade they received was composed of grades received in (1) periodic written tests given to them during the ten-week course, (2) instructors' observations, and (3) a final, written examination.

Columbus, Ohio, has conducted a study of the PPA's validity relative to the performance of recruits in the Fire Department's academy. Dr. Frederick Carleton, an employee of the Personnel Research and Development Corporation, concluded that the PPA validly predicted four measures of an applicant's performance at the training academy. The PPA test established a correlation between those who scored well on it and how they tested at the academy (their cumulative average of phase exams, teachers' observations, and final exams).

 QUESTION

1. The court's finding was in favor of _____ .

    The rationale was:

◢ SUGGESTED READINGS

Blits, Jan H., and Linda S. Gottfredson. "Employment Testing and Job Performance." *The Public Interest* 98 (Winter 1990): 18.

"Employee Privacy Rights: The Employee Polygraph Protection Act of 1988." *Clearinghouse Review* 24, no. 12 (April 1, 1991): 1367.

Feuer, Dale. "Validity and Reliability: A Very Short Course." *Training* 23 (March 1986): 89–90.

Jones, Edward W., Jr. "Black Managers: The Dream Deferred." *Harvard Business Review* 64 (March 1986): 84–93.

Kleiman, L. S., and R. H. Faley. "Assessing Content Validity: Standards Set by the Court." *Personnel Psychology* (Winter 1978): 701–713.

Novick, Melvin R. "Burden of Proof/Burden of Remedy." *Public Personnel Management* 10, no. 3 (Fall 1981): 333–342.

Schmitt, Neal, and Cheri Ostroff. "Operationalizing the 'Behavioral Consistency' Approach: Selection Test Development Based on a Content-Oriented Strategy." *Personnel Psychology* 39 (January 1986): 91–108.

Wigdor, Alexander K. "Fairness in Employment Testing." *Issues in Science and Technology* 6, no. 3 (Spring 1990): 54.

Chapter 21

Test Validation and Selection Ratios

Learning Objectives—After completion of this exercise, you should be able to:

1. Apply basic statistical techniques that can be used to validate the admissions criteri~ for the MBA program at XYZ University.

2. Understand and describe the usefulness of a scatter diagram.

3. Understand and describe the usefulness of a correlation coefficient.

4. Describe and determine the existence of adverse impact.

Time Suggested: For statistical calculation—One hour
For discussion—Thirty minutes

Procedures:

1. Individually, read the Introduction. The instructor will introduce the concept of correlation, scatter diagrrams, and correlation coefficients.

2. Individually, read the Scatter Diagram exercise.

3. Divide into groups of four or five.

4. As a group, complete the Pearson Product Moment Correlation Coefficient problem.

5. Complete the Adverse Impact problem.

6. Answer all questions.

◢ INTRODUCTION

In this exercise you will use two techniques to determine whether or not there is a relationship between a selection criterion (score on the graduate management aptitude test) and performance in school (i.e., grade point average or GPA), and whether this relationship is different for different ethnic groups. The GMAT is a test given to most applicants to MBA programs in the United States.

The two techniques are (1) the *scatter diagram* and (2) the *correlation coefficient*. Each of these techniques is a way of *validating* the selection criterion in question.

 **PROBLEMS**

SCATTER DIAGRAM

The first step in studying the relationship between two variables (called *bivariate data*) is to make a scatter diagram. Using the given data, plot the grade-point averages and GMAT scores for all students on the graph. A point is plotted for each student corresponding to his/her grade-point average and GMAT score. The vertical axis is referred to as the y-axis and the horizontal axis is called the x-axis. The dependent variable (GPA) is placed on the vertical axis and the independent variable (GMAT score) is placed on the horizontal axis. Make a scatter diagram for each ethnic group: Caucasians (use Figures 21–1a and 21–1b) and Japanese-Americans (use Figures 21–2a and 21–2b).

◢ FIGURE 21–1a   Bivariate Data for Scatter Diagram (Caucasians)

Student No.	GMAT X	Grad. GPA Y	Student No.	GMAT X	Grad. GPA Y
1	.80	3.56	16	.80	3.67
2	.99	3.28	17	.98	3.78
3	.82	3.56	18	.38	3.72
4	.63	3.56	19	.95	3.50
5	.63	3.39	20	.91	3.39
6	.95	3.22	21	.64	3.28
7	.86	3.11	22	.65	3.22
8	.78	3.88	23	.89	3.67
9	.80	3.83	24	.91	3.89
10	.77	3.50	25	.75	3.72
11	.97	3.17	26	.67	3.83
12	.70	3.11	27	.55	3.25
13	.79	3.11	28	.66	3.50
14	.66	3.28	29	.94	3.72
15	.78	3.83	30	.54	3.31

QUESTION

1. What does the amount of dispersion indicate?

FIGURE 21–1b   Grid for Scatter Diagram (Caucasians)

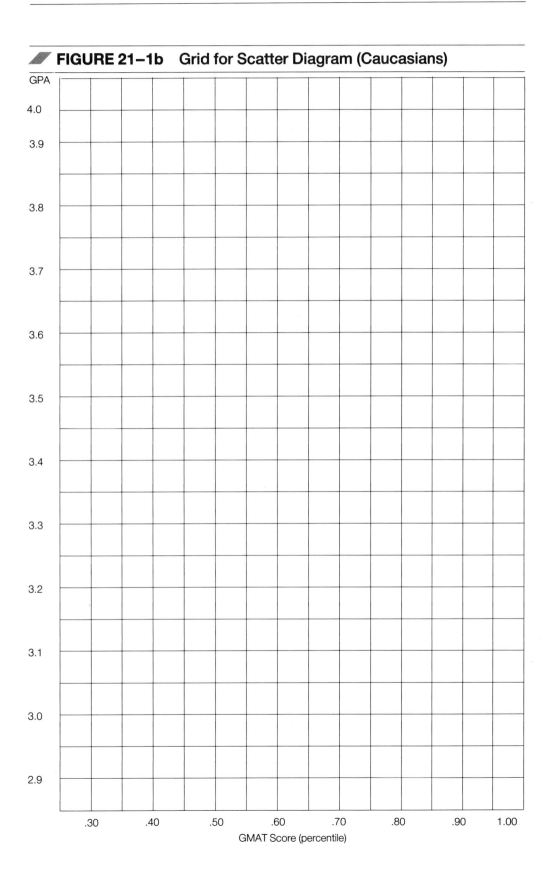

FIGURE 21–2a   Bivariate Data for Scatter Diagram (Japanese-American)

Student No.	GMAT X	Grad. GPA Y	Student No.	GMAT X	Grad. GPA Y
1	.54	3.37	16	.79	3.56
2	.54	3.50	17	.61	3.42
3	.87	3.89	18	.81	3.44
4	.73	3.39	19	.86	3.50
5	.34	3.78	20	.47	3.50
6	.67	3.72	21	.84	3.39
7	.41	3.22	22	.65	3.39
8	.75	3.61	23	.61	3.72
9	.62	3.39	24	.65	3.61
10	.85	3.17	25	.90	3.22
11	.96	3.06	26	.96	3.61
12	.62	3.00	27	.88	3.89
13	.84	3.67	28	.78	3.44
14	.97	3.67	29	.73	3.39
15	.59	3.53	30	.91	3.50

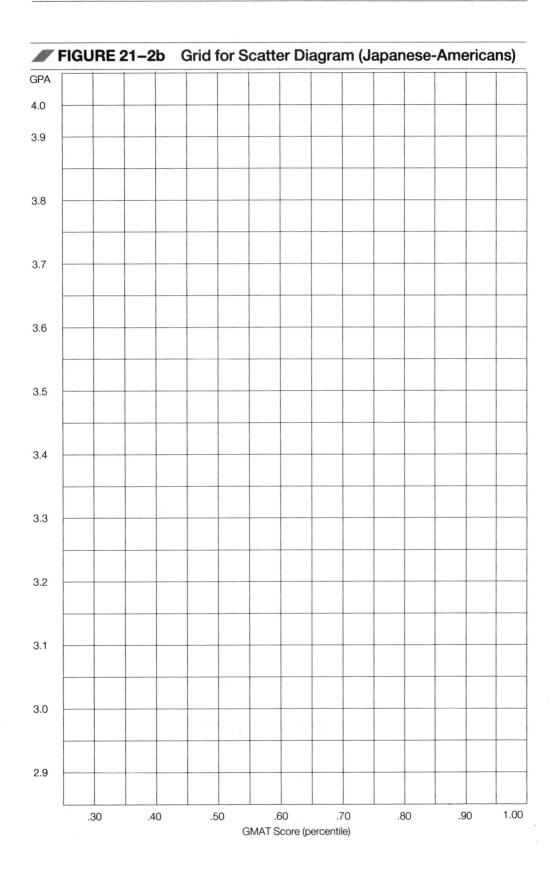

FIGURE 21–2b   Grid for Scatter Diagram (Japanese-Americans)

QUESTIONS

1. What does the amount of dispersion indicate?

2. Compare the two scatter diagrams. Is this test a valid selection criterion? Why or why not?

PEARSON PRODUCT MOMENT CORRELATION COEFFICIENT

A correlation coefficient indicates the degree of association between an independent and a dependent variable. The value of the correlation coefficient (signed by r) can vary between -1.00 and $+1.00$. The sign attached to the correlation coefficient indicates the *direction* of change in the depedent variable as the independent variable changes. Thus, a positive r indicates that as the value of the independent variable increases, the value of the dependent variable also increases. The opposite holds true as well.

For example, an r of $-.80$ indicates the degree of change in the dependent variable that is associated with changes in the independent variable. It further indicates that the relationship is inverse.

INSTRUCTIONS:

Calculate the correlation coefficient by inserting the values of X, Y, XY, X^2, Y^2 in the formula for r below. Calculate the correlation coefficient for Caucasians (use Figure 21–3) and Japanese-Americans (use Figure 21–4). Data for each group are on the following two pages.

$$r = \frac{N\Sigma XY - \Sigma X \Sigma Y}{\sqrt{N\Sigma X^2 - (\Sigma X)^2)\ (N\Sigma Y^2 - (\Sigma Y)^2)}}$$

FIGURE 21–3   Correlation Coefficient Data for Caucasians

Student No.	GMAT X	Grad. GPA Y	XY	X²	Y²
1	.80	3.56	2.848	.640	12.674
2	.99	3.28	3.247	.980	10.758
3	.82	3.56	2.919	.672	12.674
4	.63	3.56	2.243	.397	12.674
5	.63	3.39	2.136	.397	11.492
6	.95	3.22	3.059	.903	10.368
7	.86	3.11	2.675	.740	9.672
8	.78	3.88	3.026	.608	15.054
9	.80	3.83	3.064	.640	14.669
10	.77	3.50	2.695	.593	12.250
11	.97	3.17	3.075	.941	10.049
12	.70	3.11	2.177	.490	9.672
13	.79	3.11	2.457	.624	9.672
14	.66	3.28	2.165	.436	10.758
15	.78	3.83	2.987	.608	14.669
16	.80	3.67	2.936	.640	13.469
17	.98	3.78	3.704	.960	14.288
18	.38	3.72	1.414	.144	13.838
19	.95	3.50	3.325	.903	12.250
20	.91	3.39	3.085	.828	11.492
21	.64	3.28	2.099	.410	10.758
22	.65	3.22	2.093	.423	10.368
23	.89	3.67	3.266	.792	13.469
24	.91	3.89	3.540	.828	15.132
25	.75	3.72	2.790	.563	13.838
26	.67	3.83	2.566	.449	14.669
27	.55	3.25	1.788	.303	10.563
28	.66	3.50	2.310	.436	12.250
29	.94	3.72	3.497	.884	13.838
30	.54	3.31	1.787	.292	10.956
	$\Sigma X = 23.15$	$\Sigma Y = 104.84$	$\Sigma XY = 80.975$	$\Sigma X^2 = 18.254$	$\Sigma Y^2 = 368.283$

Calculations:

$r = $ _____

QUESTION

1. How highly correlated are Caucasian test scores and performance?

◢ **FIGURE 21–4** Correlation Coefficient Data for Japanese-Americans

Student No.	GMAT X	Grad. GPA Y	XY	X^2	Y^2
1	.54	3.37	1.820	.292	11.357
2	.54	3.50	1.890	.292	12.250
3	.87	3.89	3.384	.757	15.132
4	.73	3.39	2.475	.533	11.492
5	.34	3.78	1.285	.116	14.288
6	.67	3.72	2.492	.449	13.838
7	.41	3.22	1.320	.168	10.368
8	.75	3.61	2.708	.563	13.032
9	.62	3.39	2.102	.384	11.492
10	.85	3.17	2.695	.723	10.049
11	.96	3.06	2.938	.922	9.364
12	.62	3.00	1.860	.384	9.000
13	.84	3.67	3.083	.706	13.469
14	.97	3.67	3.560	.941	13.469
15	.59	3.53	2.083	.348	12.461
16	.79	3.56	2.812	.624	12.674
17	.61	3.42	2.086	.372	11.696
18	.81	3.44	2.786	.656	11.834
19	.86	3.50	3.010	.740	12.250
20	.47	3.50	1.645	.221	12.250
21	.84	3.39	2.848	.706	11.492
22	.65	3.39	2.204	.423	11.492
23	.61	3.72	2.270	.372	13.838
24	.65	3.61	2.347	.423	13.032
25	.90	3.22	2.898	.810	10.368
26	.96	3.61	3.466	.922	13.032
27	.88	3.89	3.423	.774	15.132
28	.78	3.44	2.683	.608	11.834
29	.73	3.39	2.475	.533	11.492
30	.91	3.50	3.185	.828	12.250
	$\Sigma X = 21.75$	$\Sigma Y = 104.55$	$\Sigma XY = 75.833$	$\Sigma X^2 = 16.590$	$\Sigma Y^2 = 365.727$

QUESTIONS

1. Discuss within your group some of the issues associated with using test scores to establish entrance standards into MBA programs. List three major issues below.

   a.

   b.

   c.

2. Compare the two correlation coefficients. Is this test a valid selection criterion? Why or why not?

3. Compare the conclusions made about test validity using scatter diagram and correlation-coefficient techniques. Did you reach the same conclusions? Why or why not?

ADVERSE IMPACT

There are two general approaches to charges of discrimination. The first is to show *discriminatory intent* of a particular practice. An employer treats applicants differently based on their membership or nonmembership in a minority group. The second is to show the *discriminatory effect* of a practice. *Effect* can be shown or demonstrated by statistical evidence of what is referred to as disparate or *adverse impact*. It can occur when a test is administered to *all* job applicants, yet a disproportionate number of applicants from minority groups score low on the test, as shown in the preceding exercise. Two specific statistics are used to show adverse impact—selection rate and population/workforce comparisons. These rates refer to the proportion of applicants that are actually hired in the selection process. For example, if we hired five applicants out of a total of twenty-five, the selection rate is 20 percent. These selection rates are calculated by race and sex. If the selection rates vary enough between groups, there is adverse impact. Recent government regulations suggest the 80 percent rule for comparing selection rates. For example, assume that the selection rates for whites and blacks are 40 percent and 30 percent, respectively. The 80 percent rule means that the black selection rate would have to be 80 percent of the white rate, or 32 percent (.40 × .80). A 30-percent rate in this case implies adverse impact.

The data in Figure 21–5 provide the minority status (in this case, sex) and index scores of applicants for a position in a retail store. The index score for each applicant is a composite score made of numerical weights from the application blank (years in retailing, years in children's wear, years in department manager position, and so on) plus a score from employment tests.

FIGURE 21–5   Adverse Impact Data

Applicant No.	Sex	Score	Applicant No.	Sex	Score
1	M	495	26	M	430
2	M	485	27	F	385
3	F	420	28	F	575
4	M	470	29	M	525
5	M	500	30	F	450
6	F	535	31	M	450
7	F	510	32	M	580
8	M	455	33	F	450
9	M	610	34	M	515
10	M	480	35	F	560
11	F	480	36	M	450
12	M	545	37	F	485
13	F	590	38	M	595
14	M	410	39	M	465
15	F	460	40	F	500
16	M	560	41	F	470
17	M	570	42	M	610
18	F	410	43	M	530
19	M	530	44	F	455
20	F	550	45	M	575
21	F	545	46	F	460
22	M	620	47	M	390
23	M	470	48	M	550
24	M	565	49	F	530
25	M	560	50	M	440

Only those applicants who scored 490 or higher will be further considered for employment.

AS A GROUP, CALCULATE THE FOLLOWING:

Selection rate for males   _____ %

Selection rate for females   _____ %

80 percent rule   _____ %

As a group, answer the following questions:

1. Do your calculations show that there is adverse impact?

2. What are your conclusions concerning the discriminatory effect of this selection process?

3. How might the validity of the selection test affect the selection rates?

QUESTIONS

Write group responses to each of the following questions.

1. Briefly describe the usefulness of the scatter diagram and the correlation coefficient for determining the validity of GMAT scores as a selection criterion at XYZ University.

2. Can it be assumed that GMAT scores *cause* GPAs? Summarize your discussion below.

3. Is there a difference in the relationship between GMAT scores and GPAs between Caucasians and Japanese-Americans? If so, what is the significance of the difference? Is the GMAT a "fair" selection criterion for individuals of ethnic backgrounds?

4. How much weight would you give to the GMAT score if you were the admissions officer at your university?

5. Discuss within your group what the r value you have just calculated means. Are GMAT scores a good predictor of academic success? Write a group summary below.

SUGGESTED READINGS

Norborg, James M. "A Warning Regarding the Simplified Approach to the Evaluation of Test Fairness in Employee Selection Procedures." *Personnel Psychology* 37 (March 1984): 483–486.

Pannone, Ronald D. "Predicting Test Performance: A Content Valid Approach to Screening Applicants." *Personnel Psychology* 37 (March 1984): 507–514.

Patrick, Christopher J., and William G. Iacono. "Validity of the Control Question Polygraph Test: The Problem of Sampling Bias." *Journal of Applied Psychology* 76, no. 2 (April 1, 1991): 229.

Reilly, Richard R., and Georgia T. Chao. "Validity and Fairness of Some Alternative Employee Selection Procedures." *Personnel Psychology* 35, no. 1 (Spring 1982): 1–62.

Taylor, John W. "Strategic Military Employment Operations: Theory and Application." *Comparative Strategy* 10, no. 2 (April 1, 1991): 155.

"United States Fair Employment Law in the Transitional Employment Arena: The Case for the Extraterritorial Application of Title VII of the Civil Rights Act of 1964." *Catholic University Law Review* 39, no. 4 (Summer 1990): 1109.

PART 6
Training and
Career Development

Once the hiring decision is made, new employees often are put into training programs designed to give them the specific skills necessary for performing their jobs. Training also is made available to existing employees to upgrade their skills and abilities, and to help employees plan their careers.

In Chapter 22, students will learn several approaches to training and then match each approach with the type of learning that is likely to occur. The lecture approach to training, for example, results in only certain types of learning. Managers must learn the many approaches to training and what they are designed to do before choosing a training program. Chapter 23 asks students to describe in writing their lifetime goals in terms of several important life topics. These lifetime goals are then broken down into 5-year and one-year goals to illustrate the importance of clarifying goals and specifying when they are to be accomplished. In addition, students are asked to look fifteen years into the future and describe what their lives will be like at that time and what they will have to do between now and then to accomplish their goals. This exercise in career/life planning will illustrate the value of consciously thinking through the relationship between the goals a person has and the steps necessary for achieving those goals. Finally, in Chapter 24, students are introduced to the topic of international negotiations and are asked to design a training program to help prepare individuals for the difficult task of negotiating internationally.

Chapter 22

Training and Development

Learning Objectives—After completion of this exercise, you should be able to:

1. Define training and list three types of training methods.

2. Determine which training techniques are appropriate for specific circumstances.

Time Suggested: Thirty to forty-five minutes

Procedures:

1. Read and become familiar with the Introduction to training and the three training techniques listed.

2. Complete the Problems section.

3. Answer the questions at the end of the exercise.

◢ INTRODUCTION

Training and *development* are here used synonymously and have the general characteristics of being a learning experience planned by the organization that occurs after the individual has joined the organization and that is intended to further the organization's goals.[1]

Three major training techniques will be discussed here:

1. *Information processing technique.* This is aimed at teaching facts, concepts, attitudes, and skills without requiring simulation or actual practice on the job itself. The most common methods are lectures, conferences or discussions, movies, readings, observations, closed-circuit television lectures, and teaching machines in the form of programmed instructions where the learner goes at his or her own pace through a predetermined format. The disadvantages of this type of training are numerous. Critics never fail to point out that due to a lack of feedback, the instructor never knows whether or not she or he is reaching the learners effectively. There are advantages, however, such as the fact that all of these methods have a large information-giving ability; that they are economical; that they have wide acceptance; and that there is role modeling by the teacher for the students.

2. *Simulation method.* Here, the trainee is presented with a simulated or artificial representation of some aspect of an organization and is required to react to it as if it were real. This allows the trainee to fulfill meaningful roles with a degree of realism without affecting the organization. Examples are the case method, role playing, and business games. The advantage of these methods is that there is participation and feedback for the trainees, and they learn from watching others and communicating with them. One disadvantage is that general principles cannot be taught in this manner; the trainee must be assumed to have the basic knowledge necessary. Also, this type of training is expensive and time consuming.

3. *On-the-job training.* This means practice in the real world as a manager. Examples of this method are job rotation, performance appraisal, committee assignment, and on-the-job coaching from a supervisor. The main objective of these methods is to give the trainee factual knowledge about the operations of the organization. The disadvantage is that if the trainee has poor or inadequate supervision, the lack of structure degenerates into trial and error learning.

The results of a study done by Carroll, Paine, and Ivancevich[2] show that for the purposes of developing effectiveness in problem-solving skills, 200 training directors questioned nationwide rated the case study method, business games, role playing, and the conference method as being more effective than any information presentation technique. The case study method was rated the highest.

The training directors rated role playing as being the most effective in developing interpersonal skills. When questioned on participants' acceptance, the training directors rated business games as highest, then conference method and case study. The least acceptable to participants are closed-circuit television lectures, movies, traditional lectures, and programmed instruction. Study Figure 22–1 on rating by training directors.

◢◢ FIGURE 22–1   Rating by Training Directors on Effectiveness of Alternative Training Methods for Various Training Objectives

Training Objectives *Training Method*	Knowledge Acquisition *Mean Rank*	Changing Attitudes *Mean Rank*	Problem-Solving Skills *Mean Rank*	Interpersonal Skills *Mean Rank*	Participant Accept-ance *Mean Rank*	Knowledge Retention *Mean Rank*
Case Study	2	3	1	3	2	2
Conference (Discussion)	3	2	4	2	1	4
Lecture (with questions)	8	7	8	7	7	7
Business Game	6	4	2	4	3	5
Movie	4	5	6	5	5	6
Programmed Instruction	1	6	5	6	6	1
Role Playing	7	1	3	1	4	3
Television Lecture	5	8	7	8	8	8

Source: Stephen Carroll, Jr., Frank T. Paine, and John J. Ivancevich, "The Relative Effectiveness of Training Methods—Expert Opinion and Research," *Contemporary Problems in Personnel* (New York: St. Clair Press, 1977), 195.

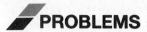 **PROBLEMS**

Your objective is to determine which training method is most appropriate for teaching a human resources management class. Given this topic, rank (1 = high, 8 = low) the eight training methods on effectiveness for the six training objectives. Use the blank table given.

Training Objectives / Training Method	Knowledge Acquisition / Expected Rank	Changing Attitudes / Expected Rank	Problem-Solving Skills / Expected Rank	Interpersonal Skills / Expected Rank	Participant Acceptance / Expected Rank	Knowledge Retention / Expected Rank
Case Study	___	___	___	___	___	___
Conference (Discussion)	___	___	___	___	___	___
Lecture (with questions)	___	___	___	___	___	___
Business Game	___	___	___	___	___	___
Movie	___	___	___	___	___	___
Programmed Instruction	___	___	___	___	___	___
Role Playing	___	___	___	___	___	___
Television Lecture	___	___	___	___	___	___

QUESTIONS

1. Given the widely accepted lack of support for the lecture method, why is it still so frequently used?

   Under what circumstances is the lecture method most appropriate? Why?

2. Think of a job you have had. What would have been the most effective method of training you for that position? Explain your answer.

3. How can the human resources department aid in determining your training needs? Explain your answer.

NOTES

1. John P. Campbell, et al., *Managerial Behavior, Performance and Effectiveness* (New York: McGraw-Hill, 1970).

2. S. J. Carroll, F. T. Paine, and J. J. Ivancevich, "The Relative Effectiveness of Training Methods—Expert Opinion and Research," *Personnel Psychology* 25 (1972): 495–509.

SUGGESTED READINGS

Bruwelheide, Laurence R., and Phillip K. Duncan. "A Method for Evaluating Corporation Training Seminars." *Journal of Organizational Behavior Management* 7 (January–February 1985): 65–115.

Bushnell, David S. "Input, Process, Output: A Model for Evaluating Training." *Training and Development Journal* 44, no. 3 (March 1, 1990): 41.

Courtney, Roslyn S. "A Human Resources Program That Helps Management and Employees Prepare for the Future." *Personnel* 63 (May 1986): 32–40.

Friedman, Paul G., and Elaine A. Yarbrough. *Training Strategies from Start to Finish.* Englewood Cliffs, NJ: Prentice-Hall, 1985.

Harkins, Philip J. "The Changing Role of Corporate Training and Development." *Training: the Magazine of Human Resources Development* 28, no. 1 (January 1, 1991): 26.

Kaye, Beverly. "Career Development Puts Training in Its Place." *Personnel Journal* 62, no. 2 (February 1983): 132–137.

Kello, John E. "Developing Training Step-by-Step." *Training and Development Journal* 40 (January 1986): 50–52.

Chapter 23

Career Planning

Learning Objectives—After completion of this exercise, you should be able to:

1. Describe any personal goals that may have an impact on your career development.

2. List your goals regarding career, family, marriage, personal life, spiritual development, and finance.

Time Suggested: One hour

Procedures:

1. Read the Introduction.

2. Complete Parts A, B, and C.

3. Divide into groups of two and share your responses to Parts A, B, and C.

4. Answer the questions at the end of the exercise.

INTRODUCTION

Intelligent managers are constantly looking for ways to retain their best employees, and the best employees are those who seek career growth and development from their employers. *Career development* refers to those management activities concerned with developing career paths in which employees progress over a period of time. From the employees' viewpoint, career development is a way of helping to utilize their utmost capabilities.

During career development planning, employees are asked to state specifically and write down what it is they want from their present job in terms of challenge, responsibility, the nature of the work to be done, and salary. What they want in the future is also discussed and specifically stated. This is difficult to do sometimes because it requires enough self-awareness to clearly know what one wants.

Self-awareness can be increased if career goals are written down. There are other advantages as well.

1. Written goals are more concrete and specific than unwritten goals. Unwritten goals tend to be vague and easily forgotten.

2. Written goals are easier to refine, analyze, and update.

3. Written goals make it easier to identify and attempt to resolve areas of conflict between goals.

The future is very important to all of us, but very few people think through and write out career goals that could help provide direction to their lives.

 **PROBLEMS**

This exercise is designed to help you determine your career goals and to help you analyze and refine these goals:

PART A: CAREER AND LIFE GOALS

I. Spend a few minutes writing down your specific answers to these questions.

    a. What are your lifetime goals in terms of:

Job	1. _____
	2. _____
	3. _____
	4. _____
	5. _____
Money	6. _____
	7. _____
	8. _____
	9. _____
	10. _____
Family	11. _____
	12. _____
	13. _____
	14. _____
	15. _____
Religion	16. _____
	17. _____
	18. _____
	19. _____
	20. _____
Social Life	21. _____
	22. _____
	23. _____
	24. _____

Marriage

25. _____
26. _____
27. _____
28. _____
29. _____
30. _____

Others

31. _____
32. _____
33. _____
34. _____
35. _____

b. What would you like to achieve in the next five years in each goal category?

Job

1. _____
2. _____
3. _____
4. _____
5. _____

Money

6. _____
7. _____
8. _____
9. _____
10. _____

Family

11. _____
12. _____
13. _____
14. _____
15. _____

Religion

16. _____
17. _____
18. _____
19. _____
20. _____

Life   **21.** _____

              22. _____

              23. _____

              24. _____

              25. _____

Marriage   **26.** _____

              27. _____

              28. _____

              29. _____

              30. _____

Others   **31.** _____

              32. _____

              33. _____

              34. _____

              35. _____

c. A year from now, what would you like to look back on as having accomplished in each goal category?

Job   **1.** _____

              2. _____

              3. _____

              4. _____

              5. _____

Money   **6.** _____

              7. _____

              8. _____

              9. _____

              10. _____

Family   **11.** _____

              12. _____

              13. _____

              14. _____

              15. _____

Religion   16. _____

                17. _____

                18. _____

                19. _____

                20. _____

Social Life   21. _____

                22. _____

                23. _____

                24. _____

                25. _____

Marriage   26. _____

                27. _____

                28. _____

                29. _____

                30. _____

Others   31. _____

                32. _____

                33. _____

                34. _____

                35. _____

PART B: CAREER DECISIONS

I. Select a critical decision that you have made in your career or that you will make in the near future. Examples of these types of career-altering decisions could be choosing a major, changing jobs, or furthering your education.

Once you have selected a decision, write below the *Best Possible Outcomes* and the *Worst Possible Outcomes*. Starting with the *Best Possible Outcomes*, make a list of these outcomes if you were to make the best decision in this situation. What would be the effects on your life, career, family, etc.? Then, list the *Worst Possible Outcomes*. What would happen if you made a bad decision?

II. Compare the best and the worst outcomes and determine if there are any inconsistencies or conflicts. Be prepared to discuss your conclusions. Are your career decisions consistent with your goals?

Best Possible Outcomes?

Worst Possible Outcomes?

PART C: FIFTEEN YEARS FROM NOW

Project your current lifestyle fifteen years into the future. What will your life be like in terms of (1) your economic status, (2) your professional/job status, (3) your family, and (4) your living environment? Write your answers here.

QUESTIONS

1. How can determining your goals help you to make career decisions?

2. What is the advantage of writing out career goals as opposed to leaving them unspecified?

3. How often should you review and update your career goals? Why?

4. How can a manager use career planning and development to increase job satisfaction and performance among employees? If you were a manager, what would you do?

SUGGESTED READINGS

Bolles, Richard N. *What Color Is Your Parachute?* Berkeley, CA: Ten Speed Press, 1991.

Crystal, John C., and Richard N. Bolles. *Where Do I Go From Here With My Life?* Berkeley, CA: Ten Speed Press, 1980.

Gardner, Phillip D. "Will the Real Prescreening Criteria Please Stand Up?" *Journal of Career Planning & Employment* 51, no. 2 (January 1, 1991): 57.

Hall, Douglas T., and Lynn A. Isabelle. "Downward Movement and Career Development." *Organizational Dynamics* (Summer 1985): 5–23.

Honeck, Jack. "IBM's Focus: On Employees' Abilities . . . Not Their Disabilities." *Journal of Career Planning & Employment* 51, no. 2 (January 1, 1991): 68.

Jackson, Tom, and Davidyne Mayleas. *The Hidden Job Market for the Eighties*. New York: Times Books, 1981.

Jacobson, Betsy, and Beverly L. Kaye. "Career Development and Performance Appraisal: It Takes Two to Tango." *Personnel* 63 (January 1986): 26–32.

Martin, Phyllis. *Martin's Magic Formula for Getting the Right Job*. New York: St. Martin's Press, 1981.

McRae, Kenneth B. "Career-Management Planning: A Boon to Managers and Employees." *Personnel* 62 (May 1985): 56–60.

Michelozzi, Betty N. *Coming Alive from Nine to Five: The Career Search Handbook*. Palo Alto, CA: Mayfield Publishing Company, 1984.

Mirabile, Richard J. "Designing CD Programs the O.D. Way." *Training and Development Journal* 40 (February 1986): 38–41.

Pederson, Paul, Alan Goldberg, and Tony Papalia. "A Model for Planning Career Continuation and Change Through Increased Awareness, Knowledge, and Skill." *Journal of Employment Counseling* 28, no. 2 (June 1, 1991): 74.

Chapter 24

Training for International Negotiations

Learning Objectives—After completion of this exercise, you should be able to:

1. Identify the skills necessary for successful international negotiations.

2. Write a job specification for an international negotiator.

3. Develop a training program designed to teach the skills of international negotiations.

Time Suggested: One hour

Procedures:

1. Divide the class into culturally diverse groups of three or four members.

2. Read "Insights into International Negotiations."

3. Based on the information learned, your group is to design a program for training people to become international negotiators. Use the form provided in "A Proposed Program for Training International Negotiators" to help identify the content of the training program.

4. Answer the questions at the end of the chapter.

INSIGHTS INTO INTERNATIONAL NEGOTIATIONS

Business negotiations are always a sensitive and complex activity involving a variety of skills, including planning for the negotiation meeting, communicating accurately and effectively with the other party, judging offers and counteroffers, and anticipating the responses of the other party. Additional skills are needed when negotiations involve people from different cultures. Differences in culture translate into different values and perceptions regarding the negotiation process. For example, Americans may value promptness, a "let's get down to business" attitude, while negotiators from other cultures may see promptness as unnecessary and the rush to get down to business as rude and overlooking social relationships. There are a set of skills that the international negotiator can use to overcome these special problems. These skills are described below (Casse, 1979):

1. To be able to view the world as others see it and to understand their behavior from their perspective. For example, mainland Chinese negotiators may need to confer often with their superiors during a negotiation meeting. They are not allowed to make major decisions without approval from their superiors. Thus, delays during the session are frequent and the time to complete a project is often viewed as excessive unless the opposing party is willing to view the world as the Chinese see it.

2. To be able to show the other party the advantages to them from accepting your proposal. For example, many American companies have established *maquiladora* (twin plants) operations in Mexico. The advantage to the American firms is obvious: the availability of low-cost Mexican labor. Parts are shipped into Mexico, assembled by hand, and the final product is then exported all over the world. American firms negotiating to locate a twin plant in Mexico must establish its advantages in the eyes of the Mexican negotiator. Stable employment, on-the-job training, and supervisory training are some items Mexican negotiators find attractive.

3. To be able to respond to unpredictable demands and ambiguous situations without undue stress. For example, American negotiators tend to focus on one issue in the negotiations at a time—providing factual support for the issue and emphasizing its merits. Syrian negotiators, however, will seek to broaden the scope of the issue into areas seemingly irrelevant to Americans, such as the historical value of their civilization. Such an ambiguous move will often generate confusion and frustration on the part of the unaware American negotiator. Rather than get upset, the appropriate response is to understand Syrians' love of their country's long history and how such a long history can make the issues in the negotiations seem small and insignificant by comparison.

4. To be able to communicate your ideas so that the other party understands them. For example, the concept of compromise is foreign to Russian culture and language. If used at all, it has a derogatory connotation. Given that Russians negotiate from an ideological as well as a practical position, to compromise means to violate their ideology. For Americans to be successful negotiating with Russians, they will have to negotiate the entire issue as a whole. If this is not possible, it may be permissible to engage in a form of bartering where there is a direct and equal exchange of goods on a quid pro quo basis.

5. To be sensitive to the cultural background of the other party. For example, when negotiating with Arab men it is insulting to inquire about the well-being of their wives—a very private matter; or to offer something to another using the left hand—the hand historically used for cleaning oneself.

However, American negotiators do not come by these skills naturally. Largely because of the economic success the U.S. has experienced in this century, Americans tend to view the world from a highly ethnocentric perspective—our way of doing business is the only way, our products are superior, and our management practices are the best. These ethnocentric behaviors on the part of American negotiators have been summarized by Graham and Herberger (1983) as follows:[2]

1. I can go it alone. Many Americans think they can handle any negotiating situation by themselves.

2. Just call me John. Americans emphasize informality and equality when dealing with others. They try to make others comfortable by playing down status distinctions.

3. Americans aren't very talented at speaking foreign languages and therefore miscommunicate frequently, not bothering to learn the language of their opposing negotiator.

4. Americans like to get to the point, lay their cards on the table, stop beating around the bush, stop wasting time.

5. Silence is not "golden" to Americans. They talk frequently and expect others to do so as well.

6. One thing at a time. Americans usually like to negotiate one issue at a time, sequentially.

7. I am what I am. Changing one's mind is unusual for Americans.

If they are insensitive to the cultural characteristics of the other party or unaware of their own cultural predispositions, international negotiators are likely to fail. To reduce the prospects of failure there is a set of negotiation skills that should be part of every negotiator's mindset. These skills were identified in a large research project (1976)[3] conducted on American negotiators, designed to distinguish between the "successful" negotiator as contrasted to the "average" negotiator. Successful negotiators were those who were rated as successful by both parties, were known to be successful based on their track record, and had a low failure rate. A total of 48 successful negotiators were studied by observing their behaviors and analyzing the recordings of 102 separate negotiating sessions.

The skills and characteristics of these successful negotiators were found to be quite different from those of the average negotiators. In terms of planning for the negotiation meetings, important findings were:

1. Successful negotiators considered a wider range of outcomes (5.1 outcomes or options per issue) than did the average negotiators (2.6 outcomes or options per issue).

2. Successful negotiators focused the negotiations on areas of common interest three times as often (38 percent of comments on areas of possible agreement or common ground) as did the average negotiators (11 percent of comments on areas of possible agreement or common ground).

3. Successful negotiators were twice as likely to emphasize the long term (8.5 percent of comments) as compared to the average negotiators (4 percent of comments).

4. Successful negotiators were significantly more likely to establish a range of possible outcomes or points of agreement than were average negotiators, who were most likely to specify a fixed outcome (e.g., "the price we want is $3.89 per unit").

5. Successful negotiators were more flexible in terms of how negotiators proceeded than were average negotiators. Negotiable items were not linked to one another as often by successful negotiators while average negotiators would attempt to make the outcome of one item contingent upon the outcome of a prior item, and so on.

Once negotiations begin, other important behavioral differences between the successful and average negotiators were found. For example, during negotiations successful negotiators were five times less likely to use irritating words or phrases (e.g., "I am making you a generous offer") than were average negotiators: 2.3 irritators per hour of face-to-face speaking time vs. 10.8, respectively.

Successful negotiators were also slower to make counterproposals than were average negotiators: 1.7 vs. 3.1 counterproposals per hour of face-to-face speaking time, respectively. A third area in which successful negotiators were found to be different from average negotiators was the number of reasons they gave to justify their position. Successful negotiators pose fewer reasons (1.8) for their position than do average negotiators (3.0). This finding runs counter to the commonly held notion that the more reasons one can produce to support a position, the better the chances for success.

Finally, successful negotiators more frequently set aside time after the negotiation meeting to review what had happened, what was learned, and what was likely to occur during the next meeting.

These findings suggest ways to behave during the negotiation process to increase the chances of having a successful negotiation outcome.

A PROPOSED PROGRAM FOR TRAINING INTERNATIONAL NEGOTIATORS

Discuss within your group and then fill in the blank spaces below. Review "Insights into International Negotiations" as much as necessary to assist you.

The *attitudes* that one must learn before interacting with business people from other cultures are:

1. _____
2. _____
3. _____
4. _____
5. _____
6. _____
7. _____
8. _____

The *skills that one must learn before engaging in international negotiations are:*

1. _____
2. _____
3. _____
4. _____
5. _____
6. _____
7. _____
8. _____

The *American cultural traits* that American negotiators must be aware of in themselves before engaging in international negotiations are:

1. _____

2. _____

3. _____

4. _____

5. _____

6. _____

7. _____

8. _____

Now describe the training approaches that would be most effective in teaching these skills. If necessary, consult a standard human resources or management training and development textbook.

For teaching *attitudes*, the most effective training approaches would be:

_____

_____

_____

_____

_____

For teaching *skills*, the most effective training approaches would be:

_____

_____

_____

_____

_____

For teaching trainees *awareness of their own cultural traits*, the most effective training approaches would be:

_____

_____

_____

_____

_____

QUESTIONS

1. How does training the international negotiator differ from training negotiators for in-country negotiations? Discuss below.

2. Write a brief job specification for a person to be hired to conduct international negotiations. Include the type of education, work experience, personal characteristics, international experiences, language capabilities, etc.

NOTES

1. Pierre Casse, *Training for the Cross-Cultural Mind* (Washington, D.C.: Society for Intercultural Training, Education, and Research, 1979).

2. John Graham, and Roy Herberger, "Negotiators Abroad—Don't Shoot from the Hip," *Harvard Business Review* (July–August 1983).

3. *The Behavior of Successful Negotiators* (Reston, VA: Huthwaite Research Group, 1976).

SUGGESTED READINGS

Adler, Nancy, and John Graham. "Cross-Cultural Interaction: The International Comparison Fallacy." *Journal of International Business Studies* 20, no. 3 (1988): 525–532.

Adler, Nancy, Theodore Schwarz, and John L. Graham. "Business Negotiations in the United States, Mexico and Canada." *Journal of Business Research* 15, no. 4 (1987): 1–19.

Fisher, Glen. *International Negotiations: A Cross-Cultural Perspective*. Chicago: Intercultural Press, 1980.

Graham, John, and Roy Herberger. "Negotiators Abroad—Don't Shoot from the Hip." *Harvard Business Review* (July–August 1983).

Lanier, Alison R. *Living in the U.S.A.*, 4th ed. Yarmouth, ME: Intercultural Press, 1988.

Nigel, C., G. Campbell, John L. Graham, Alain Jolibert, and Hans Gunther Meissner, "Marketing Negotiations in France, Germany, the United Kingdom, and the United States." *Journal of Marketing* 52 (1988): 49–62.

Stewart, Edward C. *American Cultural Patterns*. Chicago: Intercultural Press, 1972.

Tung, Rosalie L. "U.S.–China Trade Negotiations: Practices, Procedures, and Outcomes." *Journal of International Business Studies* 13 (Fall 1982): 25–38.

PART 7
Appraisal

After recruiting, selecting, and training employees, management must then appraise employee work performance in order to administer compensation and to provide feedback. Merit pay has become a widely discussed topic. Before employees can be rewarded on the basis of merit, management must be able to accurately distinguish low performers from high performers. Performance appraisal, if carried out correctly, can provide management with the necessary information for making these decisions.

Chapter 25 introduces the student to different approaches to performance appraisal and emphasizes a management by objectives approach. With this approach, employees must be clear regarding what work goals are expected of them. Once measurable goals have been clearly established, individuals can be held accountable for attaining them. Management by objectives minimizes miscommunication between employees and managers and increases the chances of employees perceiving the appraisal system as fair because expectations are clarified at the beginning of the appraisal period.

The appraisal interview is covered in Chapter 26. In this exercise, students are to role play the appraisal interview in order to learn how to conduct interviews correctly. Professionally done interviews provide management with valid information for making fair and job-related compensation decisions, which in turn minimizes the chances of fair employment questions being raised. If employees are paid based on non-job-related reasons, the organization runs the risk of litigation and serious morale problems among employees.

Chapter **25**

Performance Appraisal

Learning Objectives—After completion of this exercise, you should be able to:

1. Describe the characteristics of two basic approaches to performance appraisal.
2. Contrast management by objectives with the rating scale approach.
3. List at least two advantages and two disadvantages of management by objectives.
4. Understand basic types of rater bias.

Time Suggested: Part A—One hour
Part B—One hour

Procedures:

Part A

1. Read the Introduction to Part A.
2. Individually complete the Problems and Questions sections.

Part B

1. Read the Introduction to Part B.

2. Divide into groups of four to five for the role-playing. One member in each group is to play the role of a subordinate of P & M Manufacturing Company. Another member is to play the role of the supervisor.

3. The person playing the role of the supervisor is to read "The Role of the Supervisor."

4. The person playing the role of the employee is to read "The Role of the Employee."

5. Other members of the group are to observe the goal-setting conference.

6. Answer the questions at the end of Part B.

 INTRODUCTION—PART A

One of the most difficult management jobs is evaluating the performance of subordinates. The reason is obvious—individuals dislike receiving or giving negative feedback. Another important reason is not so obvious—it is difficult to objectively evaluate an individual's work performance. Examples will illustrate this point:

- *Example A*: A company uses profit centers to evaluate its managers. Manager "A" is considering her training budget for next year. She realizes that training costs will have negative impact on her short-term profits, which translates into a lower appraisal of her performance.

- *Example B*: Manager "B" is not popular in the organization. He does not get along with his peers, subordinates, or superiors. He tends to be very opinionated and dogmatic. Interestingly, he nearly always exceeds the company's expectations for his work. He is a producer.

Both of the above situations would contaminate the appraisal of each manager's performance. In the first example the conflict is over the long-term impact of training vs. its short-term impact on profits. Current accounting practices treat training as a current expense rather than as an asset that can be amortized. The second example illustrates one of the more common problems in appraisal—we are often biased against people we dislike and biased toward those we like. Personality is a strong contaminator of appraisal systems.

Other difficulties with appraising performance are as follows:

- *Recent behavior bias*. Appraisal tends to be based more on recent performance than on the ratee's performance over the entire rating period.

- *Rater bias*. As illustrated in the above examples, the rater's values, attitudes, or prejudices tend to distort the ratings given. Feelings of like or dislike for the ratee interfere with the rater's ability to evaluate the performance accurately.

- *Halo bias*. Raters often allow the ratee's performance on one factor to contaminate the appraisal of other factors. If the ratee is highly organized, the rater may feel that being "organized" also means that the person is "productive." In other words, high marks for "organization" lead to high marks for "productivity" even though productivity may in fact in low.

GRAPHIC RATING SCALES

The graphic rating scale is the most popular technique used to appraise performance. It is also the simplest and most easily used method. In this approach the employee (ratee) is evaluated on various dimensions of work performance using adjective descriptions that commonly range from one extreme to another—for example, weak to strong, unsatisfactory to outstanding, unacceptable to excellent. The rater chooses the adjective that best describes the performance of the ratee on each performance dimension.

Figure 25–1 is an example of a typical rating scale.

◢ FIGURE 25–1 Typical Performance Appraisal Rating Scale

Supervisor's Evaluation of Employee

A. Cooperation   Consider: Ability and willingness to work in harmony for and with others. Does he/she get along with others? Is he/she pleasant to work with?

Unknown	Unsatisfactory	Fair	Satisfactory	Satisfaction Plus	Excellent	Outstanding
☐	☐	☐	☐	☐	☐	☐

B. Job Knowledge   Consider: Technical know-how, experience. Does he/she know what to do? Does he/she know the required steps to get a job done?

Unknown	Unsatisfactory	Fair	Satisfactory	Satisfaction Plus	Excellent	Outstanding
☐	☐	☐	☐	☐	☐	☐

C. Job Accomplishment   Consider: A careful worker. A thorough worker. Works quickly. Checks his/her work. System of work displays good judgment. Does he/she finish assigned work satisfactorily?

Unknown	Unsatisfactory	Fair	Satisfactory	Satisfaction Plus	Excellent	Outstanding
☐	☐	☐	☐	☐	☐	☐

D. Initiative   Consider: Ability to accomplish job with available resources. Ability to work without frequent supervision. Does he/she go out of his/her way to do a better job?

Unknown	Unsatisfactory	Fair	Satisfactory	Satisfaction Plus	Excellent	Outstanding
☐	☐	☐	☐	☐	☐	☐

E. Supervision   Consider: Ability to plan and organize work in advance. Assumes responsibility. Uses delegated authority properly. Develops teamwork.

Not Applicable	Unknown	Unsatisfactory	Fair	Satisfactory	Satisfaction Plus	Excellent	Outstanding
☐	☐	☐	☐	☐	☐	☐	☐

F. Overall Rating   Consider: Each of the above rating factors.

	Unknown	Unsatisfactory	Fair	Satisfactory	Satisfaction Plus	Excellent	Outstanding
☐	☐	☐	☐	☐	☐	☐	

Comments of Supervisor

_____

_____

_____

_____

_____

_____

Signature of Supervisor   Date

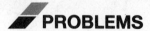 **PROBLEMS**

1. Carefully examine the graphic rating scale (Figure 25–1). Which of the dimensions on the scale would be *most* sensitive to the biases of the rater? Explain/justify your choices.

2. Which of the dimensions on the scale would be the *least* sensitive to the biases of the rater? Explain/justify your choices.

3. Rating scales have been criticized for allowing too much subjectivity on the part of the rater. What is it about the rating scale that allows for such subjectivity? How can this scale be changed to correct the problem?

4. How can the biases of recent behavior, halo, and the rater be minimized? What do you recommend?

Recent Behavior Bias

Halo Bias

Rater Bias

INTRODUCTION—PART B

MANAGEMENT BY OBJECTIVES (MBO)

Management by objectives (MBO) is actually much more than an appraisal method. It has been described as:

> a managerial process whereby organizational purposes are diagnosed and met by joining superiors and subordinates in the pursuit of mutually agreed upon goals and objectives which are specific, measurable, time bounded, and joined to an action plan; progress and goal attainment are discussed and monitored in appraisal sessions which center on mutually determined objective standards of performance.[1]

MBO has probably had more impact on management processes in the United States and Europe than any other management technique during the last quarter-century. It features increased collaboration in planning as well as communication between superior and subordinate, and it supposedly enhances acceptance of and commitment to organizational objectives. It is an organizationwide planning and control process whereby explicit objectives are defined for (1) the organization, (2) each department, (3) each manager, and (4) each employee.

The rationale behind management by objectives is that job performance should be related to organizational objectives. If such a relationship exists, a person will be viewed as a success in terms of individual performance. Objectives, therefore, are defined as those desired goals or results that the supervisor and the employee agree are achievable and worthwhile—given a certain level of performance and given a mutual understanding of the overall goals of the organization.

Because work activity takes many forms, performance objectives fall into three broad categories of work behavior. The largest number of objectives will fall into a category called *routine* or *regular objectives*. Regular objectives are those ongoing, everyday-type goals that are an integral part of any job. They provide the employee with a sense of security, predictability, and stability in reference to the job. The employee can expect these objectives always to be a part of his or her work activities. However, if regular objectives are the only type set forth, the chances of boredom setting in are increased, as most people can easily meet regular objectives.

Therefore, a second category of objectives, called *problem-solving objectives*, is needed to provide solutions to problems that often arise in the course of a typical workday. These objectives are defined in terms of trying to correct and solve problems that arise in connection with one's job. Problem-solving objectives are considered to be more sophisticated than regular objectives, as they require the worker to use his or her know-how before successful problem solving can occur.

Even with the addition of problem-solving objectives, there is yet another class of objectives that is necessary for any MBO program to be complete. These objectives are called *innovative objectives* and are defined as those activities designed to make things work better or to improve some aspect of the job. Because organizations, the people in them, and the activities associated with any job are always changing, the opportunity for improving and innovating one's job is ever present. This is brought about by our human tendency to be a bit dissatisfied with the status quo, to want to rearrange and improve situations. Oftentimes, success in reaching these kinds of objectives has a long-lasting positive effect on the organization.

In summary, we have discussed three types of objectives. They are: (1) regular objectives, (2) problem-solving objectives, and (3) innovative objectives.

HOW TO SET GOALS

1. Goals should be stated in a form that facilitates their use in measuring results at a future time.

2. Goals should be stated in a way that will affect behavior and results. They should not simply state those activities which would have been performed anyway.

3. The two basic tools for setting goals are a goal-setting conference and a memo. The goal-setting conference is explained later in the chapter. The memo is a confirmation in writing of what is agreed upon between the employee and the supervisor as a result of the goal-setting conference.

4. Goal statements should be accessible for regular review by the employee, permitting self-guidance and self-feedback. Goals are not to be etched on copper and buried.

The terms *goals* and *objectives* are used interchangeably.

HOW AND WHEN TO MEASURE PERFORMANCE

1. The following table describes how and when to measure the three types of goals:

Type	How to Measure	When to Measure
Routine or regular	When exceptional performance occurs	At specified times throughout the year
Problem-solving	Solutions as promised in time	At the point in time when a problem is solved
Innovative	By stages of commitment	When each stage is completed

2. These goals should be arranged to comprise an ascending scale of managerial excellence. Regular goals are the minimum acceptable performance, while excellent performance emerges when the subordinate begins to accomplish problem-solving and innovative goals.

ROLE-PLAYING

THE ROLE OF THE SUPERVISOR

Assume the role of the general manager of P & M Manufacturing Company. You have developed goals for the company and have asked one of your subordinates, the supervisor of the production department, to study the goals you have set and to submit goals of his or her own that will contribute to the goals of the organization.

The goals you have set for 1992 are:

1. To increase sales by 10 percent.

2. To reduce labor turnover by 5 percent.

3. To improve community relations.

4. To reduce the rate of absenteeism to the industry average of 4 percent (present rate at P & M is 6 percent).

5. To reduce the rate of defective products from 5 percent to 3 percent.

You are now ready to have a goal-setting conference with the supervisor of the production department.

THE GOAL-SETTING CONFERENCE

1. Let the subordinate know that you consider this meeting important for both of you.

2. Listen attentively. Encourage the subordinate to talk and to ask questions.

3. Ask the subordinate to discuss the goals he or she has selected for improvement. Discuss the plans for accomplishing each goal. When you both agree on what can and should be done, make notes of goals for later use.

4. Ask what you as the supervisor can do, refrain from doing, or do differently to help the subordinate do an even better job. Don't ask what is wrong with you. Don't go on the defensive or argue.

5. Avoid using or thinking in terms of "weaknesses," "faults," and "shortcomings." Concentrate on results and actions. Avoid discussion of personality traits, peculiarities, and attitudes.

6. Be careful in giving advice. Avoid such approaches as "If I were you . . .," or "If you did this . . .," or "Why don't you . . .?" Encourage each person to work out a plan for improvement.

7. Be cautious in making promises. Keep the ones you make.

8. Review the points agreed upon and make notes of the important points. Whenever possible, let the subordinate put the conclusions in his or her own words, with each of you having a copy for follow-up. End the conference on an encouraging note of confidence. Schedule a follow-up meeting and make it clear that you will be looking forward to further discussion and improvement.

In summary, your role as a supervisor is to:

1. Insist that the employee set attainable objectives that are challenging.

2. Ask how the employee arrived at the various objectives stated.

3. Question the methods proposed for reaching objectives.

4. Suggest other possible action where needed.

THE ROLE OF THE EMPLOYEE

Assume that the general manager of P & M Manufacturing Company has determined the following goals for 1992:

1. To increase sales by 10 percent.

2. To reduce labor turnover by 5 percent.

3. To improve community relations.

4. To reduce the rate of absenteeism to the industry average of 4 percent (present rate at P & M is 6 percent).

5. To reduce the rate of defective products from 5 percent to 3 percent.

You are to assume the role of the supervisor of the production department. You have complete responsibility for its overall operations.

The organization's yearly goals (just listed) have been given to you by the general manager. You must now develop goals for your department that will contribute to the organizational goals. Once you finish writing your goals, you have a goal-setting conference with your supervisor. During that conference be prepared to:

1. Set performance standards for the various objectives you set.

2. Define how results are to be measured.

3. Explain in detail how you intend to achieve the objectives you set forth.

4. Suggest alternative courses of action.

Use the information that follows to assist you in setting goals, then write your goals on the forms provided.

INSTRUCTIONS FOR FILLING OUT GOAL-SETTING FORMS

1. Begin identifying each of the three types of goals.

2. Consider how each of the goals is to be measured, and the time dimensions associated with each one.

3. Study the examples of poor and better statements of goals that appear in Figure 25–2.

4. Study Figure 25–3, which gives examples of how goals are expressed.

5. Write goals for yourself.

■ **FIGURE 25–2   Examples of Goals**

Poor	Better
High quality production	The reject rate equal to less than 2% of total cost
100% of budget standards	+ 5% of labor cost
	+ 4% material
	+ 6% overhead
Participate in training program	Enroll 60 employees in training program during next 6 months
Maintain high productivity	Produce 5,000 units per shift
Improve quality	Reduce number of defects in finished product by 10%
Maintain morale	Reduce absenteeism by 10% and turnover by 6%
Improve safety	Bring frequency and severity rate of accidents in line with industrial averages

FIGURE 25–3   Examples of How Goals Are Expressed

	Examples
Raw data	Number of units produced per shift
	Number of shipments per week
	Number of accidents per month
Ratios	95% time departures within 5% of budget standards
	98% defect-free
	Overtime no greater than 100% of regular time
Scales	How would you rate this job?
	Skill 1 2 3 4 5 6 7 8
	Hazards 1 2 3 4 5 6 7 8
	Seniority 1 2 3 4 5 6 7 8
	Education 1 2 3 4 5 6 7 8
Adjectives, adverbs	A clean work area reduces accident proneness.
Verbs	*Develop* a training program.
	Mop the floor.
	Conduct quality inspections.

P & M MANUFACTURING COMPANY

REGULAR OBJECTIVES—TYPE I

This form is to be used to record regular objectives that can be quantitatively measured.

Objectives	How Measured	Time Dimension
Example: Produce 5,000 units per shift	By exceptional performance, when over 5,000 units are produced	Monthly
Example: Clean work area when shift ends	By inspection	Daily

P & M MANUFACTURING COMPANY

PROBLEM-SOLVING OBJECTIVES—TYPE II

On this form include those objectives that identify problem areas and proposed solutions.

Statement	Dimensions of Problem	Desired Solution	Timetable
Example: Bring absenteeism to the industry average of 4%	Year-long problem involving counseling with employees with high absentee-ism rates	4% or less	Reports will be made every quarter

P & M MANUFACTURING COMPANY

INNOVATIVE, GROWTH, OR IMPROVEMENT GOALS—TYPE III

On this form include those projects that are designed to bring about application of new technology, new systems and programs, or self-development.

Objectives	Stages or Steps Necessary	Time Dimensions	Necessary Input (money material, etc.)
Example: Install a training program on employee motivation for all first-line supervisors	1. Design the program 2. Contract with qualified trainers 3. Schedule and conduct the program	One year	1. $15,000 2. Clerical assistance ¼ time

QUESTIONS

1. How can compensation be tied to MBO? Discuss within your group and write a group response.

2. What behavioral consequences does MBO have for both the supervisor and the subordinate? Discuss within your group and write a group response.

3. What should management do if a labor strike occurs and disrupts the employee in his or her striving to meet specified objectives?

4. How is MBO advantageous to an organization that makes it work successfully? Discuss within your group and write a group response.

5. What might be some of the potential problems and difficulties associated with an MBO program? Discuss within your group and write a group response.

6. How does MBO as a philosophy of management differ from traditional management philosophy? Discuss within your group and write a group response.

7. As a group describe three characteristics of poorly stated objectives and three characteristics of properly stated objectives.

   Poorly Stated Objectives:

   a.

   b.

   c.

   Properly Stated Objectives:

   a.

   b.

   c.

8. Which appraisal method would you prefer—graphic rating scale or management by objectives? As a first-line supervisor? As a general manager? Why?

NOTE

1. M. C. McConkie, "A Clarification of the Goal Setting and Appraisal Processes in MBO," *Academy of Management Review* 4 (1979): 29.

SUGGESTED READINGS

Carson, Kenneth P., Robert L. Cardy, and Gregory H. Dobbins. "Performance Appraisal as Effective Management of Deadly Management Disease: Two Initial Empirical Investigations." *Group & Organization Studies* 16, no. 2 (June 1, 1991): 143.

Giblin, E. J., and S. F. Sanfilippo. "MBO: Misunderstood Goal for Creative Planning." *Managerial Planning* (May 1978): 4–10.

Goodson, Jane R., and Gail W. McGee. "Enhancing Individual Perceptions of Objectivity in Performance Appraisal." *Journal of Business Research* 22, no. 4 (June 1, 1991): 283.

Guinn, Katherine A. "Putting a Price on Performance." *Personnel Journal* 70, no. 5 (May 1, 1991): 72.

Ivancevich, J. M. "Subordinates' Reaction to Performance Appraisal Interviews: A Test of Feedback and Goal-Setting Techniques." *Journal of Applied Psychology* 67 (1982): 581–587.

Kearney, W. J. "Behaviorally Anchored Rating Scales—MBO's Missing Ingredient." *Personnel Journal* (January 1979): 20–25.

Lathan, G. P., and E. A. Locke. "Goal Setting—A Motivational Technique That Works." *Organizational Dynamics* (Autumn 1979).

Lowe, Terry R. "Eight Ways to Ruin a Performance Review." *Personnel Journal* 65 (January 1986): 60–62.

Milliman, John. "Interpersonal Relations as a Context for the Effects of Appraisal Interviews on Performance and Satisfaction: A Longitudinal Study." *Academy of Management Journal* 34, no. 2 (June 1, 1991): 352.

Oliver, John E. et al. "Adapting Performance Appraisal Systems to Changed Technologies." *Human Resources Management* 5 (April 1985): 323–331.

Smith, David E. "Training Programs for Performance Appraisal: A Review." *The Academy of Management Review* 11 (January 1986): 22–40.

Chapter 26

Appraisal Interview

Learning Objectives—After completion of this exercise, you should be able to:

1. Identify and describe three possible problem areas in an appraisal interview.

2. Identify and describe three ways of conducting a proper appraisal interview.

3. Develop an interview plan.

Time Suggested: One hour

Procedures:

1. Read the Introduction

2. Two members from the class are selected—one to role-play the supervisor who conducts the appraisal interview and the other to role-play the employee being interviewed.

3. All other members act as observers.

4. All participants read the "General Instructions."

5. The participant who will conduct the interview studies the role of George Stanley. The participant who is to be interviewed studies the role of Tom Burke. Both should role-play their parts without referring to their role sheets.

6. The observers read "Instructions for Observers."

7. The scene is set up: a table in front of the room to represent the interviewer's desk and two chairs arranged by the desk in such a way that the participants can talk to each other comfortably and still have their faces visible to the observers.

8. Go to the "Process Instructions."

9. When the interview is over, all participants should read "Comments and Implications."

10. Answer the questions at the end of the exercise.

◢ INTRODUCTION

When a supervisor conducts appraisal interviews with her subordinates, the results are often ill feelings and misunderstandings rather than improved relations and employee development. The subordinates often feel there is undue emphasis on deficiencies and they become defensive. When the superior, as a result, feels compelled to justify her point of view, she also becomes defensive. As a consequence, the interview frequently creates conflict and new problems rather than solves existing problems.

A common cause of difficulty is the difference in frames of reference between the supervisor and her subordinates. The supervisor's situation tends to make her sensitive to deficiencies in job performance because these create problems for her; she is likely to take adequate performance more or less for granted. The employee, on the other hand, is aware of the little extras she does and is likely to blame poor results on inadequate or unclear assignments, poor training, or someone else's failure to cooperate. Thus, the interview tends to contain highly divergent views.

Because difficulties are encountered in interviews of this kind, supervisors are reluctant to conduct them. If a company program requires periodic evaluations, there is a marked tendency among supervisors to avoid mentioning unfavorable points, thereby defeating the purpose of the evaluation. The success or failure of an employee developmental program largely depends on the skill with which employees are interviewed by their superiors.

The purpose of this exercise is to develop sensitivity toward communication problems in this type of interview. This will be carried out through a role-playing procedure.

The Introduction is reprinted from N. R. F. Maier, A. R. Solem, and A. A. Maier, *The Role-Play Technique: A Handbook for Management and Leadership Practice*, San Diego, CA: University Associates, 1975. Used with permission.

ROLE-PLAYING

GENERAL INSTRUCTIONS

George Stanley is the head of the electrical section in the engineering department at the American Construction Company. The work in the department includes designing, drafting, making cost estimates, keeping maps up to date, checking standards and building codes, doing field inspection and follow-up, and so on. Eight first-line supervisors report to Stanley. Their duties are partly technical and partly supervisory. The organizational chart for Stanley's section is shown in Figure 26–1.

FIGURE 26–1   Organizational Chart of the Electrical Section

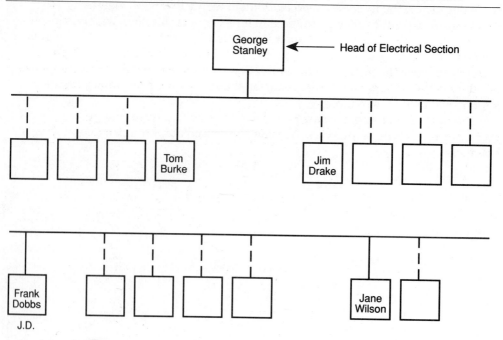

The "General Instructions" and "Comments and Implications" sections are based on an exercise taken from *Psychology in Industrial Organizations*, 5th ed., by Norman R. F. Maier and Gertrude Casselman Verser, 579–581. Copyright © 1982 by Houghton Mifflin Company. Used by permission of the publisher.

Company policy requires that each section head interview his or her supervisors once a year. The purpose is to: (1) evaluate the supervisor's performance during the year; (2) give recognition for jobs well done; and (3) correct weaknesses.

The evaluation interviews were introduced because the company believes that employees should know how they stand and that everything should be done to develop management personnel. Today, Stanley will conduct an evaluation interview with Tom Burke, one of the supervisors reporting to him.

Tom Burke has a college degree in electrical engineering; in addition to his technical duties—which often take him to the field—he supervises the work of one junior designer, six draftsmen, and two clerks. He is highly paid, as are all the supervisors in this department, because of the job's high requirements in technical knowledge. Burke has been with the company for twelve years, and has been a supervisor for two years. He is married and has two children. He owns his home, and is active in the civic affairs of his community.

ROLE SHEET: GEORGE STANLEY, SECTION HEAD

You have evaluated all the supervisors who report to you and during the next two weeks you will interview each of them. You hope to use these interviews constructively. Today you have arranged to interview Tom Burke, one of the eight first-line supervisors who report to you. Burke's file contains the following information and evaluation:

> Twelve years with the company, two years as supervisor, college degree, married, two children. Highly creative and original, exceptionally competent technically.

His unit is very productive and during the two years he has supervised the group, there has been steady improvement. Within the past six months, you have given him extra work, and it has been done on schedule. As far as productivity and dependability are concerned, he is your top supervisor.

His cooperation with other supervisors in the section, however, leaves much to be desired. Before you made him a supervisor, his originality and technical knowledge were available to your whole section. Gradually he has withdrawn, and now acts like a lone wolf. You have asked other supervisors to talk over certain problems with him, but they tell you that he offers no suggestions. He tells them he is busy, listens without interest to their problems, kids them, or makes sarcastic remarks, depending on his mood. On one occasion, he caused Jim Drake, one of the supervisors in another unit, to make a mistake that could have been forestalled if Burke had let Drake know the status of certain design changes. It is expected that supervisors will cooperate on matters involving design changes that affect them.

Furthermore, during the past six months, Burke has been unwilling to take two assignments. He said that they were routine, and that he preferred more interesting work, and he advised you to give the assignments to other supervisors. To prevent trouble, you followed his suggestion. However, you feel that you cannot give him all the interesting work and that if he persists in this attitude, there will be trouble. You cannot play favorites and still keep up morale in your unit.

Burke's failure to cooperate has you worried for another reason. Although his group is highly productive, there is more turnover among his draftsmen than in other groups. You have heard no complaints yet, but you suspect that he may be treating his group in an arbitrary manner. Certainly if he is demanding with you and other supervisors, he is likely to be even more so with his employees. Apparently the high productivity in his group is not due to high morale, but to his ability to use his employees to do the things for which they are best suited. You do not want to lose good draftsmen. You hope to discuss these matters with Burke in such a way as to recognize his good points and, at the same time, correct some of his weaknesses.

ROLE SHEET: TOM BURKE, SUPERVISOR

One junior designer, six draftsmen, and two clerks report to you. You feel that you get along fine with your group. You have always been pretty much of an "idea" man, and apparently have the knack of passing on your enthusiasm to others in your group. There is a lot of "we" feeling in your unit, because it is obvious that your group is the most productive.

You believe in developing your employees, and always given them strong recommendations. You think you have gained the reputation of helping your employees grow, because they frequently go out and get much better jobs. Since promotion is necessarily slow in a company such as yours, you think that the best way to stimulate morale is to develop new personnel, and demonstrate that a good worker can get somewhere. The two women in your unit are bright and efficient, and there is a lot of good-natured kidding. Recently one of your employees, Jane Wilson, turned down an outside offer that paid thirty-five dollars a month more, because she preferred to stay in your group. You are going to get her a raise the first chance you get.

The other supervisors in George Stanley's section do not have your enthusiasm. Some of them are dull and unimaginative. During your first year as supervisor, you used to help them a lot, but you soon found that they leaned on you, and before long you were doing their work. There is a lot of pressure to produce. You got your promotion by producing, and you don't intend to let other supervisors interfere. Since you no longer help the other supervisors, your production has gone up, but a couple of them seem a bit sore at you. Frank, your junior designer, is a better worker than most, and you would like to see him made a supervisor.

Stanley ought to recognize the fact that the company has some deadwood in it and assign the more routine jobs to those units. Then they wouldn't need your help, and you could concentrate your efforts on jobs that suit your unit. At present, George Stanley passes out work pretty much as he gets it. Because you are efficient, you get more than your share of jobs, and you see no reason why the extra work shouldn't be in the form of "plums." This would motivate units to turn out work. When you suggested to Stanley that he turn over some of the more routine jobs to other supervisors, he did it, but he was very reluctant about it.

You did one thing recently that bothers you. There was a design change in a set of plans and you should have told Jim Drake (a fellow supervisor) about it, but it slipped your mind. Drake was out when you had it on your mind, and then you got involved in a hot idea of Frank's and forgot all about Drake. As a result, Drake had to make a lot of unnecessary changes and he was quite sore about it. You told him you were sorry and offered to make the change, but he turned down the offer.

Today you have an interview with George Stanley. It's about this management development plan in the company. It shouldn't take very long, and it's nice to have the boss tell you about the job you are turning out. Maybe there is a raise in it; maybe he'll tell you something about what to expect in the future.

INSTRUCTIONS FOR OBSERVERS

1. Observe the manner in which Stanley begins the interview.

   a. What does the interview do, if anything, to create a permissive atmosphere?

   b. Does the interviewer state the purpose of the interview early in the session?

   c. Is the purpose of the interview stated clearly and concisely?

2. Observe how the interview is conducted.

   a. To what extent does the interviewer learn how Burke feels about the job in general?

   b. Does the interviewer use broad, general questions at the outset?

   c. Does Stanley criticize Burke?

   d. Does Stanley praise Burke?

   e. Does he accept Burke's feelings and ideas?

   f. Which one talked the most?

3. Observe and evaluate the outcome of the interview.

   a. To what extent did Stanley arrive at a fairer and more accurate evaluation of Burke as a result of the interview?

   b. What things did Stanley do, if any, to motivate Burke to improve?

   c. Were relations better or worse after the interview? If worse, why?

   d. In what ways might the interviewer have done a better job?

PROCESS INSTRUCTIONS

1. When everybody is ready, George Stanley enters his office and sits at his desk. A moment later, Tom Burke enters the office and the scene begins.

2. The amount of time needed to complete the interview will vary, but twenty to thirty minutes usually is adequate. The interview is carried to the point of completion unless an argument develops and no progress is evident after ten or fifteen minutes of conflict.

3. If an interview ends too quickly, alternative approaches suggested by observers may be tested briefly.

4. One or two new pairs of participants may role-play in order to permit comparison of different interview styles and their outcomes.

5. A Stanley and a Burke exchange roles and role-play the case. Observers read the role instructions for both players.

COMMENTS AND IMPLICATIONS

Stanley will usually begin the interview by praising Burke for certain aspects of his performance such as his originality, productivity, and technical competence. Since this is a form of recognition for good work and involves no area of misunderstanding, the early part of the interview generally proceeds quite smoothly.

However, there are several areas of Burke's performance that Stanley is led to interpret in an unfavorable way. If Stanley proceeds with the interview on the basis of this interpretation, he is likely to make a number of criticisms that seem unjustified to Burke. If Burke feels that he is being treated unfairly, he will become defensive and even hostile. When this occurs, the interview will lead to further misunderstandings and bad feelings.

As in most performance appraisal situations, there is a built-in source of misunderstanding because the two persons involved are looking at the employee's job from two different points of view. In this case, both are aware of certain facts about Burke's unit, but they interpret the facts differently because of the differences in their perspectives.

To Stanley, the facts add up to an evaluation that Burke's strengths lie in his technical qualifications, while his weaknesses lie in his interpersonal relationships. Burke apparently has problems with his peers (the Drake incident), with his superior (resisting assignments), and with his subordinates (highest turnover).

To Burke, however, the same facts add up to the feeling that he successfully develops his employees to their best potential, which accounts for the unit's productivity. He takes pride in the fact that a number of his employees have been offered better jobs. In his opinion, this is partially because of the team spirit that exists within the unit, the fact that he has shared his technical knowledge with his employees, and the enthusiasm that he has generated for the challenges of the job. (It was mainly due to his own enthusiasm and absorption in the challenges that he forgot to see Drake.) Burke feels that he needs even more of the challenging jobs in order to develop and stimulate his employees if he is to be expected to keep them working for the company without wage increases.

Since the known facts are seen as faults by Stanley and as virtues by Burke, the problem is obviously one of interpretation. Each man views his interpretation as the correct one. In order to have a basis for problem solving and the development of solutions, each must learn to respect differing interpretations.

In order to conduct this interview satisfactorily, it is necessary for Stanley to create a supportive climate so that Burke will feel free to express his ideas and feelings. In this way, Stanley will learn Burke's frame of reference toward various aspects of the work, and he should discover that many of Burke's actions can be seen in a more favorable light. He is then unlikely to make unjustified criticisms and put Burke on the defensive. Thus, the first thing Stanley must learn is how Burke views his own performance.

In general, the best way for the interviewer to proceed is to begin the interview with a general question about how things are going. Frequently, Burke's comments will furnish leads that can be explored later on. The interviewer should than lead into a discussion of the things that Burke feels are going well for him. These aspects of the job are not only easy for Burke to discuss, they also give the interviewer a good opportunity to praise Burke for the things he has done well.

The next area of discussion should center around the things that are causing Burke some difficulties. By listening and accepting complaints, Stanley may learn some of the problems as they appear to Burke. There will be no feeling on Burke's part that he must try to cover up deficiencies (the Drake incident) or defend his actions if he finds that Stanley wants to be helpful. Burke may mention his desire to obtain a greater share of the challenging assignments as a reward for his productivity. Stanley will tend to reject this idea because it poses a problem for him. Nevertheless, the problem of how this can be accomplished without showing favoritism is capable of being solved through discussion.

In the final phase of the interview, mutual understanding and problem solving will be aided if the interviewer asks Burke what he or the company can do to help Burke with his problems. This not only produces constructive problem-solving behavior, but also motivates Burke to develop and carry out solutions to his work problems.

In typical solutions, some Burkes are given consulting assignments, some trade a superior draftsman for an unskilled one (in order to obtain a raise in pay for the better draftsman), others influence Stanley to hold group meetings to give out assignments, and many others begin to seek work elsewhere.

It should not matter if all an employee's apparent deficiencies are not brought up in one interview, since the objective is to develop his potential. It is obvious that a person cannot correct all his faults after one interview. The hope is to obtain some improvement after each interview. Of course, if the objective of an appraisal interview is to warn an employee rather than to develop him, this does not apply.

This case is typical of conflict situations that may be resolved innovatively if both sides work toward a mutually satisfactory solution. Such situations require that differences be respected and explored. A good deal of research indicates that disagreement can lead either to hard feelings or to innovation, depending on the skills utilized by the concerned parties.

 **QUESTIONS**

1. Develop your own interview plan using the material in this exercise.

Interview Plan

2. Describe at least three errors that might be made by an interviewer during an appraisal interview.

   a.

   b.

   c.

3. Describe at least three ways to conduct a good appraisal interview.

   a.

   b.

   c.

SUGGESTED READINGS

Alewine, Thomas C. "Performance Appraisal and Performance Standards." *Personnel Journal* 61, no. 3 (March 1982): 210–213.

Banks, Christina G., and Kevin R. Murphy. "Toward Narrowing the Research-Practice Gap in Performance Appraisal." *Personnel Psychology* 38 (February 1985): 335–346.

Burchett, Shelley R., and Kenneth P. De Meuse. "Performance Appraisal and the Law." *Personnel* 62 (July 1985): 29–37.

Burke, R. J., et al. "Characteristics of Effective Employee Performance and Development Interviews: Replication and Extension." *Personnel Psychology* (Winter 1978): 908–919.

Carson, Kenneth P., Robert L. Cardy, and Gregory H. Dobbins. "Performance Appraisal as Effective Management of Deadly Management Disease: Two Initial Empirical Investigations." *Group & Organization Studies* 16, no. 2 (June 1, 1991): 143.

Deets, Norman R., and D. Timothy Tyler. "How Xerox Improved Its Performance Appraisals." *Personnel Journal* 65 (April 1986): 50–52.

Fellner, Denise J., and Beth Sulzer-Azaroff. "Occupational Safety: Assessing the Impact of Adding Assigned or Participative Goal-Setting." *Journal of Organizational Behavior Management* 7 (January–February 1985): 3–24.

Guinn, Kathleen A. "Putting a Price on Performance." *Personnel Journal* 70, no. 5 (May 1, 1991): 72.

Kaye, Beverly, and Shelley Krantz. "Performance Appraisal: A Win/Win Approach." *Training and Development Journal* 37, no. 3 (March 1983): 32–35.

Kirkpatrick, Donald L. "Performance Appraisal: When Two Jobs Are Too Many." *Training* 23 (March 1986): 65–69.

Lannal, Peggy. "Team Appraisals." *Personnel Journal* 64 (March 1985): 46–51.

Savage, Adrian. "Reconciling Your Appraisal System With Company Reality." *Personnel Management* 14, no. 4 (May 1982): 31–33.

PART 8
Compensation

The management of compensation has implications for employee morale, employee productivity, and the financial health of the organization. In a modern market economy, compensation is the means by which individuals participate in the marketplace. If employees perceive their compensation to be either inadequate or unfair for the amount of work they perform, they are likely to leave the organization or engage in unproductive and costly behaviors such as showing up late for work or calling in sick. On the other hand, if the organization pays too much for the work performed, it is not being managed efficiently and may lose out to competitors, or lose customers, or both.

Compensation has other social connotations as well. For example, twenty-five years ago, women were making sixty cents for every dollar men made. Today, while some gains have been made, inequities remain. These must be addressed if sexism and discrimination toward women are to be eliminated. The question of fair or equal compensation is addressed in Chapter 27. Employers are legally required to give equal pay for equal work, an issue that arose from the traditional practice in this country of paying women less than men when both were performing the same job. With the passage of the Equal Pay Act of 1963, such practices became unlawful. In this chapter students examine several equal-pay cases to learn the various conditions by which the equal pay principle can be contested.

In Chapter 28 the concept of equal pay is extended to cover a more controversial issue known as comparable worth. In this exercise students learn what *comparable worth* means and analyze several cases concerning the issue. Comparable worth addresses the question of whether jobs of similar or comparable (not equal) value should receive comparable pay. This concept provides a basis for comparing the pay of a secretarial position with that of a mechanic for the purposes of determining their pay fairness. The former is typically held by women, the latter by men.

Many of the problems caused by the poor management of conpensation can be eliminated or minimized through the use of job evaluation. In Chapter 29 students study the two most common types of job evaluation and compare their relative weaknesses and strengths. They also become aware of how different jobs can be compared in terms of responsibility, skill, and other characteristics necessary to get the job done. Once these job characteristics are evaluated, management has a logical basis for determining their relative worth compared to other jobs in the organization.

The final exercise in this part of the book, Chapter 30, relates various compensation practices to a theory of work motivation called expectancy theory. After working through this exercise, students will begin to see the connection between rewards (compensation is the most important type of organization reward) and the employee's motivation to work.

Chapter 27

Equal Pay Act of 1963

Learning Objectives—After completion of this exercise, you should be able to:

1. Describe the requirements of the Equal Pay Act.

2. Identify possible areas of pay discrimination in actual work situations.

3. Understand the importance of job evaluation in implementing equal pay.

Time Suggested: One hour

Procedures:

1. Individually read the Introduction, which includes "Facts about the Equal Pay Act of 1963" and "Comparable Pay for Comparable Worth."

2. Individually, read and underline the important points in the three case briefs, *Hodgson* v. *City Stores, Inc., Dunlop* v. *Allegheny County Institution District*, and *Lemons* v. *City and County of Denver*.

3. Form into sexually mixed groups of four or five, and answer the questions at the end of each case brief.

4. The instructor will lead a discussion based on the group responses.

 **INTRODUCTION**

FACTS ABOUT THE EQUAL PAY ACT OF 1963 AS AMENDED BY EDUCATION AMENDMENTS OF 1972 (HIGHER EDUCATION ACT)

Who Is Covered?	Industries engaged in interstate commerce (same as Fair Labor Standards Act coverage).
What Is Prohibited?	Discrimination in salaries (including almost all fringe benefits) on the basis of sex. Differentials based on any other factor are not affected.
Exemptions from Coverage	Local, state, and federal governments. Industries exempted from Fair Labor Standards Act.
Who Enforces the Provisions?	Equal Employment Opportunity Commission (EEOC).
What Are Wages?	It encompasses all rates, whether calculated on time, piece, incentive, or other basis.
Record-Keeping Requirements and Government Access to Records	Institution must keep and preserve specified records relevant to the determination of whether violations have occurred. Government is empowered to review all relevant records.
What Employers Are Covered?	Employers covered by Fair Labor Standards Act. Since 1972, Act broadened to include professionals, executives, and outside-sales persons.
Enforcement Power and Sanctions	If voluntary compliance fails, EEOC may file suit. Court may prevent respondent from engaging in unlawful behavior, and order salary raises, back pay, and interest.
Affirmative Action Requirements	Affirmative action, other than salary increases and back pay, is not required.
Coverage of Labor Organizations	Labor organizations are prohibited from causing or attempting to cause an employer to discriminate on the basis of sex.
Is Harassment Prohibited?	Institutions are prohibited from discharging or discriminating against any employee or applicant because she/he has made a complaint, assisted with an investigation, or instituted proceedings.
Test of "Equal Wages"	Initially, the EPA made it illegal for unequal pay for "same" work; now it is for the same "general" work, determined in terms of skill, effort, and responsibility.

COMPARABLE PAY FOR COMPARABLE WORTH

As far back as the 1880s, there were organizations calling for equal pay. During the time of World War I and again in World War II, the United States and Europe practiced a policy of nondiscrimination in wages as women moved in to take over factory jobs vacated by men. However, as the wars ended, national debate arose over whether or not to continue this practice during peacetime.

Despite wartime legislation, some companies such as General Electric and Westinghouse classified their jobs on the basis of necessary skill, effort, and responsibility and consistently paid 18 to 30 percent less to women if they performed a specified job. This practice of setting women's rates below men's rates continued as late as the mid-1960s. Many union contracts up until that time still contained separate male and female pay rates. It was not uncommon for the lowest male rate to be higher than the highest female rate, despite similar job specifications.

The Equal Pay Act (EPA) calling for equal pay for equal or closely similar work became law in 1963. This was a result of women's groups and labor unions becoming particularly active. The EPA was followed in 1964 by Title VII of the Civil Rights Act. This prescribed general equal employment opportunity for minorities and women, including equality in compensation. Title VII had a broader jurisdiction than the EPA and prohibited a broader range of discrimination.

Currently, in an effort to broaden the approach to equal compensation, the term "comparable worth for comparable value" has been adapted.

The issue is now for equal pay both within the same general job classification and across job classifications, especially in fields that are predominantly female. Characteristically, women's jobs are generally lower paid with little outlook for upward mobility or any hope of on-the-job training. The persistent assignment of women to stereotypical jobs has not changed much since the 1950s. This fact of segregation and the concomitant lack of equal job opportunities motivated the adoption of Title VII of the Civil Rights Act.

A look at the historical rates paid to men and women shows that the wage differential between women and men is increasing despite legislation. For example, in 1955 women earned 64 percent of men's income; in 1973, they earned only about 57 percent. Findings by the Bureau of Labor Statistics, in looking at the twenty highest-paid occupations of men and women, found that the highest weekly median male earnings were $619 while the highest female earnings were only $422. Also, all twenty of the highest-paying male occupations were above the highest-paying female occupations.

There are numerous explanations used to support the findings of female segregation. For example, economists assume women are less committed to work, that they prefer the jobs with less responsibility and skill, that women excel in finger dexterity, which is less demanding and therefore less well paid than jobs requiring more mental or physical exertion, and that women are only secondary earners without full family responsibilities. Responses to these types of traditional arguments come from many directions. Some observers believe that women's and minorities' low wage rates are a result of their segregation into a limited number of occupations within which they are overcrowded, and therefore are competing against one another to drive down women's wages.

How do we achieve the goal of pay equity? There are many ways, each depending on the unique situation. The first step, however, is to get the workers to have an accurate picture of where they are in the present situation, so they can set realistic goals for achievement.

CASE STUDIES

Hodgson v. City Stores, Inc.
U.S. District Court
332 F.Supp. 942 (M.D.Ala.1971)

Injunction action by the Secretary of Labor against department store that has allegedly violated equal pay provisions of Section 6(d)(1) of the Fair Labor Standards Act.

PLAINTIFF'S POSITION:

Plaintiff has alleged that female salespersons engaged as regular employees to sell women's and children's clothes and related items have been and continue to be paid less than men with substantially equal amounts of retail sales experience who sell men's suits. The Secretary, having concluded that the work of these male and female employees was and is equal within the meaning of the Act, contends that violations have been and are occurring. Plaintiff further alleges violations as to a female seamstress who alters women's clothing and is paid less than a male tailor who alters men's clothing.

As is true of similar employees in any department store, the primary duty of each salesperson is to sell merchandise. This requires knowledge of the stock and its location and of how to meet the public, analyze customer needs, present the merchandise with understanding, close the sale, help select for the customers and overcome their objections, trade up in quality of merchandise, sell more than one item of what the customer initially wants, and see that the merchandise is delivered in the proper state, form, and fit.

Both men and women salespeople in their respective departments are responsible for the successful presentation of items to their customers. Each must assist in selecting the item of the size and material most appropriate to fit a customer's needs. Both bear the responsibility for suggesting a garment's alterations which will enhance the customer's appearance. There is no greater responsibility of one group over another for the maintenance and procurement of proper inventory.

DEFENDANT'S POSITION:

The defendant denies generally that it has violated the Act. It alleges that jobs within a department store cannot be equated equitably with other sales jobs within the same store. Rather, it contends that jobs within its store must be compared with sales jobs in other specialty shops selling a similar product within the market area. In explaining the wage disparities between various sales personnel, defendant claims that "merit adjustments are made to all sales personnel based upon their cost of sales for the previous year." This adjustment is computed by dividing yearly salary by yearly net sales, and awarding minor increases in salary if it is sufficiently small in comparison to sales.

The defendant further claims that there is a wide range of wage rates throughout the store dependent upon the individual employee, the department to which the employee is assigned, and the product sold. Finally, it is alleged that the wages have been based upon the rate prevailing in the labor market for the selling of particular products, and are not based upon sex.

As to the actual comparison of these positions, defendant seeks to defend the apparent differential between these groups of employees by characterizing those who work in the men's department store as "specialists," on the theory that the sort of marking and fitting required in altering men's suits is materially more difficult and complex than that required for women's and children's clothes. The defendant further contends that men are more difficult customers than women, since they seldom know what they desire or need. Thus, it is incumbent upon the salesmen or "specialists" that they select that which will best meet the customers' needs. On the other hand, defendant portrays women as more discerning shoppers with much more definite concepts of style and fabric. Accordingly, they are easier to cater to than men since they know what they want.

QUESTIONS

1. The employer claimed that a salesclerk's wages in one department could not be compared to the wages of a salesclerk in another department, but should be compared to the wages of salesclerks in similar departments in other stores. Do you agree? Why?

2. Do you agree with the defendant that men are more difficult customers than women? Why?

3. If you wanted to pay your salespersons by their sales performance rather than by time (hourly wages), what pay system would you use? Why?

If this resulted in a pay difference between males and females, would it be legal? Explain your answer.

CASE STUDIES

Dunlop v. Allegheny County Institution District
U.S. District Court
410 F.Supp. 501 (W.D.Pa.1975)

The action was instituted by the Secretary of Labor, U.S. Department of Labor, under the provisions of the Fair Labor Standards Act. John J. Kane Hospital is a geriatric hospital operated by the Allegheny County Institution District, a political subdivision of the Commonwealth of Pennsylvania. The plaintiff alleged that the defendant had violated the Equal Pay Act by paying its female beauticians at a lower rate than it paid its male barbers for performance of work which required equal skill, effort, and responsibility, and which was performed under similar working conditions.

PLAINTIFF'S POSITION:

All beauticians work from 7:30 a.m. to 3:30 p.m. Monday through Friday. The work of the beauticians is divided between the floors in the women's section of the hospital and the beauty shop. Between 50 percent and 75 percent of the time is spent cutting hair, and the remaining time is spent in the beauty shop. The beauticians are required to wear a uniform purchased with their own funds. The female beauticians are engaged in basic hair care for female patients, and are licensed by the Pennsylvania Bureau of Licensing.

All the male barbers work from 8:00 a.m. to 4:00 p.m. Monday through Friday. Usually in the morning, the barbers work on the floors of the hospital in the men's sections. In the afternoon, one barber works in the barbershop, while the others work on the floor. The barbers wear aprons provided by the hospital, and are licensed by the Pennsylvania Bureau of Licensing.

Both barbers and beauticians perform their work under similar conditions. Both report scalp diseases to hospital nurses. Both perform their respective skills for bedridden patients and those in geriatric chairs. At the end of each day, both clean their tools and do some light cleaning of their respective shops.

During the period in which violations are alleged to have occurred, the female beauticians were paid $165.00 a month less than male barbers.

DEFENDANT'S POSITION:

Barbers and beauticians belong to separately licensed professions, they are trained by different courses of study, and their jobs require unequal skill, effort, and responsibility.

The duties performed by barbers and beauticians are different in that the occupations are different; each craft has different duties and different work performance, expectations, effort, and responsibilities, as classified; each requires a special independent course of study, and a separate license from the Commonwealth of Pennsylvania.

Not only do barbers and beauticians at the hospital perform different duties involving different skills, they also expend different amounts of effort in performing their different techniques. Unlike the barbers, the beauticians use several tools in addition to the basic scissors, clippers, and combs, the use of which requires more effort in performance. In addition, barbers on the average spend ten to twenty minutes cutting the hair of a male patient, whereas the beautician spends thirty to forty minutes to complete a hair straightening process, and one hour to an hour and fifteen minutes to give a hair set. The time spent by the two crafts per patient is clearly unequal, thus requiring unequal effort in performing different work.

The responsibility of barbers is to cut the hair of over 700 male patients. The responsibility of the beauticians is to cut hair and perform additional beauty skills on the female patients who need or request their services. The beauticians, unlike the barbers, do not have the responsibility to serve every female patient in the hospital.

The barbers are not trained to give permanents and hair sets. They are not trained to straighten hair. They do not shampoo or manicure patients or use chemical lotions. They are not trained to cut female hair or to apply beauty techniques. Cutting the hair of women requires a substantially different skill than cutting the hair of men.

QUESTIONS

1. If we evaluated these two jobs in terms of skill requirements, responsibilities, and job conditions, which would receive the highest evaluation? Why?

2. In the *Hodgson* v. *City Stores, Inc.* case, the court's decision leads to the conclusion that in retail stores, salesclerks are salesclerks—toy salesclerks are no different from clothes salesclerks. Would that case's decision have bearing on this case? Why?

CASE STUDIES

Lemons v. The City and County of Denver
620 F.2d 288 (10th Cir. 1980)

The issue was one of wage discrimination under Title VII of the Civil Rights Act of 1964. A nurse was trying to gain a higher pay scale based on the fact that the nurses' wages compared unfavorably to those of a sign painter, tree trimmer, tire service-man, and parking meter repairman. All these male-dominated occupations were paid at a much higher rate than the nurses, a predominantly female profession. The nurses endeavored to show that on every count of skill, effort, responsibility, and working conditions, nurses were entitled to higher remuneration.

PLAINTIFF'S POSITION:

Nurses have historically been underpaid because their work has not been properly recognized and because they almost universally have been women, and therefore their positions should be reclassified into the classification of "General Administrative Series" for purposes of comparing their salary with that of nonnursing positions that are of equal worth to the City.

DEFENDANT'S POSITION:

The value of any job to the employer represents but one factor affecting wages. Other factors may include the supply of workers willing to do the job and the ability of the workers to band together to bargain collectively for higher wages. Nothing in the text and history of Title VII suggests that Congress intended to change the laws of supply and demand or economic principles that determine various wage rates for various kinds of work. The City of Denver did not interpret Title VII as requiring an employer to ignore the market in setting wage rates for genuinely different work classifications.

QUESTIONS

1. How will cases similar to this one affect employers?

2. How does the market rate of a job reflect the built-in and often covert sex discrimination in our society? How can this be changed?

SUGGESTED READINGS

Cook, A. H. "Equal Pay: Where Is It?" *Industrial Relations* 14 (May 1975): 158–177.

Kuraitis, Vytenis. "Analyzing the Equal Pay Equation." *Management World* 10, no. 9 (September 1981): 8ff.

Madigan, Robert M., and David J. Hoover. "Effects of Alternative Job Evaluation Methods on Decisions Involving Pay Equity." *Academy of Management Journal* 29 (March 1986): 84–100.

Newman, Winn. "Pay Equity Emerges as Top Labor Issue in the 1980s." *Monthly Labor Review* 105, no. 4 (April 1982): 49–51.

Pratt, Leila J., Stephanie A. Smullen, and Ben L. Kyer. "The Macroeconomics of the Equal Pay Act." *Journal of Macroeconomics* 12, no. 4 (Fall 1990): 675.

Remick, Helen (ed.). *Comparable Worth and Wage Discrimination: Technical Possibilities and Political Realities*. Temple University Press, 1984.

Sape, George P. "Coping with Comparable Worth." *Harvard Business Review* 63 (March 1985): 145–152.

Chapter 28

Comparable Worth

Learning Objectives—After completion of this exercise, you should be able to:

1. Describe the issues surrounding comparable worth.
2. Contrast the concept of comparable worth with the concept of equal pay.

Time Suggested: 45 minutes

Procedures:

1. Read the Introduction.
2. Individually, read and note the important points in the two case briefs, *Gunther v. County of Washington* and *Biggs v. City of Madison.*
3. Form into sexually mixed groups of four or five and answer the questions at the end of each case.
4. As a group, discuss the questions at the end of the exercise and write a group response.

◢ INTRODUCTION

In an effort to extend the Equal Pay Act of 1963 beyond the concept of equal pay for equal work, the term *comparable worth* was introduced. The major problems facing employers and employees today in terms of this concept are the *definitions* of comparable worth, its *legal status* in terms of the Equal Pay Act, and its *implications* for human resource management.

Many definitions have been used to explain comparable worth. An especially clear definition comes from Nancy Perlman, chair of the National Committee on Pay Equity, who testified before the House Subcommittee on Compensation and Employee Benefits:

> Simply stated, [comparable worth] involves correcting the practice of paying women less than men for work that requires comparable skill, effort, responsibility, and working conditions. This is done by raising the wages of underpaid female-dominated jobs. It is important to note that comparable worth is a fairness issue. It doesn't involve giving special consideration to special people. It simply means paying people a fair wage for their contribution.[1]

Most jobs typically held by women are generally lower paid, have limited upward mobility, and fewer opportunities for on-the-job training. According to the U.S. Census Bureau, 80 percent of all female workers are found in only 20 of 427 occupations currently listed by the Bureau. These conditions have not changed much since the 1950s. The fact of this continued segregation and concomitant lack of pay equity across job positions has given birth to the comparable worth movement.

Opponents of comparable worth argue that Title VII is limited by the narrow interpretations of the Equal Pay Act of 1963. This act requires that in cases of sex-based wage discrimination, the job positions in question *must be equal* in terms of skill, effort, and responsibilities and must be performed under similar conditions. These requirements must be met before a case of sex-based wage discrimination will be heard by the courts. Proponents of comparable worth argue that Title VII is not limited by the Equal Pay Act and its broader scope is applicable in cases of sex-based wage discrimination, even if jobs are dissimilar. If jobs are comparable and women are paid less than men, then Title VII forms a basis for legal action.

Presently, charges of sex-based wage discrimination will be heard by the courts if the employee can show, by means of job evaluation, that an employer has determined a female-dominated job position to be equal to a male-dominated position, yet continues to pay the female-dominated job less than its evaluated value. However, an employer can defend him/herself by showing that the female-dominated job is paid less because of "any other factor other than sex." A currently acceptable defense includes the market rate. The market rate is the salary or wage paid by other employers for similar jobs in the same market. Under current legal interpretations, even if a nurse's job is determined by a job evaluation to be of greater value to the hospital than that of a gardener, the hospital is legally sanctioned to compensate the gardener more if the market rate sets a higher wage for the gardener.

Because women earn approximately seventy-five cents for every dollar earned by men, proponents of comparable worth propose that jobs be priced according to internal job evaluations. They argue that market rate contains an inherent bias that will perpetuate pay inequities if organizations continue to use it. They also contend that the "wage gap" or disparity in wages between men and women will narrow if job compensation is based on internal job-evaluation studies rather than on market rates alone.

Opponents of comparable worth argue that job evaluations are subject to biases and the subsequent results are not a justifiable basis for a compensation system. They argue that the forces of supply and demand must be used when making job-pricing decisions. In short, the market rate must not be disregarded.

Today, the future of comparable worth is uncertain. However, employers and managers should look at their own job evaluation and compensation systems for sources of possible wage discrimination that could result in paying comparable jobs differently.

CASE STUDIES

The following is a landmark case concerning comparable worth. For the first time since the passage of Title VII in 1964, the Supreme Court recognized gender-based wage discrimination under less restrictive Title VII applications. Proponents of comparable worth saw it as a move by the courts in the direction of their cause.

Gunther v. County of Washington
U.S. Supreme Court
452 U.S. 161 (1981)

The Supreme Court considered the claims of four females employed as jail matrons by the Washington County jail in Oregon. The plaintiffs, who guarded inmates in the female section of the jail, were employed at a lower rate than men who guarded inmates in the male section of the jail. Even though the duties of these two segregated job positions were not equal, the plaintiffs sought to prove wage discrimination.

PLAINTIFF'S POSITION:

The plaintiffs claimed that the County discriminated in setting wages based on the gender of the guards. They sought to prove this by showing that only the wages of the female guards—not the male guards—were set at a level lower than the determinations of the employer's own internal job evaluation and survey of outside markets. This internal and external study indicated that female guards should have been paid 95 percent as much as the male guards. The female guards, however, were paid only 70 percent as much as the male guards.

DEFENDANT'S POSITION:

The defendant argued that because the two job positions in question were not substantially equal, this case could not be heard because of the Equal Pay Act restrictive requirements. The male guards supervised up to ten times as many prisoners per guard as did matrons, and the matrons spent a greater deal of their time on clerical duties. Because their jobs were unequal, the wages of the male and female guards should remain unequal.

QUESTIONS

1. Based on the evidence presented, predict how the Court ruled in this case. Explain your decision.

2. Do you believe it is fair to price a job based only on an internal evaluation? Why or why not? Is it fair to price a job based only on market rates? Why or why not?

CASE STUDIES

Briggs v. City of Madison
District Court of Wisconsin
526 F.Supp. 435, 445 (1982)

The decision in this case spelled out the circumstances under which market rate could be used as a defense.

PLAINTIFF'S POSITION:

The plaintiffs, the city's public health nurses who were all female, filed a claim against the city alleging their jobs were of at least, if not more, value than the higher paid all-male sanitation workers. The plaintiffs supported their claims by referring the court to a 1963 job evaluation study performed for the city by a consulting firm. This study recommended that the pay-rate levels of each job position be approximately equal. Initially the city adhered to these recommendations, but eventually deviated from them by raising the wages of sanitation workers to a higher rate.

DEFENDANT'S POSITION:

The employer refuted these claims of discrimination by offering the market rate as a defense. The employer deviated from the job evaluation study because the wages the city offered for the sanitarians were below the prevailing market rate. This caused the city difficulty because the job positions would often remain unfilled for months. The city produced additional supporting evidence in the form of written requests by the public health director to pay a higher rate in order to be competitive with other employers who hired sanitarians.

QUESTIONS

1. Based on the evidence presented, predict how the court ruled. Explain/justify your decision.

2. Is the use of market rates only in this case a fair defense? Explain/justify your answer. Is the use of job evaluation data a fair claim to make? Explain/justify your answer.

QUESTIONS

1. Why years, have women's wages persistently remained less than men? Discuss this question within your group and write your answers here. Justify those reasons that are due to sexism or discrimination and those that are due to defensible, business-related decisions.

   Reason:

   Reason:

   Reason:

   Reason:

   Reason:

   Reason:

   Reason:

2. Assume you have been given the responsibility of implementing comparable worth in your organization. Propose a plan that will bring about comparable pay for comparable worth. Be sure not to ignore market rates. You have five years to implement your plan. Discuss it with your group and write a group response here.

NOTE

1. N. D. Perlman, and B. J. Ennis, "Preliminary Memorandum on Pay Equity: Achieving Equal Pay for Worth of Comparable Value," Institute for Government and Policy Studies, Rockefeller College, State University of New York at Albany, 1982.

SUGGESTED READINGS

Buchele, R., and M. Aldrich. "How Much Difference Would Comparable Worth Make?" *Industrial Relations* 24 (Spring 1985): 222–233.

Cook, A. H. "Comparable Worth: Recent Developments in Selected States." *Labor Law Journal* 34 (August 1983): 494–503.

Freed, M. G., and D. D. Polsby. "Comparable Worth in the Equal Pay Act." *University of Chicago Law Review* 51, no. 4 (Fall 1984): 1078–1111.

Golper, J. B. "The Current Legal Status of 'Comparable Worth' in the Federal Courts." *Labor Law Journal* 34 (September 1983): 563–580.

Hurd, S., P. Murray, and B. Shaw. "Comparable Worth: A Legal and Ethical Analysis." *American Business Law Journal* 22 (Fall 1984): 407–427.

Koziara, K. S., D. A. Pierson, and R. E. Johannesson. "The Comparable Worth Issue: Current Status and New Directions." *Labor Law Journal* 34 (August 1983): 504–509.

Krauthammer, C. "From Bad to Worth." *New Republic* (July 30, 1984): 16–18.

Legler, J. I. "City, County and State Government Liability for Sex-Based Wage Discrimination after *County of Washington* v. *Gunther* and *AFSCME* v. *Washington*." *Urban Law* 17, no. 2 (Spring 1985): 229–275.

Lorber, L. "Job Segregation and Wage Discrimination under Title VII and the Equal Pay Act." *Personnel Administration* 25, no. 5 (May 1980): 31–34.

Meng, George J. "All the Parts of Comparable Worth." *Personnel Journal* 69, no. 11 (November 1, 1990): 89.

Nelson, Bruce A., Edward M. Opton, and Thomas E. Wilson. "Wage Discrimination and Title VII in the 1980s: The Case against 'Comparable Worth.'" *Contemporary Problems in Personnel.* New York: John Wiley and Sons, 1983, 66–82.

Ost, E. "Comparable Worth: A Response for the '80s." *Personnel Journal* 64 (February 1985): 64–69.

Perlman, N. D., and B. J. Ennis. *Preliminary Memorandum on Pay Equity: Achieving Equal Pay for Work of Comparable Value.* Institute for Government and Policy Studies, Rockefeller College, State University of New York at Albany, 1982.

Tompkins, Jonathan, Joyce Brown, and John H. McEwan. "Designing a Comparable Worth–Based Job Evaluation System: Failure of an A Priori Approach." *Public Personnel Management* 19, no. 1 (Spring 1990): 31.

Waldauer, C. "The Non-Comparability of the 'Comparable Worth Doctrine.' " *The Collegiate Forum* (Fall 1985).

Whatley, G. "Controversial Swirls over Comparable Worth Issue." *Personnel Administrator* (April 1982): 51–61.

Wiedenbaum, M. L. " 'Comparable Worth' Theory for Gaining Equal Pay Has Its Flaws." *Christian Science Monitor* (July 24, 1984): 19.

Chapter **29**

Job
Evaluation

Learning Objectives—After completion of this exercise, you should be able to:

1. Evaluate jobs by the ranking method and the point method.

2. Describe the differences between the ranking and point methods of job evaluation.

3. Describe at least two advantages and two disadvantages of each of the two methods of job evaluation.

Time Suggested: One hour

Procedures:

1. Read the Introduction.

2. Read the job descriptions of computer operators A–E.

3. In groups of four or five, rank the jobs as described, using Figure 29–1.

4. Study "The Point Rating Method of Job Evaluation" (Figure 29–2). As a group, rate each job using the five forms that follow.

5. Complete the "Ranking on the Basis of Points" exercise.

6. Answer the questions at the end of the chapter.

 **INTRODUCTION**

THE RANKING METHOD OF JOB EVALUATION

Evaluating jobs by the ranking method is the simplest method known. As the name implies, all the jobs in the organization are "ranked" from high to low on the basis of one or several factors. A general factor such as the overall importance of the job can be used; or several specific factors such as skill, effort, and responsibility can be the basis for the evaluation. Visualize, if you can, the difficulty of ranking several hundred different jobs. It would be almost impossible. Therefore, the ranking method of job evaluation is well suited for smaller organizations.

Several advantages and disadvantages of this method are as follows:

ADVANTAGES

1. It is the simplest of all the evaluation procedures and requires little time or paperwork. The direct cost of application is negligible.

2. It can eliminate personalities and is thus superior to guesswork.

3. It is practical, although crude, and avoids any hypocrisy of seeming to be scientific.

DISADVANTAGES

1. Equal differentials are sometimes assumed between adjacent ranks, and such assumptions are frequently incorrect.

2. Appraising each job as a whole does not facilitate analysis and cannot be expected to give an accurate measurement of worth.

3. It is difficult to use in organizations with large numbers of jobs.

THE POINT RATING METHOD OF JOB EVALUATION

The underlying idea of the point method of job evaluation is that a number of evaluation factors can be found to some degree in all jobs. After these evaluation factors have been identified, each is given an overall number of points, and the points are often subdivided into a number of degrees. In this way, each job can be measured in terms of the various factors by assigning points, the sum of which gives an overall value of the job.

Several advantages and disadvantages of the point method are as follows:

ADVANTAGES

1. The point rating method is the most widely used throughout industry, permitting comparisons on a similar basis with other firms.
2. The point rating plan is relatively simple to understand.
3. A well-conceived point rating plan has considerable stability—it is applicable to a wide range of jobs over an extended period of time.

DISADVANTAGES

1. Any method whose objectivity depends on relative weights, degree values, and fixed factors can be confusing to the average worker, thus causing resistance when implemented.
2. A large amount of time is consumed putting this approach into practice.

COMPUTER OPERATOR A

DESCRIPTION OF WORK

- *General duties.* Serves as an operator of a computer and associated peripheral devices and processes input and output materials associated with automated data processing.
- *Supervision received.* Works under general supervision of an administrative superior.
- *Supervision exercised.* Exercises supervision over personnel as assigned.

EXAMPLE OF DUTIES

Performs normal, routine duties in the operation of consoles, magnetic tape and disk units, printers, card readers, card punches, plotters, other peripheral equipment, and communication equipment; works in support functions such as input/output offices and file storage libraries and performs necessary housekeeping functions such as stocking of supplies and minimal maintenance and upkeep of equipment and facilities; performs related work as assigned.

MINIMUM QUALIFICATIONS

- *Knowledge.* Good knowledge of: computers and peripheral equipment; computer software and control languages and the theory of operation of computer hardware; input/output processing and file storage library operation.
- *Skills.* Skill in: typing or the use of keyboards as data entry devices; operating complex data processing equipment.
- *Abilities.* Ability to: work overtime and weekend shifts on a regular basis and with short notice; work in a cold, controlled environment; understand and follow written and oral instructions; lift and carry 50-lb. cartons for an extended period of time and stand for long periods of time while working under strenuous conditions; work with associates in a team effort; communicate both orally and in writing; make and implement decisions regarding priorities and computer utilization; give technical instructions to less qualified operators; establish and maintain effective working relationships with associates.
- *Education.* Graduation from high school or GED certificate.
- *Experience.* Six (6) months' experience in computer operations or related data processing field.

  or

- Any equivalent combination of education and experience.

COMPUTER OPERATOR B

DESCRIPTION OF WORK

- *General duties.* Serves as senior or key operator to coordinate computer activity during normal operation; provides guidance and instructions to other operators to assure that computer operations function in accordance with established priorities and procedures and for maximum efficiency, or serves as specialist on small computer system or terminal.

- *Supervision received.* Works under general supervision of an administrative superior.

- *Supervision exercised.* Exercises supervision over personnel as assigned.

EXAMPLE OF DUTIES

Serves as coordinator of computer activity to assure that requirements are being met and that work is flowing through the computer system in a smooth manner; monitors operation and takes corrective action to keep processing on schedule; follows established priorities and procedures where possible and alerts supervisor and users when adjustments in procedures are necessary; calls appropriate maintenance or systems personnel when problems develop; takes corrective action to recover from computer failures; coordinates checkout activity with systems and maintenance personnel; provides training for other operations personnel and assists supervisor in evaluating their performance; answers questions from the users and assists them in solving problems with their jobs; inventories supplies and requests replacements as necessary; performs minimal maintenance and upkeep on equipment and facilities; may serve as coordinator of input/output processing and as file storage library operator; performs related work as assigned.

MINIMUM QUALIFICATIONS

- *Knowledge.* Considerable knowledge of: all computer equipment work flow and processing requirements applicable to the position; computer software and control languages and hardware operations; input and output processing and file storage library operations; the relationship of the computer processing function to the mission of the organization; the principles of supervision.

- *Skills.* Skill in: typing or the use of keyboards to enter commands into the computer; operating complex data processing equipment.

- *Abilities.* Considerable ability to: work in a cold, controlled environment; understand and follow written and oral instructions; lift and carry 50-lb. cartons for an extended period of time and stand for long periods of time while working under strenuous conditions; work with associates in a team effort; communicate both orally and in writing; quickly make and implement decisions regarding priorities and computer utilization; give technical instructions to other operators; interface with users and personnel from other areas; work overtime and weekend shifts on a regular basis and on short notice; establish and maintain effective working relationships with associates.

- *Education*. Graduation from high school or GED certificate.

- *Experience*. One (1) year in data processing field to include at least six (6) months of computer operations and some experience with input/output processing and file storage library operation.

  or

- Any equivalent combination of education and experience.

COMPUTER OPERATOR C

DESCRIPTION OF WORK

- *General duties*. Performs supervisory and operational duties as a shift leader of a computer system including all hardware operations, input/output processing, and file storage library functions.

- *Supervision received*. Works under general supervision of an administrative superior.

- *Supervision exercised*. Performs full range of supervision over personnel assigned to the shift; provides the level of supervision as specified for Computer Operator(s) "A", Computer Operator(s) "B", and other shift crew members.

EXAMPLE OF DUTIES

Carries out normal supervisory duties such as assignment scheduling, evaluating, training, discipline, counseling, and interviewing; monitors all phases of computer systems operation for the shift and takes corrective action as necessary; keeps proper authorities and other shifts informed of problems and work load status; assists users with special requirements and solutions to problems; works with customers and users to determine daily schedule and priorities; reviews procedures to assure that they are adequate to meet needs and maintains records of operation performance; assures that adequate supplies and resources are available; determines the proper staffing and makes recommendations to the next level of supervision; performs related work as assigned.

MINIMUM QUALIFICATIONS

- *Knowledge*. Extensive knowledge of: all computer equipment, work flow and processing requirements applicable to the position; computer software and control languages and hardware operation; input and output processing and file storage library operation; relationship of the computer processing function to the mission of the organization; principles of supervision; procedures necessary for the proper protection of sensitive information and critical plant facilities.

- *Skills*. Skill in typing or the use of keyboards to enter commands into the computer; good skill in the operation of complex data processing equipment.

- *Abilities*. Considerable ability to: work in a cold, controlled environment; understand and follow written and oral instructions; lift and carry 50-lb cartons for an extended period of time and to stand for long periods of time while working under strenuous conditions; lead and promote team spirit on the shift; train crew members; interface with users and personnel from other areas; communicate both orally and in writing; work overtime and weekends on a regular basis and on short notice; establish and maintain effective working relationships with associates.

- *Education*. Graduation from high school or GED certificate.

- *Experience*. Two (2) years of progressively responsible experience in data processing field to include at least one (1) year of experience in computer operations.

  or

- Any equivalent combination of education and experience.

COMPUTER OPERATOR D

DESCRIPTION OF WORK

- *General duties*. Performs supervisory and complex computer operations work.
- *Supervision received*. Works under general supervision of an administrative supervisor.
- *Supervision exercised*. Exercises supervision over technical, clerical, and other personnel as assigned.

EXAMPLE OF DUTIES

In coordination with Computer Operator(s) "E", supervises the planning, scheduling, and work flow of the day-to-day operation of an electronic computer system on an assigned shift; prepares programs and tests new and revised programs; develops operating methods to process data; aids subordinates in locating and overcoming error conditions; revises operating schedules to adjust for delays; prepares or reviews records and reports of production, operating, and downtime; trains, assigns, and evaluates duties of computer operators; confers with and makes recommendations to supervisor; performs related work as assigned.

MINIMUM QUALIFICATIONS

- *Knowledge*. Considerable knowledge of the principles, capabilities, and operation of electronic computer systems and related peripheral equipment; tabulating machine, keypunch, and control functions. Working knowledge of electronic computer programming documentation techniques.
- *Skills*. Skill in the operation of electronic computer equipment.
- *Abilities*. Ability to plan, organize, and direct the operation of an electronic computer system; develop forms and procedures; recognize and work out solutions for operational problems; work effectively with others; supervisory ability.
- *Education*. Graduation from high school or GED certificate.
- *Experience*. Three (3) years of progressively more responsible experience in operating electronic computer systems.

  or

- Any equivalent combination of education and experience.

COMPUTER OPERATOR E

DESCRIPTION OF WORK

- *General duties*. Performs supervisory and complex computer operations work.

- *Supervision received*. Works under general supervision of an administrative supervisor.

- *Supervision exercised*. Exercises supervision over technical personnel, clerical personnel, and others as assigned.

EXAMPLE OF DUTIES

Supervises the planning, scheduling, and work flow of the day-to-day operation of an electronic computer system on an assigned shift; coordinates such activities across all shifts; prepares programs and tests new and revised programs; develops operating methods to process data; aids subordinates in locating and overcoming error conditions; revises operating schedules to adjust for delays; prepares or reviews records and reports of production, operating, and downtime; trains, assigns, and evaluates duties of computer operators; confers with and makes recommendations to supervisor; develops and maintains procedures manuals for machine room operations and training; recommends, develops, and supervises implementation of improvements in hardware, software, operational procedures, and physical arrangements; stocks and maintains inventory of expandables, letting responsible persons know of needed materials to order or what supplies are running low; performs related work as required.

MINIMUM QUALIFICATIONS

- *Knowledge*. Extensive knowledge of the principles, capabilities, and operation of electronic computer systems and related peripheral equipment; tabulating machine, keypunch, and control functions; working knowledge of electronic computer programming documentation techniques.

- *Skills*. Skill in the operation of electronic computer equipment.

- *Abilities*. Considerable ability to plan, organize, and direct the operation of an electronic computer system; develop forms and procedures; recognize and work out solutions for operational problems; work effectively with others; supervisory ability.

- *Education*. Graduation from high school or GED certificate.

- *Experience*. Five (5) years of progressively more responsible experience in operating electronic computer systems.

  or

- Any equivalent combination of education and experience.

THE RANKING METHOD

Instructions: Using Figure 29–1, compare the first job in the first column with each job in the slant columns. Wherever the job in the first column is considered to have greater value to the firm than the job in the slant column, place a check mark (√) in the box below the job in that slant column. Repeat the process until all jobs have been compared. Tally check marks to find ranks of jobs. The highest ranked job would be number 1, the lowest ranked job would be number 5.

◢ FIGURE 29–1   Comparison of Jobs by Ranking Method

Jobs	Computer Operator A	Computer Operator B	Computer Operator C	Computer Operator D	Computer Operator E	Total (checks)	Rank
Jobs							
Computer Operator A	██						
Computer Operator B		██					
Computer Operator C			██				
Computer Operator D				██			
Computer Operator E					██		

THE RATING METHOD

Figure 29–2 provides sample points for use in evaluating jobs by the point rating method. For each job, determine the number of points appropriate for each subfactor. Then multiply the number of points by the give weight.

◢ FIGURE 29–2 The Point Rating Method of Job Evaluation

Factors and Subfactors	Points						Weight in Percent
Skill	**Low**					**High**	
1. Education and Job Knowledge	12	24	36	48	60	72	12
2. Experience and Training	24	48	72	96	120	144	24
3. Initiative and Ingenuity	14	28	42	56	70	84	14
							50%
Effort							
4. Physical Demand	10	20	30	40	50	60	10
5. Mental and/or Visual Demand	5	10	15	20	25	30	5
							15%
Responsibility							
6. Equipment or Tools	6	12	18	24	30	36	6
7. Material or Product	7	14	21	28	35	42	7
8. Safety of Others	3	6	9	12	15	18	3
9. Work of Others	4	8	12	16	20	24	4
							20%
Job Conditions	**Good**					**Poor**	
10. Working Conditions	10	20	30	40	50	60	10
	Few					**Many**	
11. Unavoidable Hazards	5	10	15	20	25	30	5
							15%
Total possible points and weights						600	100%

JOB TITLE: COMPUTER OPERATOR A

FACTORS AND SUBFACTORS

Skill	*Weight in %* *(from Fig. 29–2)*		*Points (from Fig. 29–2)*	
1. Education and Job Knowledge	.12	× _____	=	_____
2. Experience and Training	.24	× _____	=	_____
3. Initiative and Ingenuity	.14	× _____	=	_____
Effort				
4. Physical Demand	.10	× _____	=	_____
5. Mental and/or Visual Demand	.05	× _____	=	_____
Responsibility				
6. Equipment or Tools	.06	× _____	=	_____
7. Material or Product	.07	× _____	=	_____
8. Safety of Others	.03	× _____	=	_____
9. Work of Others	.04	× _____	=	_____
Job Conditions				
10. Working Conditions	.10	× _____	=	_____
11. Unavoidable Hazards	.05	× _____	=	_____
			TOTAL	

JOB TITLE: COMPUTER OPERATOR B

FACTORS AND SUBFACTORS

Skill	Weight in % (from Fig. 29–2)		Points (from Fig. 29–2)	
1. Education and Job Knowledge	.12	× _____	=	____
2. Experience and Training	.24	× _____	=	____
3. Initiative and Ingenuity	.14	× _____	=	____

Effort

4. Physical Demand	.10	× _____	=	____
5. Mental and/or Visual Demand	.05	× _____	=	____

Responsibility

6. Equipment or Tools	.06	× _____	=	____
7. Material or Product	.07	× _____	=	____
8. Safety of Others	.03	× _____	=	____
9. Work of Others	.04	× _____	=	____

Job Conditions

10. Working Conditions	.10	× _____	=	____
11. Unavoidable Hazards	.05	× _____	=	____

TOTAL

JOB TITLE: COMPUTER OPERATOR C

FACTORS AND SUBFACTORS

Skill	Weight in % (from Fig. 29–2)	Points (from Fig. 29–2)
1. Education and Job Knowledge	.12	× _____ = ____
2. Experience and Training	.24	× _____ = ____
3. Initiative and Ingenuity	.14	× _____ = ____

Effort

4. Physical Demand	.10	× _____ = ____
5. Mental and/or Visual Demand	.05	× _____ = ____

Responsibility

6. Equipment or Tools	.06	× _____ = ____
7. Material or Product	.07	× _____ = ____
8. Safety of Others	.03	× _____ = ____
9. Work of Others	.04	× _____ = ____

Job Conditions

10. Working Conditions	.10	× _____ = ____
11. Unavoidable Hazards	.05	× _____ = ____

TOTAL

JOB TITLE: COMPUTER OPERATOR D

FACTORS AND SUBFACTORS

Skill	Weight in % (from Fig. 29–2)		Points (from Fig. 29–2)	
1. Education and Job Knowledge	.12	× _____	=	____
2. Experience and Training	.24	× _____	=	____
3. Initiative and Ingenuity	.14	× _____	=	____

Effort

4. Physical Demand	.10	× _____	=	____
5. Mental and/or Visual Demand	.05	× _____	=	____

Responsibility

6. Equipment or Tools	.06	× _____	=	____
7. Material or Product	.07	× _____	=	____
8. Safety of Others	.03	× _____	=	____
9. Work of Others	.04	× _____	=	____

Job Conditions

10. Working Conditions	.10	× _____	=	____
11. Unavoidable Hazards	.05	× _____	=	____

TOTAL

JOB TITLE: COMPUTER OPERATOR E

FACTORS AND SUBFACTORS

Skill	*Weight in %* *(from Fig. 29–2)*		*Points (from Fig. 29–2)*
1. Education and Job Knowledge	.12	× _____ =	_____
2. Experience and Training	.24	× _____ =	_____
3. Initiative and Ingenuity	.14	× _____ =	_____
Effort			
4. Physical Demand	.10	× _____ =	_____
5. Mental and/or Visual Demand	.05	× _____ =	_____
Responsibility			
6. Equipment or Tools	.06	× _____ =	_____
7. Material or Product	.07	× _____ =	_____
8. Safety of Others	.03	× _____ =	_____
9. Work of Others	.04	× _____ =	_____
Job Conditions			
10. Working Conditions	.10	× _____ =	_____
11. Unavoidable Hazards	.05	× _____ =	_____

TOTAL

RANKING ON THE BASIS OF POINTS

The job with the most points receives a ranking of 1, the second most points a ranking of 2, and so on.

Job Title	Total Points	Ranking
Computer Operator A	_____	_____
Computer Operator B	_____	_____
Computer Operator C	_____	_____
Computer Operator D	_____	_____
Computer Operator E	_____	_____

QUESTION

1. What does the point system tell you that the ranking system does not? Explain.

**QUESTIONS**

1. Describe some of the ranking method's weaknesses not listed in the exercise.

2. What are the advantages of the point method over the ranking method?

3. How would you tie compensation to each of these two methods? Speculate, if you don't know for sure.

4. Discuss with the other members in your group how a job evaluation program can be beneficial for establishing a fair plus equitable compensation program. Write a group response.

5. Is it possible for job evaluation to be biased? How could such biases be minimized? Discuss it within your group and write a group response.

◢ SUGGESTED READINGS

Fonda, N., et al. "Job Evaluation Without Sex Discrimination." *Personnel Management* (February 1979): 34–37.

King, Donald L., and Pierre M. Vallee. "Job Evaluation: You Can Compare Apples and Oranges." *Canadian Business Review* 9, no. 1 (Spring 1982): 54–57.

Madigan, Robert M., and David J. Hoover. "Effects of Alternative Job Evaluation Methods on Decisions Involving Pay Equity." *Academy of Management Journal* 29 (March 1986): 84–100.

Murlis, Helen. "Job Evaluation in a Changing World." *Personnel Management* 23, no. 5 (May 1, 1991): 39.

Murlis, Helen, and Derek Pritchard. "The Computerized Way to Evaluate Jobs." *Personnel Management* 23, no. 4 (April 1, 1991): 48.

Scholl, Richard W., and Elizabeth A. Cooper. "The Use of Job Evaluation to Eliminate Gender-Based Pay Differentials." *Public Personnel Management* 20, no. 1 (Spring 1991): 1.

Wallace, M. J., and C. H. Fav. In *Compensation Theory and Practice*, 145–169. Boston: Kent Publishing, 1983.

Chapter **30**

Compensation and Work Motivation

Learning Objectives—After completion of this exercise, you should be able to:

1. Distinguish between a content and a process model of motivation.
2. Understand simple relationships between motivation theories and compensation.
3. Describe Maslow's need hierarchy and Vroom's expectancy theory.
4. Be aware of your need level.

Time Suggested: One and one-half hours

Procedures:

1. Read "Approaches to Motivating the Human Resource."
2. Complete the "Motivation Profile" exercise.
3. Complete the "Compensation and Expectancy Theory Matrix."
4. Answer the questions at the end of the exercise.

APPROACHES TO MOTIVATING THE HUMAN RESOURCE

Getting people at work to do what is expected of them is the art and science of motivation. The manager of a L'eggs panty hose factory in the southwest is successful at motivating quality work, low turnover and absenteeism, and good relationships among her employees. She maintains close, personal contact with the over 800 employees by walking around the factory floor. In addition, the manager sponsors annual picnics involving employees and their families, provides excellent fringe benefits, and often makes personal loans to employees in emergency situations. All of these motivational techniques work with this particular semiskilled workforce. But would they work in other organizations? It is difficult to predict which motivation theory will work in a given situation because every individual is motivated differently.

Because motivation is a complex topic it is useful to organize our thoughts into categories of motivation theories. Two of the most popular categories will be presented here, along with an example of a theory in each category. The first category is *content* theories with Maslow's need hierarchy as an example. The second category is *process* theory. An example of a process theory is expectancy theory.

CONTENT THEORY: MASLOW'S NEED HIERARCHY

Content theories focus on individual needs as a way to understand people's work behavior. It is through the identification of these needs that the manager can respond to satisfy them. An obvious example is people working in a dangerous environment. Their need for safety is paramount; an unsafe environment is likely to lead to accidents, turnover, and distractions from the tasks at hand. In this situation the manager, having identified the unmet human need for safety, can begin to remove the unsafe conditions in the workplace.

The best known example of a content theory is Abraham Maslow's need hierarchy.

Abraham Maslow theorized that experienced needs are the primary influences on an individual's behavior. When a particular need emerges, it determines the individual's behavior in terms of motivation, priorities, and action taken. Thus, motivated behavior is the result of the tension—either pleasant or unpleasant—experienced when a need presents itself. The goal of the behavior is the reduction of this tension or discomfort, and the behavior itself will be appropriate for facilitating the satisfaction of the need. Only unsatisfied needs are prime sources of motivation.

Understanding behaviors and their goals involves gaining insight into presently unsatisfied needs. Maslow developed a method for gaining insight by providing categories of needs in a hierarchical structure. He placed all human needs, from primitive or immature (in terms of the behaviors they foster) to civilized or mature needs, into five need systems. He believed that there is a natural process whereby individuals fulfill needs in ascending order from most immature to most mature. This

---

Data for diagram based on Hierarchy of Needs in "A Theory of Human Motivation" in *Motivation and Personality*, 2d ed. by Abraham H. Maslow, copyright © 1970 by Abraham H. Maslow. By permission of Harper and Row.

progression through the need hierarchy is seen as the climbing of a ladder, where the individual must have experienced secure footing on the first rung in order to experience the need to step up to the next higher rung. The awareness of the need to climb farther up the ladder is a function of having fulfilled the need of managing the preceding rung, and only satisfactory fulfillment of this need will allow the individual to deal with the new need or rung. Inability to fulfill a lower-order need or difficulty in fulfilling a lower-order need may result in an individual's locking in on immature patterns, or may produce a tendency to return to immature behaviors under stress any time any individual feels a lower-order need is not fulfilled satisfactorily. The individual may also revert to behaviors that fulfilled lower-order needs when the satisfaction of higher needs is temporarily blocked. That is not to say that any need is ever completely satisfied; rather, Maslow indicates that there must be at least partial fulfillment before an individual can become aware of the tensions manifested by a higher-order need and have the freedom to pursue its fulfillment.

The Maslow Need Hierarchy is presented in Figure 30–1. The Basic level represents needs that reflect physiological and survival goals. At this level are such factors as shelter, clothing, food, sex, and other necessities. In a culture such as ours, where these Basic needs are almost automatically met, there is not likely to be any need tension concerning the fulfillment of Basic needs. However, individuals adapt this Basic level upward to include such needs as avoidance of physical discomfort, pleasant working environment, or more money for providing creature comforts.

The second level of the hierarchy consists of Safety needs. When the individual has at least partially fulfilled the Basic needs, he or she will experience the tensions relating to the needs of security, orderliness, protective rules, and general risk avoidance. These needs are often satisfied by an adequate salary, insurance policies, a good burglar alarm system, a doorman for the apartment building, etc.

FIGURE 30–1   Maslow's Need Hierarchy

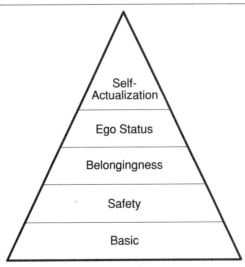

When Safety needs have been met, the individual will become less preoccupied with self, and will endeavor to form interpersonal relationships. The relative success of this need for Belongingness will result in his or her feeling accepted and appreciated by others. Thus, the third-level needs concern family ties, friendship, and group membership.

When an individual feels secure in relationships with others, he or she will probably seek to gain special status within the group. His or her need tensions will be associated with ambition and a desire to excel. These Ego-Status needs will motivate the individual to seek out opportunities to display his or her competence in an effort to gain social and professional rewards.

Because Ego-Status fulfillment is greatly dependent upon the ability of others to respond appropriately to the individual's effort to perform in a superior way, they are the most difficult to fulfill satisfactorily. However, if the individual has gained satisfaction on level four, he or she may be able to move to level five—Self-Actualization. At this level, the individual is concerned with personal growth and may fulfill this need by challenging himself or herself to become more creative, demanding greater achievement, and, in general, directing himself or herself to measure up to his or her own criteria of personal success. Self-Actualizing behaviors must include risk taking, seeking autonomy, and developing freedom to act.

PROCESS THEORY: VROOM'S EXPECTANCY THEORY

Process theories attempt to explain human motivation by focusing on the thought or cognitive processes of people as these processes influence work behaviors. They are more directly linked to behaviors than content theories. For example, individuals who *think* that they are not being compensated fairly are likely to *behave* differently from those who think they are being compensated fairly. They may start coming to work later than usual, or they may begin to work less hard, or be less concerned with the quality of their work. One of the most popular examples of a process theory of motivation is Vroom's expectancy theory.

Expectancy theory assumes that employees try to maximize their desired satisfaction in the workplace. According to expectancy theory, individuals will be motivated to perform their jobs if three perceptions occur. The first perception is called expectancy perception. It refers to the degree to which the employee perceives he or she has the ability to perform the job. The stronger the expectancy perception an individual has, the higher the motivation toward that behavior.

The second characteristic of expectancy theory is called instrumentality perception. This perception refers to the degree to which the employee sees a relationship between effort expended and rewards for that effort. If there is a clear perception that certain behaviors will be rewarded, the motivation to produce those behaviors will be greater. The reverse is also true: if there is a clear perception that certain behaviors will not be rewarded, there will be little motivation to produce them.

The third characteristic of expectancy theory is called valence perception. Perceptions about the desirability of rewards, whether they are positive, neutral, or negative, also determine how motivated the individual will be to perform. For example, an employee may perceive peer-group approval to be neutral, a promotion to be positive, and a job transfer to be negative.

In summary, these three perceptions—expectancy, instrumentality, and valence—combine to determine an employee's motivation in any given situation. Figure 30–2 illustrates these relationships.

FIGURE 30–2   A Model of Expectancy Theory

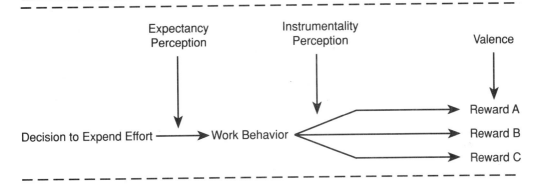

MOTIVATION PROFILE

PART I

Directions

The following statements have seven possible responses.

Strongly Agree	Agree	Slightly Agree	Don't Know	Slightly Disagree	Disagree	Strongly Disagree
+3	+2	+1	0	−1	−2	−3

Please mark one of the seven responses by circling the number that corresponds to the response that fits your opinion. For example: if you "Strongly Agree," circle the number "+3."

Complete every item. You have about 10 minutes to do so.

1. Special wage increases should be given to employees who do their jobs very well. +3 +2 +1 0 −1 −2 −3

2. Better job descriptions would be helpful so that employees will know exactly what is expected of them. +3 +2 +1 0 −1 −2 −3

3. Employees need to be reminded that their jobs are dependent on the Company's ability to compete effectively. +3 +2 +1 0 −1 −2 −3

4. A supervisor should give a good deal of attention to the physical working conditions of his employees. +3 +2 +1 0 −1 −2 −3

5. The supervisor ought to work hard to develop a friendly working atmosphere among his people. +3 +2 +1 0 −1 −2 −3

6. Individual recognition for above-standard performance means a lot to employees. +3 +2 +1 0 −1 −2 −3

7. Indifferent supervision can often bruise feelings. +3 +2 +1 0 −1 −2 −3

8. Employees want to feel that their real skills and capacities are put to use on their jobs. +3 +2 +1 0 −1 −2 −3

9. The Company retirement benefits and stock programs are important factors in keeping employees on their jobs. +3 +2 +1 0 −1 −2 −3

Reprinted from J. E. Jones and J. W. Pfeiffer (Eds.), *The 1973 Annual Handbook for Group Facilitators*, San Diego, CA: University Associates, 1973. Used with permission.

10. Almost every job can be made more stimulating and challenging.

    $+3$ $+2$ $+1$ 0 -1 -2 -3

11. Many employees want to give their best in everything they do.

    $+3$ $+2$ $+1$ 0 -1 -2 -3

12. Management could show more interest in the employees by sponsoring social events after-hours.

    $+3$ $+2$ $+1$ 0 -1 -2 -3

13. Pride in one's work is actually an important reward.

    $+3$ $+2$ $+1$ 0 -1 -2 -3

14. Employees want to be able to think of themselves as "the best" at their own jobs.

    $+3$ $+2$ $+1$ 0 -1 -2 -3

15. The quality of the relationships in the informal work group is quite important.

    $+3$ $+2$ $+1$ 0 -1 -2 -3

16. Individual incentive bonuses would improve the performance of employees.

    $+3$ $+2$ $+1$ 0 -1 -2 -3

17. Visibility with upper management is important to employees.

    $+3$ $+2$ $+1$ 0 -1 -2 -3

18. Employees generally like to schedule their own work and to make job-related decisions with a minimum of supervision.

    $+3$ $+2$ $+1$ 0 -1 -2 -3

19. Job security is important to employees.

    $+3$ $+2$ $+1$ 0 -1 -2 -3

20. Having good equipment to work with is important to employees.

    $+3$ $+2$ $+1$ 0 -1 -2 -3

MOTIVATION PROFILE

PART II

Scoring

1. Transfer the numbers you circled in Part I to the appropriate places in the following chart:

Statement No.	Score
10	____
11	____
13	____
18	____
Total	____

(Self-Actualization Needs)

Statement No.	Score
2	____
3	____
9	____
19	____
Total	____

(Safety Needs)

Statement No.	Score
6	____
8	____
14	____
17	____
Total	____

(Esteem Needs)

Statement No.	Score
1	____
4	____
16	____
20	____
Total	____

(Basic Needs)

Statement No.	Score
5	____
7	____
12	____
15	____
Total	____

(Belonging Needs)

2. Record your total scores in the chart below by marking an "X" in each row next to the number of your total score for that area of needs motivation.

	−12	−10	−8	−6	−4	−2	0	+2	+4	+6	+8	+10	+12
Self-Actualization													
Esteem													
Belonging													
Safety													
Basic													
	Low Use												High Use

Once you have completed this chart, you can see the relative strength of your use of each of these areas of needs motivation.

There is, of course, no "right" answer. What is right for you is what matches the actual needs of your employees and that, of course, is specific to each situation and each individual. In general, however, the "experts" tell us that today's employees are best motivated by efforts in the areas of Belonging and Esteem.

3. The instructor will assist the class is calculating a class profile. It is established by taking a poll of the class members in terms of each individual's strongest motivational factor (the factor with the highest score).

A. *Strongest Motivator*   *%**   *rank*

	%*	rank
Self-Actualization	_____	_____
Esteem	_____	_____
Belonging	_____	_____
Safety	_____	_____
Basic	_____	_____

A. *Weakest Motivator*   *%**   *rank*

	%*	rank
Self-Actualization	_____	_____
Esteem	_____	_____
Belonging	_____	_____
Safety	_____	_____
Basic	_____	_____

---

* % is determined by number of students giving that factor the highest score for A (lowest score for B), divided by the number of students in the class.

COMPENSATION AND EXPECTANCY THEORY MATRIX

Instructions: Discuss within your group whether or not each of the various compensation techniques affects each of the three aspects of expectancy theory. Based on your group discussion, place an N for No, an S for Sometimes, and an O for Often, as appropriate.

Compensation Techniques	Expectancy Perception	Instrumentality Perception	Valence Perception
Hourly Wage	_____	_____	_____
Cost-of-Living Increase	_____	_____	_____
Length-of-Service Increase	_____	_____	_____
Individual Incentive Plans			
Measured Day Work	_____	_____	_____
Time Standard Plans (Halsey & Rowan Plans)	_____	_____	_____
Merit Increases	_____	_____	_____
Bonuses	_____	_____	_____
Group Incentive Plans			
Profit Sharing	_____	_____	_____
Scanlon Plan	_____	_____	_____
Small Group Incentives	_____	_____	_____
Fringe Benefits			
Retirement Programs	_____	_____	_____
Medical Benefits	_____	_____	_____
Life Insurance	_____	_____	_____

Source: This matrix is adapted from Harold F. Rothe, "Does Higher Pay Bring Higher Productivity?" *Personnel* 37 (July–August 1960), 25.

QUESTIONS

1. In small groups of 3–5, discuss how management can use rewards to motivate employees who are behaving at each of the five levels of Maslow's need hierarchy. Remember that management can use either monetary or nonmonetary approaches to reward people. Write a group response for each need level.

   a. Basic needs

   b. Safety needs

   c. Belonging needs

   d. Esteem needs

   e. Self-actualization needs

2. Japanese organizations tend to stress longevity rather than performance in their compensation and promotion systems. What sorts of productive behaviors are motivated by using longevity as a reward? What sorts of unproductive behaviors can result from using longevity as a reward? Explain using expectancy theory. Discuss within your group and write a group answer below.

3. Many U.S. organizations pay their blue-collar and clerical workers hourly wages. What aspects of expectancy theory are violated by using this type of reward scheme? Discuss within your group and write a group answer below.

4. Merit pay systems are receiving considerable attention today. Explain merit pay from an expectancy theory point of view. Are there any weaknesses in merit pay systems? Discuss within your group and write a group answer below.

5. Which of the five needs is the strongest motivator for you, based on your score on the Motivation Profile exercise? _____ The second strongest? _____ Based on this information, briefly speculate on the type of job and the type of organization that would best satisfy these needs for you.

Type of job

Why?

Type of organization

Why?

SUGGESTED READINGS

Bushardt, Stephen C., and Aubrey R. Fouler. "Compensation and Benefits: Today's Dilemma in Motivation." *The Personnel Administrator* 27, no. 4 (April 1982): 23–28.

Compensation and Benefits Review 23, no. 1 (January 1, 1991): 39.

Freedman, Sara M., Robert T. Keller, and John R. Montanari. "The Compensation Program: Balancing Organizational and Employee Needs." *Compensation Review* 14, no. 2 (Summer 1982): 47–53.

Hampson, H. Anthony. "Tying CEO Pay to Performance: Compensation Committees Must Do Better." *The Business Quarterly* 55, no. 4 (Spring 1991): 18.

Jordan, Paul C. "Effects of Extrinsic Reward on Intrinsic Motivation: A Field Experiment." *Academy of Management Journal* 29 (June 1986): 405–411.

Kaponya, P. G. "Salaries for All Workers." *Harvard Business Review* (May–June 1962).

Kearney, W. J. "Pay for Performance? Not Always." *MSU Business Topics* (Spring 1979): 47–53.

Leefeldt, E. "Profit-Sharing Plans Reward Productivity." *Wall Street Journal*, November 5, 1984, p. 27.

Maslow, A. H. "A Theory of Human Motivation." *Psychological Review* 50 (1943): 370–396.

―――. *Motivation and Personality*. New York: Harper & Row, 1954.

Newsom, Walter B. "Motivate, Now!" *Personnel Journal* 69, no. 2 (February 1, 1990): 50.

Pinder, Craig C. *Work Motivation—Theory, Issues, and Applications*. Glenview, IL: Scott, Foresman, 1984.

Schneider, Eileen. "A Matter of Motivation." *Graphic Arts Monthly* 63, no. 5 (May 1, 1991): 78.

Tapper, Gordon A., and Dale E. Miller. "Building a Sound Salary Program." *Management World* 11, no. 5 (May 1982): 16ff.

Weber, Caroline L., and Sara L. Rynes. "Effects of Compensation Strategy on Job Pay Decisions." *Academy of Management Journal* 34, no. 1 (March 1, 1991): 86.

Wickenden, D. "Merit Pay Won't Work." *The New Republic*, November 7, 1983, 12–15.

Winstanley, Nathan B. "Are Merit Increases Really Effective?" *The Personnel Administrator* 27, no. 4 (April 1982): 37–42.

PART 9

Labor Law and Termination at Will

Modern human resource managers face legal issues other than those brought about by Title VII. If an organization is unionized, managers must honor the labor contract and learn to negotiate effectively with union officials. Chapter 31 gives students, through role playing, practical experience in negotiating a labor contract. The fine line between negotiating from too hard a position, which leads to a strike, and too soft a position, which leads to inefficiencies, is difficult to agree on. Students will experience just how difficult this task can be.

Chapter 32 ends the book with another controversial topic that is increasingly impinging on management's traditional prerogatives. Historically, the employee/employer relationship was bound by a common-law doctrine known as termination at will. Essentially, this doctrine held that either party could terminate the employment relationship whenever one of the parties decided to do so. Recently, however, this doctrine has been challenged on the grounds that termination is often more injurious to the employee than to the employer and therefore the doctrine doesn't hold if the employer has implied a long-term employment relationship. In this exercise, students will learn about the basic questions regarding termination at will and how management can act to prevent these problems from arising.

Chapter **31**

Industrial
Relations
Law

Learning Objectives—After completion of this exercise, you should be able to:

1. Provide an overview of U.S. industrial relations law.

2. Recognize the employment ramifications of U.S. industrial relations law.

Time Suggested: One hour

Procedures:

1. Read the section on federal industrial relations legislation.

2. In groups of five, answer the questions in the "Test Your Labor Know-How" section.

3. The instructor will provide the correct answers to items on the test and lead a discussion of the issues.

FEDERAL INDUSTRIAL RELATIONS LEGISLATION

The legal rights of workers and management are defined in large part by legislation passed nearly sixty years ago during the Great Depression. Those laws and subsequent laws passed just after World War II and in the late Fifties basically approved and encouraged the process of collective bargaining in the United States.

Two laws passed in the 1930s gave tremendous power to unionization. The Taft-Hartley Act, passed in 1947, shifted the power equilibrium by defining some union activities as "unfair labor practices" and giving the states the opportunity to have "right to work" legislation. This law came at a time when union strikes were having an impact on the national economy.

The Landrum-Griffin Act (1959), was passed at a time when unions were perceived as being undemocratic and being taken over by criminal elements. The law attempted to correct these abuses by establishing election and representation procedures and also by requiring the disclosure of the union's financial records.

What follows is a summary of the major industrial relations laws in the United States. Carefully study each law and the content of Figure 31–1.

▰ **FIGURE 31–1** Principal Labor Laws

Law	Major Thrust	Coverage
Railway Labor Act (1926)	Gave employees the right to organize and bargain collectively	Railroads Airlines
Norris-LaGuardia Act (1932)	Prohibited federal courts from enjoining strikes and from enforcing yellow dog contracts	Private-sector employment
Wagner Act (1935)	Established the right to organize and engage in other concerted activities; declared certain employer actions to be unfair labor practices; established procedures for employees to elect a union; regulated collective bargaining; established the National Labor Relations Board (NLRB)	Private-sector employment • businesses • nonprofit hospitals and nursing homes • private colleges and universities • performing arts
Taft-Hartley Act (1947)	Established the right to refrain from the activities protected in the Wagner Act; declared certain union actions to be unfair labor practices; provided for passage of state right-to-work laws; established the Federal Mediation and Conciliation Service (FMCS)	Same as Wagner Act
Landrum-Griffin Act (1959)	Established standards for union treatment of union members; regulated internal union affairs	Same as Wagner Act and Taft-Hartley Act
Title VII, Civil Civil Service Reform Act (1978)	Established the right to collective bargaining; required arbitration of impasses and grievances; prohibited strikes and other disruptions	Federal employment

Source: Scarpello, V. G. and S. Ledvinka, *Personnel/Human Resource Management*. PWS-Kent Publishing Company, 1988, p. 582.

SUMMARY OF INDUSTRIAL RELATIONS LAWS

NORRIS-LAGUARDIA ACT, 1932

1. Restricts federal courts from issuing injunctions that are used to discourage collective bargaining.

2. Made "yellow dog" contracts (in which the employee agreed not to engage in or be represented by collective bargaining) illegal.

WAGNER ACT (NATIONAL LABOR RELATIONS ACT), 1935

Section 7 expresses the spirit and sentiment of the law defining the rights of the employee:

> Employees shall have the right to self-organization, to form, join, or assist labor organizations, to bargain collectively through representatives of their own choosing, and to engage in other concerted activities, for the purpose of collective bargaining or other mutual aid and for protection.

The next section of the law identifies five management practices that were deemed to be unfair:

1. Modification of section 7 to include the right of employees to refrain from union activity as well as engage in it.

2. Prohibiting the closed shop (the arrangement requiring that all workers be union members at the time they are hired) and narrowing the freedom of the parties to authorize the union shop (the employer may hire anyone he or she chooses, but all new workers must join the union after a stipulated period of time).

3. Broadening of the employer's right of free speech.

4. Provision that employers need not recognize or bargain with unions formed by supervisory personnel.

5. Giving employees the right to initiate decertification petitions.

6. Provision for government intervention in "national emergency strikes."

A significant change in the Act extended the concept of unfair labor practices to unions. Labor organizations were to refrain from:

1. Restraining or coercing employees in the exercise of their guaranteed collective bargaining rights.

2. Causing an employer to discriminate in any way against an employee in order to encourage or discourage union membership.

3. Refusing to bargain in good faith with an employer regarding wages, hours, and other conditions of employment.

4. Engaging in certain types of strikes and boycotts.

5. Requiring employees covered by union-shop contracts to pay initiation fees or dues "in an amount which the Board finds excessive or discriminatory under all circumstances."

6. "Featherbedding," i.e., requiring that an employer pay for services not performed.

TAFT-HARTLEY ACT, 1947

This law amended the NLRA and also (1) gave management certain rights, (2) provided for right-to-work laws, (3) set up the Federal Mediation and Conciliation Service, and (4) provided for national emergencies. It gave management the following rights:

1. To refuse to bargain with supervisory personnel.

2. To have freedom of speech as long as there is no threat or force during a representation election.

3. To seek a representation election if it believes the union does not represent the workers.

4. To sue the union for breach of contract when it engages in unlawful strikes and boycotts.

5. To receive a sixty-day notice of the union's intent to terminate a contract.

Another restriction was the closed-shop agreement to limit the union shop in states that prohibited it (Section 14(b)). Twenty states have *right-to-work laws* that take priority over federal law. This portion of the Taft-Hartley Act has been very controversial by making some states union states and others nonunion. Figure 31–1 lists the principal labor laws.

TEST YOUR LABOR KNOW-HOW

1. Company A, a shoe manufacturer, and Company B, a retailer of A's products, are owned by the same stockholders and operated by the same directors and officers. When a union seeks to organize the employees of Company B, the company discharges and refuses to reinstate employees who join the union. The union files a complaint with the labor board against both companies. If back pay is awarded to the employees, is Company A liable as a result of Company B's unlawful acts?

     Yes _____   No _____

2. An auto mechanic applied for a job with a manufacturer of nationally distributed automobiles. Because she was known to be an active union member, the company refused to hire her. The mechanic then asked the federal labor board to force the company to give her a job. The company claims that she is not protected by federal labor relations laws, since she is not an "employee" but merely an applicant for employment. Is this reasoning correct?

     Yes _____   No _____

3. When Mr. Watts's son finished school, Mr. Watts gave him a job in the family-owned manufacturing business. The son, dissatisfied with the wages his father was paying him, joined the union, hoping to force his father to raise the wage scale. Instead, the father promptly fired him. Is the son entitled to the protection of federal labor relations laws?

     Yes _____   No _____

4. Although the owner of a manufacturing plant did all his own hiring and firing, he appointed John Foreman to oversee employees and report on the progress of the work. If Foreman made a complaint about any employee's work or conduct, the owner investigated the matter personally and decided whether the employee should be fired, disciplined, or let alone. When a union organizer began signing up members, Foreman joined. The owner then fired him, claiming that Foreman, as a supervisor, is not protected by federal labor relations laws. Is the owner right?

     Yes _____   No _____

5. An international union employs several organizers to solicit members for the union. The organizers, dissatisfied with their vacation plan and promotion system, form their own union and demand that the international bargain with their representative. Must a union bargain with another union?

     Yes _____   No _____

6. When a union seeks to act as bargaining agent for all employees of a metals processing plant, the boilermakers object. In the absence of a history of bargaining, they claim that, because they are skilled workers in a recognized craft requiring apprenticeship or experience, they are entitled to form their own separate bargaining group. Are the boilermakers right?

Yes ＿＿＿　　　No ＿＿＿

7. The only employee of a firm is too timid to ask for the raise he thinks he deserves. He therefore joins a union and asks the union to bargain with the employer for him. The employer refuses to deal with the union agent. Is the employer violating the law?

Yes ＿＿＿　　　No ＿＿＿

8. An employer is willing to bargain with any union her employees choose to represent them. However, she doubts that the union claiming to be their choice has the support of most of the workers. She refuses to bargain unless the union wins a majority of the votes in an election sponsored by the federal labor board. Is the employer within her rights?

Yes ＿＿＿　　　No ＿＿＿

9. When a union claimed to represent a majority of employees of Company A, the federal labor board held an election among the employees. A majority of them, however, rejected the union and voted for "no union." Six months later a rival union, which had not appeared on the ballot in the earlier election, claimed that in the six months after the election most of the employees had signed up with that union. Is the rival union entitled to an election to prove its majority?

Yes ＿＿＿　　　No ＿＿＿

10. Negotiations between Company Y and Union M, the certified bargaining agent of the company's employees, were speeded up when a rival union produced membership cards showing that a substantial number of employees had switched to that union. Fourteen months after the Union M's certification, the company signed a contract with the certified union, over the rival union's protest. Does the contract bar another election during its term?

Yes ＿＿＿　　　No ＿＿＿

11. A few years after Union E was certified as bargaining agent of the employees of Company R, the employees became dissatisfied with the union, and a substantial number of them asked the federal labor board to withdraw the certification of Union E. The union protested that its certification could not be withdrawn unless and until the employees chose another union to replace it. Is the union correct?

Yes ＿＿＿　　　No ＿＿＿

12. In a bitterly contested election to choose a bargaining agent for a company's employees, Union A defeated Union B by a narrow margin of votes. Employees who were members of the defeated union told the employer that they would rather have no union agent than be represented by Union A. The employer then agreed to bargain with Union A as agent for its own members only. Was the employer justified?

Yes ＿＿   No ＿＿

13. When a union was selected as bargaining agent by employees of a manufacturer, the union insisted that it had a right to be consulted on several matters other than wage rates and hours of work. The union demanded that the employer bargain on pensions, retirement and group insurance plans, and prices at which the company's products were sold. The company claimed that it had a right to decide such matters without consulting the union. Must the company bargain on such matters?

Yes ＿＿   No ＿＿

14. A corporation allowed its employees a ten-minute coffee break every morning and afternoon. When a union became bargaining agent of the employees, the union demanded that the coffee breaks be extended to fifteen minutes each. The company pointed out that, since no work was done during the breaks, and the employees were being paid for that time, the breaks amounted to a gift and their length should be determined by management. Must the company bargain with the union on coffee breaks?

Yes ＿＿   No ＿＿

15. When an office clerk snagged her sixth pair of nylons on her office chair, she stormed into the personnel manager's office and demanded not only a new chair, but also the price of half a dozen pairs of nylons. The managers decided to adjust the grievance by complying with the employee's demands. He then notified the bargaining agent for the company's employees of his decision. The union protested, claiming that the employee should have presented the grievance through the union, instead of directly to the employer. The employer replied that, although the union was welcome to be present at the adjustment conference with the aggrieved employee, no other concessions would be made to the union, since the adjustment did not violate the terms of the union's contract. Was the employer right?

Yes ＿＿   No ＿＿

16. The price of a corporation's stock rose steadily after the corporation bought a controlling interest in another company. The union, acting as bargaining agent of the corporation's employees, asked the employer to discuss a plan for giving the employees options to buy the corporation's stock. The corporation refused to negotiate on the matter, pointing out that the union had not brought up the subject when its present contract, still in effect, was negotiated. Must the employer bargain on the stock option plan before the present contract expires?

Yes ＿＿   No ＿＿

17. For a number of years, a company had been experiencing a decline in sales. When the union acting as bargaining agent for the company's employees demanded an increase in wages, the company replied that it could not afford to give an increase and still remain in business. The union demanded proof of the company's financial condition. Must the company furnish the proof?

Yes _____   No _____

18. When a company refused the demand of a union for a wage increase, the union called a strike. The company then called a halt to further negotiations with the union on the wage increase. Was the company justified?

Yes _____   No _____

19. A company and the union bargaining agent of its employees finally reached agreement on a contract. Although the contract provided for no increase in wages, it did contain provisions for longer vacations and more holidays. Fearful that a sudden spurt in demand for its product might find most of its employees on vacation or enjoying holidays, the company refused to put the agreement in writing. Although none of the union's previous contracts with the company had been in writing, the union insisted that the present contract be written and signed. Must the company comply with the union's demand?

Yes _____   No _____

20. Union A maintained a hiring hall for the convenience of its members and of employers in need of their services. Company X customarily hired its employees through the hiring hall. When Jane Doe applied for a job at Company X, she was told to register at the hall. Doe, who was not a member of the union, claimed that the company was violating the law by hiring through the hall, offering positive proof that the union referred only union members to jobs. Is Doe right?

Yes _____   No _____

21. A contract between a company and a union required employees to join the union after 30 days of employment and required the company to fire any employee who failed to do so. Is the contract lawful?

Yes _____   No _____

22. When a company notified its employees that it had signed a union-shop contract with a union, several employees protested that the union had been given no authorization to make such a contract. Are the protests sound?

Yes _____   No _____

23. When the president of a company discovered that a union was attempting to organize his employees, he made no secret of his feelings. He told employees that the union officers were "racketeers" who were trying to shake him down, that the organizers were "big stinkers" and "cheaper than dirt," that the members were "a bunch of radicals," and that any employee who joined the union "ought to have his head examined." Are the employer's comments protected as "free speech"?

     Yes _____   No _____

24. When the union called a strike at the company, some of the employees denounced the strike and refused to quit work. Although pickets stationed near the plant entrance did not try to keep nonstrikers from entering, they did subject each nonstriker to a barrage of name-calling. The pickets shouted "Scab!", "Strike-breaker!", and other epithets at the nonstrikers. Are the pickets' remarks protected as "free speech"? May strikers who engage in such conduct be denied rein-statement?

     Yes _____   No _____

25. When one of the employees suggested to the company president that the em-ployees form a union, the president enthusiastically endorsed the idea. He ordered his supervisors to sign up members, gave union officers time off from work to handle union business, and donated money to the union treasury to buy necessary supplies. Was the employer's aid to the union lawful?

     Yes _____   No _____

26. In a representation election among employees of the X Company, Union A, the only union on the ballot, was rejected as bargaining agent. Six months later, Union B signed up most of the employees as members and asked the company to recognize Union B as bargaining agent. When the company refused, the union picketed the plant. Is the picketing lawful?

     Yes _____   No _____

27. A year after employees of the company rejected Union A as their bargaining agent, they voted to have Union B represent them. When the company refused a demand for a wage increase, Union B called a strike and picketed the plant. Large numbers of pickets gathered at plant entrances and blocked the doors. Was the picketing lawful?

     Yes _____   No _____

28. Company Y customarily bought the gears it used in making alarm clocks from Company Z. When the union called a strike against Company Z, the union posted pickets at Company Y's plant, hoping to stop delivery of supplies to Company Y and thus force it to stop doing business with Company Z. Is the picketing lawful?

     Yes _____   No _____

SUGGESTED READINGS

Baxter, Ralph H., Jr. "Avoiding Liability in Firing Employees." *National Law Journal* 5, no. 51 (August 29, 1983): 20.

———. "Managing the Risks in Firing Employees." *National Law Journal* 6, no. 1 (September 12, 1983): 20.

Berger, Brian F. "Defining Public Policy Torts in At-Will Dismissals." *Stanford Law Review* 23 (November 1981): 153–172.

Bluen, S. D. "Some Consequences of Labor-Management Negotiations: Laboratory and Field Studies." *Journal of Organizational Behavior* 11, no. 2 (April 1, 1990): 105.

Elias, Nabil. "The Effects of Financial Information Symmetry on Conflict Resolution: An Experiment in the Context of Labor Negotiations." *Accounting Review* 65, no. 3 (July 1, 1990): 606.

"Employment Practices and Wrongful Discharge." *Labor Relations Reporter* 113, no. 11 (June 6, 1983): 116–118.

Isaacson, William J., and George B. Axelrod. "Employment at Will: An Idea Whose Time Is Done?" *Legal Times of New York* (June 20, 1983): 14.

Jenkins, William R. "Federal Legislative Exceptions to the At-Will Doctrine: Proposed Statutory Protection for Discharges Violative of Public Policy." *Albany Law Review* 47 (1983): 466–524.

Olsen, Theodore A. "Wrongful Discharge Claims Raised by At Will Employees: A New Legal Concern for Employers." *Labor Law Journal* (May 1981): 265–297.

Post, Frederick R. "Collaborative Collective Bargaining: Toward an Ethically Defensible Approach to Labor Negotiations." *Journal of Business Ethics* 9, no. 6 (June 1, 1990): 495.

"Protecting At Will Employees against Wrongful Discharge: The Duty to Terminate Only in Good Faith." *Harvard Law Review* 93 (1980): 1816–1844.

Waters, Craig R. "The New Malpractice." *Inc.* (June 1983): 136–140.

Chapter **32**

Termination at Will

Learning Objectives—After completion of this exercise, you should be able to:

1. Describe what is meant by termination at will.

2. List several of the circumstances in which termination at will is unlawful.

3. Develop a plan to avoid wrongful terminations.

4. Describe several important issues surrounding termination at will.

Time Suggested: Forty-five minutes

Procedures:

1. Individually read the Introduction and "Common Sources of Wrongful Discharge."

2. Complete the "Termination at Will" exercise.

3. Answer the questions at the end of the exercise.

INTRODUCTION

Legal issues surrounding the workplace have grown rapidly during the last twenty-five years. One of the most controversial topics to emerge recently is the common-law doctrine known as termination at will. Historically, employers and employees had the right to terminate the employment relationship "at will" unless union or other contractual agreements were present. For example, an employer could fire an employee with twenty-five years of service for no reason, and the employee would be without legal remedy. On the other hand, an employee could quit without notice. Recently, however, some employees have claimed that termination at will causes unequal harm to employees. They argue that the employee is more affected by termination than the organization is by an employee quitting.

In recent years, legislatures have passed laws to protect employees from arbitrary termination under certain circumstances. Courts have gotten involved by allowing employees to recover damages for "wrongful discharge." Terminations that are contrary to "public policy" or that are conducted in "bad faith" could be found unlawful. Obviously, judges have wide discretion in deciding when a termination at will is or is not unlawful. The trend is clearly toward more intensive scrutiny of employers' decisions, especially when basic questions of fairness are concerned.

Because of this trend, human resource managers must be aware of the new standards and become sensitive to the dangers inherent in employment relationships that could be deemed unlawful if a terminated employee brings charges of wrongful discharge.

COMMON SOURCES OF WRONGFUL DISCHARGE

Employees who have blown the whistle on employers for activities in violation of the law can usually count on some protection, depending on the circumstances of the case. For example, Title VII of the Civil Rights Act of 1964 prohibits dismissal of employees on the basis of their race, color, religion, sex, or national origin, and prohibits dismissal of employees who have filed a complaint with the Equal Employment Opportunity Commission. Similar protection is extended under the Occupational Safety and Health Act (OSHA) of 1970. If employees expose a violation of either of these laws, they are protected against termination for having done so. They cannot be fired, disciplined, or harassed to the point of quitting without the organization risking a lawsuit. Even if the employer did not violate the law, employees cannot be terminated for having made charges in good faith.

Employees are also afforded legal protection from termination at will if they exercise a legal right related to their employment. For example, employees who file claims for workers' compensation cannot be fired. In the future, this logic might be applied to other legal rights. Terminating an employee who has declared bankruptcy or who is politically active, for example, could be found unlawful.

A third situation in which termination at will could be potentially unlawful involves the "implied" contract. An implied contract occurs when the employer's actions "imply" a contractual relationship. For example, an implied contract could be established when a policy manual states that employees can have jobs as long as their work is acceptable. Contractual employment relationships could also be implied from application blanks, job descriptions, orientation materials, and grievance procedures. Statements made during the personnel interview might also be binding in a termination case. For example, an interviewer may state to an interviewee that "in two years you will have increased duties and responsibilities" and thus imply at least a two-year relationship with the organization.

MANAGING TO AVOID CHARGES OF ILLEGAL TERMINATION

Modern managers must develop strategies that will prevent unlawful terminations from occurring. Several steps can be taken.

1. Avoid implying that any job is "permanent." Review policy and personnel manuals and other organizational documents and omit phrases such as "long-term employment," "tenure," "permanent position," and "career position."

2. Maintain accurate records. Employees with poor performance records who are terminated at will are less likely to contest such a firing, and if they do contest it, they are less likely to win the case.

3. Install a progressive discipline system. Employees who have been disciplined several times before being fired are not likely to succeed in court. Managers who terminate an employee for having committed a minor offense for the first time (for example, showing up two hours late for work without notice) will have a difficult time succeeding in court because the employee was not given a second chance.

4. Educate supervisors about termination at will. Ignorance on the part of supervisors is rarely a defense for unlawful management actions.

TERMINATION AT WILL EXERCISE

In groups of three to five, review the following situations and discuss within your group whether or not they are justifiable terminations at will. Write a group response explaining your decision.

1. Mrs. Gonzales had been employed for four years as manager of a large religious organization when she was discharged in 1985. She maintained that during her initial job interview she was told that her employment was to be a series of five one-year contracts and that her termination in her fourth year denied her the fifth year of employment. The management maintained that Mrs. Gonzales had been hired for an indefinite length of time and therefore she could be fired at any time under the "at-will" doctrine. Management did admit to having described the job as a series of five one-year contracts but views such an arrangement as an indefinite period.

   Was the firing justifiable under the termination-at-will doctrine? Explain.

2. In 1982, Mr. Grauer was assistant to the president of a large textile company where he earned $18,000 per year based on an oral agreement. Late in 1982, his boss sent him a memo entitled "Your 1983 Salary" which guaranteed him a minimum of $32,500 for 1983. He was asked to sign the memo and return it to his boss. He did so and was congratulated by his boss for his past performance and was told to "keep up the good work." Six weeks later he was fired for an unannounced reason. Mr. Grauer argued that the employer intended an employment contract for 1983 and therefore he was unfairly fired. The company maintained that it had the right to terminate Mr. Grauer whenever it chose, just as he had the right to quit the company whenever he chose.

   Was the firing justifiable under the termination-at-will doctrine? Explain.

3. Collette Toussaint was hired as an EEO/Affirmative Action officer. Unknown to the employer, she began to make anonymous complaints to the Equal Employment Opportunity Commission (EEOC) about the company's EEO policy. She also conducted secret meetings with minority employees, away from the plant and during her personal time, where she encouraged them to file EEO complaints. When these complaints led to an EEO investigation, she denied knowing about them, even though she had filed several of them herself.

   When this deception was discovered, she was fired. She immediately brought suit, charging that the company was retaliating for her having made an EEO complaint. Management argued that she was hired to help the company comply with EEO laws and that it was her job to bring EEO issues to their attention for correction. Her failure to do so meant that she was not performing her job, and therefore termination was justified.

   Was the firing justifiable under the termination-at-will doctrine? Explain.

 **QUESTIONS**

1. Within your group, draft a set of procedures designed to deal with unlawful terminations at will. Extend your thinking beyond the ideas presented in this exercise. Many of your procedures could be based on common sense. For example, could you motivate supervisors to be concerned about how they manage termination decisions by including such decisions in their annual performance reviews? Use the following space to draft the procedures your group wants to adopt. Be prepared to justify your procedures.

2. Discuss within your group the following statement: "Termination at will causes unequal harm to employees." Do you agree or disagree? Why? List the points discussed in support of this statement and the points against this statement.

◢ SUGGESTED READINGS

Barbash, Jack. "Do We Really Want Labor on the Ropes?" *Harvard Business Review* 63 (April 1985): 10–20.

Bucalo, John P., Jr. "Successful Employee Relations." *Personnel Administrator* 31 (April 1986): 63–84.

Cappelli, Peter. "The Changing Face of Labor-Management Relations." *Management Review* (March 1986): 28–30.

Coil, III, James H. "The Model Uniform Employment Termination Act: A Cure or a Pox?" *Employment Relations Today* 17, no. 3 (Fall 1990): 201.

Kruse, Scott A. "Giveback Bargaining: One Answer to Current Labor Problems?" *Personnel Journal* 62, no. 4 (April 1983): 286–292.

Mauk, William L. "Model Employment Termination Act is Flawed." *Trial* 27, no. 6 (June 1, 1991): 28.

Mills, D. Quinn. "Reforming the U.S. System of Collective Bargaining." *Monthly Labor Review* 106, no. 3 (March 1983): 18–22.

Mondy, R. Wayne, and Shane R. Preameaux. "The Labor-Management Power Relationship Revisited." *Personnel Administrator* 30 (May 1985): 51–55.